Praise for *The New Pioneers*

"I predicted years ago that the idiotic and unreformable over-burden of building and zoning codes would eventually have to be ignored by anyone seeking to rebuild this country at the small scale and the fine grain. That outcome has now been realized in Lean Urbanism, a set of ingenious work-arounds for those determined to rescue our dying towns and cities. This book is the first herald of that momentous revolution."

—JAMES HOWARD KUNSTLER, author of
The Geography of Nowhere and *The Long Emergency*

"This book is one of the few collections of real world case studies showing that if you reduce regulations and move toward a more libertarian model, huge creative energies will be released and wealth created. This book tells that story in a highly readable and concrete way that makes the abstract principles of a free society very real and immediate."

—JENNIFER GROSSMAN, CEO of The Atlas Society

The
New
Pioneers

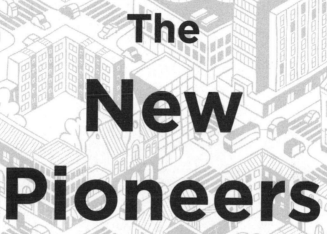

The
New
Pioneers

HOW ENTREPRENEURS
ARE DEFYING THE SYSTEM
TO REBUILD THE CITIES
AND TOWNS OF AMERICA

J.P. FABER

BenBella Books, Inc.
Dallas, TX

BenBella Books, Inc.
10440 N. Central Expressway, Suite 800
Dallas, TX 75231
www.benbellabooks.com
Send feedback to feedback@benbellabooks.com

Printed in the United States of America
10 9 8 7 6 5 4 3 2 1

Library of Congress Cataloging-in-Publication Data
Names: Faber, J. P. (James Paris), 1954- author.
Title: New pioneers : how entrepreneurs are defying the system to rebuild the
   cities and towns of America / J.P. Faber.
Description: Dallas, TX : BenBella Books, Inc., 2017.
Identifiers: LCCN 2016057462 (print) | LCCN 2017014638 (ebook) | ISBN
   9781944648312 (electronic) | ISBN 9781944648305 (trade cloth)
Subjects: LCSH: Urban renewal—United States. | Community development—United
   States. | Entrepreneurship—United States.
Classification: LCC HT175 (ebook) | LCC HT175 .F324 2017 (print) | DDC
   307.3/4160973—dc23
LC record available at https://lccn.loc.gov/2016057462

Editing by Debbie Harmsen
Copyediting by Scott Calamar
Proofreading by Kim Broderick and Lisa Story
Indexing by Amy Murphy Indexing & Editorial
Cover design by Connie Gabbert
Jacket design by Sarah Avinger
Text design and composition by Silver Feather Design
Printed by Lake Book Manufacturing

Distributed by Perseus Distribution
www.perseusdistribution.com

To place orders through Perseus Distribution:
Tel: (800) 343-4499
Fax: (800) 351-5073
E-mail: orderentry@perseusbooks.com

Special discounts for bulk sales (minimum of 25 copies) are available.
Please contact Aida Herrera at aida@benbellabooks.com.

This book is dedicated to the love of my life,
Lesley Fonger Faber, who taught me that the only worlds
worth creating are those you can share with others.

CONTENTS

THE BIRTH OF
LEAN URBANISM

There was a time in this country when young, energetic people could get things done, and that time was not long ago. When I began my career as an architect we could actually get things built—and fast. My colleagues and I, then in our mid-twenties, did not know how good we had it. We thought it was perfectly normal that people of our age, with some training, could get on with it.

That was forty years ago, when nothing could stop young, energetic people. My partner Elizabeth and I had been driven to the Sunbelt by the recession of 1974, and within four years we were building high rises in Miami. The local zoning code was less than half an inch thick and the planning department inhabited wooden WWII barracks, each office entered from a long porch. There were no hurdles to getting permits.

In the early 1980s, when we designed a whole new town called Seaside in the Florida Panhandle—one of the places visited in this book—Walton County didn't even have a bureaucracy to submit the plan to. It was enough to notify the county of commencement of construction, and so long as we followed the codes, we could call in the bulldozers and start to build. As it happened, the developer, Robert Davis, had to help set up a county planning office so that he could get an approval stamp—to show the bankers who were anxious about giving him a loan. Robert was thirty-five years old.

In that same Walton County, the most recent of our town plans took a year of bureaucratic wrangling by an army of lawyers and consultants. It had become almost impossible—at least for young, inexperienced people—to get anything done, even if they were energetic. That was only twenty years later.

Such a weight of regulation, back when Seaside started, would have crushed us. And in Miami today, the bureaucracy is housed in an enormous labyrinth of high-rise office space; the codebook they administer is ten times as thick. If I handed it to one of our young colleagues at the office today they would smirk with millennial sarcasm, "Really?"

I understand them perfectly. At their age I would not have picked up that bloated monster either.

But the young are not sitting still. One of my youngest colleagues, Mike Lydon, went off to start a movement called Tactical Urbanism. It was a method through which small, evident things could get done, bypassing the bureaucracies, the impediments, and the hurdles—few of which existed in my time. Mike and other tactical urbanists like Tony Garcia are marvelous, sanctioned or unsanctioned, at getting stuff done.

And yet, as I compare them with us at their age, their projects are too small and too temporary for such bright young minds. We are no longer enabling the energy of youth. We have forgotten that WWII was won by twenty-year-olds.

The architects, builders, and urban planners of my generation lived through the gradual growth of red tape, and we absorbed it as a slow drip. We never leapt out of the pot as it warmed. Now, it seems, the new generation will not step into the scalding situation. They actually can't.

So a movement called Lean Urbanism has emerged. This is what J.P. Faber has latched on to: the folks who have figured out—and can teach us—how it is possible to bypass the impediments.

The phenomenon of the young encountering the codified world (as New Pioneers) has an interesting parallel that we noticed in Miami (and across America): that construction crews consist largely of immigrants. Many of them are extraordinarily skilled, the kind of workers who would have built their own houses in their native countries; here they are just labor for subcontractors.

They are also more than that. In Miami and other US cities, they build and modify their own houses without permits. They can't navigate the permits, nor do they need to. Imagine if the thirty million penniless immigrants who in the nineteenth century pioneered the west had required permits! We would not have crossed the Appalachians.

Our new immigrants now operate in a gray market, hoping not to be noticed as they build for themselves and start informal businesses. And our youth—what are they doing? An inordinate number now channel their energy into the arts and the Internet, among the few areas where you can do things without a permit. But a pioneering few are not asking for permission to build or make things. Like new immigrants to America, they are just doing it.

For me personally, the moment of insight was my fifth visit to Detroit. Within that oceanic ruin, Mark Nickita showed me an archipelago of success. Hundreds of young people were renovating buildings, starting businesses, and opening restaurants—without engaging the bureaucracy. It seems that when Detroit went bankrupt it wasn't just the police the city couldn't pay; it couldn't pay the bureaucracy either. The young and the energetic emigrated from cities like Brooklyn, Chicago, and San Francisco—all places where getting anything done was difficult, if not impossible.

The head of the James L. Knight Foundation heard me raving about this and suggested that I apply for a grant to study the phenomenon. This study would become the study of Lean Urbanism.

The first year of the grant was dedicated to finding out where people were getting things done and how they were doing it. What were the workarounds, the techniques, and the ways to circumvent impossibly oppressive situations? That is what J.P. Faber is reporting on here.

The second year was dedicated to formalizing these techniques, while the third year has been dedicated to half a dozen pilot projects. These areas are called Pink Zones: sectors where the red tape has been lightened.

Please remember that the mission of Lean Urbanism is for permanent, growing projects, in between the demonstration pop-ups of Tactical Urbanism and the long-term commitment to reform of New Urbanism. Lean Urbanism works cunningly on the real with the art of the possible.

There are many Lean bumper sticker slogans, among them "Making the small possible." But in the end it will be the weight of many stories where frustration has led to heightened wit—more and more stories like those of the people described in this book, people dancing in the sheer delight of overcoming stupid impediments. That is what will drive Lean Urbanism to the mainstream. And it is inevitable. The energy of the American youth and of the new American immigrant will not be strangled by red tape. The mission of Lean Urbanism is to allow the coming generations to breathe free.

—Andrés Duany

THE NEW PIONEERS AND THE LESSONS OF LEAN URBANISM

When I was a student at New York University, my best friend and I rented an industrial loft in an old brick building. The entire loft was 4,000 square feet and occupied the whole floor. We only wanted half of it, the front half that had huge circular windows straight out of Captain Nemo's *Nautilus* submarine.

Unfortunately, the half we wanted had no bathroom. The loft was a commercial space used previously as a sweatshop for seamstresses. All of the bathrooms were clustered at the far end.

It was not legal for us to live in the loft. The zoning was strictly for industrial use. But why should we care? We were in our twenties and had what you would call an extremely high tolerance for risk. We had nothing invested so we had nothing to lose. If someone showed up to evict us, we would simply move on.

As for the lack of bathroom, we hired a maverick plumber named Leo Press. He was a slovenly man who lived illegally in his basement shop on Houston Street. He arrived one day with a bag of tools and an assistant who spoke no English. They punched holes in the wall until they found the requisite pipes. Leo and his subaltern then

1

installed a toilet, a sink, and eventually a bathtub. We were in business, living in a run-down business district used by egg wholesalers, odd-lot jobbers, rag sellers, and cardboard manufacturers.

Others soon joined the community—students, artists, musicians, and bohemians of all stripes—attracted by incredibly low rents and huge spaces. We rode up and down in freight elevators, our heat in winter was questionable, and we sometimes shared electricity by dropping extension cords out the windows to friends above and below.

As the years went by, we slowly improved the places in which we lived. We added walls and kitchens and carpets. We spackled and painted and insulated. We turned a raw and edgy neighborhood into a coven of galleries and studios and artists' lofts. Today this neighborhood—dubbed SoHo because it lies south of Houston Street—is among the city's most trendy and expensive, including in its midst a Trump hotel.

What I didn't realize at the time was that this phenomenon—the arrival of risk-oblivious urban pioneers, willing to rebuild forgotten neighborhoods with nothing but elbow grease and youthful energy—was a blueprint for creating new businesses and revitalizing dead zones. What we saw was opportunity. What we didn't comprehend was the overarching principle at hand: that the absence of oversight and code enforcement makes it possible for young, under-capitalized urban homesteaders to build their dreams.

America has always cherished the idea that any individual, given sufficient freedom, can create wealth and personal prosperity. We call it the American Dream. Hand that immigrant an axe and a bag of seeds, open the frontier, and just watch as the ingenuity and hard work of the lone citizen creates a new world.

The reality is that America today is a highly regulated country. There are laws that control virtually everything we do. You can't set up a lemonade stand these days without violating local and state ordinances. The land of the free? Not so much anymore. The land of Lincoln is now the land of litigation.

In 2014, I was approached by a group of architects who were exploring an idea called Lean Urbanism. It was based on a simple premise: half a century ago the building regulations in the average American city were minimal, whereas today they are, relatively speaking, "the size of a room compared to the size of a pea," said the group's leader, architect Andrés Duany.

What Lean Urbanism sought to understand and solve, he explained, was the deadening effect of overregulation, especially for small new builders and businesses. He felt that young entrepreneurs were being gamed out of the system and needed help to overcome the odds.

Lean Urbanism puts it this way: Whereas our ancestors could build as they pleased on any land they owned, today it is against the law to build anything anywhere without first satisfying a panoply of city, state, and federal regulations, along with their various permits and fees. These requirements have grown so complicated that only highly paid professionals can steer us through the morass. Indeed, builders no longer present their plans to city officials; they hire lawyers to do that.

Backed by a grant from the Knight Foundation, Duany and his cohorts set out to provide entrepreneurs with a toolbox of tactics to overcome, escape, or work around the worst of the regulations that were killing small-scale enterprises. For my part, they asked me to visit ten places in the US—five large cities and five small towns—where examples of Lean Urbanism were already under way.

I am not an architect, which is why the proponents of Lean Urbanism wanted me to travel to these locations. They didn't want someone weighed down by architectural theory and jargon. They wanted a journalist practiced in the art of observation. They wanted me to experience Lean Urbanism up close.

What I discovered over the better part of two years were clutches of people, mostly young but not always, who were bending, breaking, or ignoring the rules in order to homestead the forgotten corners of our towns and cities. They were creating wealth from this new wilderness—our broken municipal landscape—by building or rebuilding under the radar, in bubbles where regulation was lean.

I also discovered something not on the lean agenda, at least not consciously: That these urban (and sometimes rural) homesteading entrepreneurs were driven by the same passions as the early pioneers in America. They were bushwhackers of a new frontier, hungry for the same things as our first immigrants—a level playing field where hard work and ingenuity, free from the shackles of the Old World, could pay off. They were our nation's New Pioneers.

The dream of the lone pioneer has never really left America. It persists today in our love affair with small business. While most Americans think poorly of the federal government, financial institutions, and large corporations, the vast majority harbors positive feelings about small businesses. According to public opinion surveys, Americans think more highly of small businesses than they do of universities, churches, or tech companies.

Despite this sentiment—and the pledges of innumerable politicians to help "the little guy"—our world is, as Duany declared, gamed in favor of the large. From Apple to Walmart, massive corporations dominate the economic landscape.

Nowhere is the reign of the large more apparent than in the context of small builders and small businesses in an urban setting. On the streets of our cities, and even in the commercial centers of suburbia, small businesses—especially start-ups and small-scale developers—are at a big disadvantage compared to national chains and large-scale developers.

The upper hand enjoyed by big business has numerous foundations. An obvious one is access to capital. Banks and investment groups tend to favor larger clients. It's much easier to lend $100 million to a single borrower than it is to lend one million dollars to 100 different borrowers.

Less obvious but of greater significance is the regulatory environment. Small entrepreneurs and start-ups are far more vulnerable to suffocation by excessive regulations. This is truer today than ever before. Our regulatory codes, from business permits to worker compensation requirements, have blossomed out of control. In this dense regulatory environment, only those armed with professional expertise can navigate the thickets. Large businesses with sufficient scale can field an army of experts, but the individual is outgunned.

Our cult of hypercoding affects everything today, from banking and finance to education, health care, and the environment. But it is in the urban setting, the tangible world where we work, live, and play, where the suffocating blanket of overregulation is easiest to observe and understand.

It is arguable that young professionals can start a "business" without too much cost, especially if they are among the millions of self-employed, single proprietors, like a consultant, an accountant, a freelance designer, or an online word processor. These are the proverbial denizens of the home office.

What we are talking about here are the four million small US businesses that hire employees, and require a physical space—anything from an art gallery or café to a bookstore or bakery. These are the small retail enterprises that make our towns and cities interesting places to live. "A lively city scene is lively largely by virtue of its enormous collection of small elements," wrote Jane Jacobs in her seminal *The Death and Life of Great American Cities*. "Wherever we find a city district with an exuberant variety and plenty in its commerce, we are apt to find that it contains a good many other kinds of diversity also, including variety of cultural opportunities, variety of scenes, and a great variety in its population and other users."

The danger that Lean Urbanism points out is how our regulatory environment is killing the small in favor of the large, with a consequent loss of individuation on our city streets. Towns and cities are appealing not because of massive developments. Intricate streetscapes created by individual builders and small businesses are what make these areas attractive and interesting. A world usurped by the oversized is a boring world of sameness—cities filled with look-alike buildings and brands.

The painful fact is that it's extremely expensive for young entrepreneurs to start a business if they intend to play by the rules. The combination of business and occupational licenses, compulsory insurance, OSHA compliance, building permits, fire codes, tax requirements, municipal ordinances—the whole parade of prerequisites and layered costs—makes it prohibitively expensive for a small business to establish itself. And this does not include the process itself, the often arcane and typically time-consuming grind through the bureaucracy of city hall.

Lean Urbanism intends to provide a solution to the straitjacket of excess regulation. Their pundits and theorists have already identified the problems blocking "The Young, the Small, the Maker, and the Immigrant" from "small-scale, incremental community building." The process, they say:

- Takes too long
- Costs too much
- Requires experts
- Requires certification
- Privileges high-tech

The Lean Urbanism solutions for these impediments are:

- Pink Zones
- Thresholds
- Work-arounds
- Apprenticeship
- Vernacular Systems

Pink Zones are places with few restrictions, where only the most critical safety regulations are enforced. In cities like Detroit, New Orleans, and Miami, and in towns like Starkville, Mississippi, and Seaside, Florida, I saw the energies of the people released when entire areas became Pink Zones.

Thresholds are the levels that trigger additional code enforcement. They are tipping points for cost and complexity. If you stay below these levels, you don't trigger the next avalanche of regulations. In San Diego, for example, if you build a four-unit condominium, it triggers a requirement for a parking garage. Instead, you build a couple of side-by-side, two-unit condominiums.

Work-arounds are solutions based on the use of language to foil restrictions. In Ocean Springs, Mississippi, Orange Beach, Alabama, and Phoenix, Arizona, I saw the simple magic of how calling a certain kind of structure something else freed it from excessive regulations. Don't call it a penthouse. Call it a covered roof terrace.

Apprenticeship is a key part of creating a new generation of citizen builders, especially for young professionals (architects and developers) who would otherwise be regimented into the corporate system of gigantism. In Newbern, Alabama, and San Diego, California, I saw the importance of teaching the next generation the forgotten art of self-reliance.

Vernacular systems are the DNA of the local environment, the solutions that have been developed by residents over time in order to build affordably and sustainably. In New Orleans, Seaside, and Ocean Springs, I saw the importance of using the simple lessons of the past rather than imposing futuristic high-tech solutions.

Using this framework, I traveled to five towns and five cities to see how these solutions were being implemented. I talked to the people who were on the ground, already practicing Lean Urbanism without being aware of it, and in the process, discovered the individuals I call the New Pioneers.

Similar to Lean Urbanism, these New Pioneers manifest certain characteristics and live according to their own distinct playbook. Here's what I discovered about these New Pioneers:

New Pioneers are risk oblivious. They jump into new (and sometimes scary) areas without a guarantee of success. They are followed by settlers and professionals.

New Pioneers seek the new wilderness—the broken cityscapes and the places regulators have forgotten because these areas are too worthless, too poor, too rural.

New Pioneers are not practicing gentrification. They work from the ground up, not the top down. They don't invade with wealth; they create wealth from the wreckage.

New Pioneers are yesterday's homesteaders dropped into the present world, time traveling from prairies and forests to urban jungles, from sod busting to code busting.

New Pioneers possess the revolutionary spirit of our forefathers, the same bristle of "Don't Tread on Me" and don't bleed me with your taxes, forms, and fees.

The architects of Lean Urbanism sent me out in search of a theory on how to make small building possible, but what I found was a larger principle that applied to all new ventures, to all small businesses. And it applied to people all over America in search of the same thing that our forefathers (and mothers) sought—a place where they were free to create their destiny without interference. That is why the early pioneers hiked into the wilderness, and that is what the New Pioneers are looking for today.

chapter one

DETROIT: DAWN OF THE DEAD

Urban Destruction Creates a New Wilderness

No city in America has come close to the carnage of Detroit, with half the metropolis in ruins and two thirds of its population uprooted. Now it is experiencing a true renaissance, especially in the downtown area. The media gives credit to the arrival of new employers, most notably billionaire Dan Gilbert and his company Quicken Loans. But the reason his and other corporations relocated to Detroit is because thousands of millennial pioneers had already relocated there, starting new businesses, planting urban farms, and rebuilding houses. Why they migrated to Detroit had far more to do with the bankrupt city's inability to enforce its ordinances than any top-down investments from corporate America.

Detroit epitomizes the potential for New Pioneers, when the landscape returns to wilderness, offering a level playing field for anyone with the energy to homestead new ideas—or simply start a new business without overbearing regulations. Detroit is still a postapocalyptic city, slowly emerging from decades of devastation. But the silver lining is that the city is so stripped of resources that it can no longer enforce its own restrictive regulations. The result has been an influx of millennial urban pioneers in search of liberty from the shackles of the old order. Their unfettered energy is creating a new city.

Detroit illustrates the explosive power of Lean Urbanism and lower thresholds for the young, the small, the new, and the undercapitalized. The waning of barriers has attracted scores of start-up companies, especially in high-tech sectors like software design, app development, computer-assisted engineering, and online commerce. The catchword everywhere is "opportunity," and that opportunity has encouraged risk-oblivious entrepreneurs to inhabit places without licenses, permits, or even the payment of taxes. They are the New Pioneers of Detroit's urban frontier.

After the Apocalypse: Millennials in Detroit are starting new businesses, often without permits, in the abandoned warehouses of the old downtown.

THE POSTAPOCALYPTIC CITY

For anyone who has not visited Detroit, Michigan, the utter destruction of this once-great American city is almost unimaginable. With the exception of the core downtown, the city is checkered with architectural cadavers. Abandoned apartment buildings stand like zombies—the name given them by locals—their windows black holes that stare as blankly as the eyes of the dead. Residential streets are lined with burned-out homes, twisted and tortured as they slowly collapse. Factories and municipal buildings are abandoned, riddled with holes and stripped of all wiring and plumbing. And everywhere—everywhere—there are gaps, empty lots, and open fields where housing and commercial buildings once stood, now razed in the ongoing process of clearing the debris.

To get an idea of how vast and complete the devastation of Detroit has been, consider this: the Black Plague, remembered fearfully as the greatest single catastrophe in recorded human history, killed between 30 percent and 60 percent of Europe's population. Detroit, by comparison, has lost 65 percent to 70 percent of its population since its peak in 1950.

The destitution is omnipresent. Entire sections of the city have been lost, left crumbling in spectacular architectural graveyards or simply erased. City blocks not five minutes from the GM Renaissance Center, where only one or two houses remain standing, have reverted to grassland. In places it feels far more like rural Vermont than the urban core of a formerly vibrant metropolis.

These empty pastures of neighborhoods just east of GM's gargantuan downtown complex are soothing, however, compared to neighborhoods to the north and northwest, where more than 75,000 blighted structures are slated for demolition. These streets are not pastoral in appearance but apocalyptic, as though a firestorm had swept through, or a pandemic. Residents who roam the worst areas appear deranged and impoverished, like drugged extras in a science-fiction film about the end of the world. The desolate Packard plant in the city's northeast section, at 3.5 million square feet, is the single largest abandoned factory in the world. It is such a spectacular ruin that local entrepreneurs operate a "spelunking tour" of the cavernous wreckage.

How Detroit arrived at this destination of destruction is not essential except that it created a lean urban environment where New Pioneers could thrive. Pundits place the blame primarily on the loss of jobs that ensued when the major automakers—Ford, GM, and Chrysler—relocated their factories to other US locales with lower taxes and less tolerance for unions. The loss of employment started a downward spiral of reduced services and higher taxes, leading to the wholesale departure of the white middle class after World War II, many fleeing to the suburbs. A string of corrupt municipal governments compounded the problems and accelerated the city's depopulation, which bottomed out with the real estate collapse of 2007–2008.

As of the 2010 census, a once-mighty Detroit of nearly two million souls had shrunk to 700,000 residents. Some twenty-four square miles of the 139-square-mile city were completely vacant; another nine square miles were occupied by abandoned buildings. Of its original 380,000 properties, 114,000 had been razed. As of 2013, the situation had become untenable, and the city filed the largest municipal bankruptcy in US history.

Detroit's collapse received reams of mainstream media press. It also spawned a series of radical solutions, the most prominent of which was *Detroit Future City*. This massive document, produced in 2013 by prominent urban consultants and funded by the Kresge Foundation, envisioned repurposing huge areas of the city as urban farms, solar fields, forests, carbon buffers, and rainwater retention ponds. The remaining population would condense into districts that could be efficiently administered by the city's diminished municipal services.

While such top-down utopian solutions are mesmerizing, they require enormous investments, prolonged political will, and many years to execute. Before any come to pass—if indeed any ever do—the city will already have been reborn in the cauldron of Lean Urbanism. For, while the city's dwindling resources have attenuated the protection provided by police, fire, and rescue personnel, they have also evaporated the enforcement of zoning regulations, ordinances, and permits. And rather than enfeeble new business development, this absence of oversight has allowed it to blossom.

DETROIT'S NEW PIONEERS

On a dead-end street about half a mile from the central business district of Detroit stands a 30,000-square-foot warehouse called Ponyride. It's a block from Rosa Parks Boulevard, a once-grand avenue in the Corktown neighborhood that has given way to empty lots and cheap commercial storage spaces.

Ponyride is an incubator of sorts, a sprawling complex occupied by forty small businesses. The building has an official front entrance, but on the north side, in the middle of a gray wall decorated with graffiti and a few second-story windows, you can find a single doorway with no signs.

Inside is raw, unfinished space. A stack of bulging canvas bags, each stamped GUATEMALA, fills one corner of the room. On the wall next to the bags hangs a chalkboard inscribed with large cursive letters that read ANTHOLOGY COFFEE. Underneath those words, another scrawled sentence declares: COFFEE IS A UNIVERSAL LANGUAGE.

The walls and ceilings are unpainted wallboard, smeared with white Spackle and framed by exposed piping and aluminum ductwork; the floor is raw concrete. Four tables with chairs line one wall. At the first table, a young woman peers into a laptop. At the next, a young man scrutinizes his iPhone. Two tables down, a woman coos to her baby in its carriage. Everyone in the room is clearly under thirty.

A long table with a copper Italian espresso machine and flasks of coffee beans sits in the center of the room. A young man wearing a vest and Panama hat, and sporting a mustache curled at both ends, is talking to the operator; with muttonchop sideburns, he also looks like an outcast from the nineteenth century, a lost Grover Cleveland or Chester A. Arthur.

The operator takes beans from one of the jars, grinds them, and then decants the grinds into a beaker lined with a paper filter. He gingerly pours hot water into the beaker. It looks like a chemistry experiment. He pours the newly brewed coffee into a short glass, and the man with the Snidely Whiplash moustache smells it first, like he is drinking fine wine. He samples it and discusses the taste intently with the brewmaster, whom he then slips three dollars.

Welcome to a coffee shop on the pioneer fringe of future Detroit. The raw space of Anthology Coffee is a café that operates outside the world of regulations. Except for the chalkboard, easily erasable, there are no signs. There are no menus, no cash registers, no exit signs, no sprinklers, and no certificates of occupancy. Yet everyone seems to know just what to do.

The proprietor of Anthology is Josh Longsdorf, a thirty-three-year-old entrepreneur. While his barista sells coffees by the cup, the main business of Anthology is wholesale. Longsdorf supplies beans and ground coffee to a dozen restaurants in Detroit, another half dozen in Ann Arbor, and a handful more scattered in New York, London, and Portland, Oregon.

"We buy large quantities of coffee, then roast them in a way that shows off their properties," says Longsdorf proudly. "The best way to say it is that we try to not mess up what we have." He buys only "single-farm coffees," which means directly sourced from one farmer rather than from a conglomerate.

Longsdorf, who moved to Detroit in the fall of 2010 with his wife, a baby, and a few thousand dollars in his pockets, exemplifies Detroit's new pioneers. Having learned the coffee business in Portland, he came to Detroit because he "heard there was opportunity." Translation: an unregulated environment with low thresholds for entry, the equivalent of an earlier American frontier long since disappeared. He was able to start a business with no license, no permits, and no taxes. He bought a home out of foreclosure for $4,350 in cash and put in less than $5,000 to make it sparkle. He bicycles to work ("we are all avid cyclists here") from his new home, where he lives with his wife and (now) three small children.

"We moved here after our first kid was born, because we knew we had opportunity. We knew we could get a business started," says Longsdorf. "They [Ponyride] said, 'Move in. You can do whatever you want.'"

After tearing out a drop-down ceiling to raise the room height, Longsdorf and crew started their pop-up coffee shop. "We can't have a real café because someone will catch wind and shut us down," he says. "I started by roasting in another place, and we made enough money to get this going. We just started operating. When I started wholesaling, that was licensed. But when I came in here to sell cups, no one [in the city government] knew we were here. We took the money and put it back into the business."

Like Longsdorf, twenty-six-year-old barista Derek Craig is another pioneer who arrived in Detroit because he heard of the opportunity. A California native, Craig met Longsdorf in San Francisco and followed him to Detroit two years later.

Craig lives just a few blocks from Anthology Coffee in a three-bedroom row-house apartment, which he shares with two roommates. Their total rent is six hundred dollars. "I'm like a claim jumper," he says about his apartment hunting. "I'm always looking for a better deal, and when I find one I move there."

Despite Detroit's reputation as America's murder capital, Craig says he's never experienced any violence there. He shops at a downtown Whole Foods supermarket, put there as an urban experiment in 2013. For entertainment, he goes to underground music performances. "You go to what someone else is putting on. There is lots of that. I can't even keep up," he says. As for the absence of city inspectors: "If you're not doing anything bad, no one bothers you . . . It's sort of like living on a frontier." His brewing philosophy is parallel with his take on living in Detroit under the radar: "Just don't mess it up."

Anthology Coffee is kind of a side pocket in Ponyride. The remaining maze of businesses ensconced in the incubator/warehouse can be reached through the proper main entrance, or through a small side door from Anthology.

In this warren are more start-ups—projects cultivated by millennial pioneers in a low-barrier environment provided by local developer Phillip Cooley and his brother Ryan. The Cooley siblings purchased the building out of tax foreclosure at the bottom of the market in 2011 for $100,000, and decided to use it to nurture small, new businesses by offering what Phillip Cooley calls "depression-era" rents.

"Ponyride is a study in how foreclosure can have a benefit on our community," he says. "We're offering inexpensive rents to social entrepreneurs and artists so that they can focus on what they do. When you give people space, amazing things happen."

Ponyride is a jumbled showcase for some of those "things." Adjacent to Anthology is a dance studio, with mirrors on one wall and, on the other, a black-and-yellow mural of a Chinese woman leaping from a huge star, rifle aimed at an unseen enemy—very Chairman Mao.

"This is an important space because there are no dance studios in Detroit, except at the schools," says Daron Simon, an intern and local college student who acts as my tour guide, dressed in a gray hoodie and black T-shirt with a skull etched on it. The next space she shows is where the Cooleys keep the equipment they need for Slows Bar Bq, a local favorite the Cooley family launched in 2005—the success of which funded Ponyride. Their storage area looks like a carpentry shop, with sawhorse tables, stacked firewood, high ceilings, and extension cords snaking across the floor. Through an interior window, you can see a small internal space where a tiny two-person company makes and markets "beard balm," apropos for the hirsute millennial generation.

The Cooley storage space opens onto what appears to be a blacksmith shop, where metal workers are producing kitchen utensils and iron bracelets from old nails extracted from demolished Detroit buildings. Clusters of naked lightbulbs hang from the ceiling; medieval-looking tools and welder masks abound.

And so it goes throughout the labyrinth of Ponyride, one room leading to the next. Climb a narrow flight of stairs and you find the home of Detroit Denim, where the owners make high-quality jeans designed to last a lifetime for $250. These are the clothes of the new frontier, built to last through the worst of conditions. The proprietors decline to give their names and block photos with their hands, annoyed by the attempted breach of their anonymity. A customer emerges from a tiny changing room, also taken aback by the intrusion, wearing a pair of the forever denims they manufacture.

Through another door appears The Dirt Label T-shirt company. Its icon is a little man with Xs for eyes, a helmet, a jumpsuit, and a flag that says DIRT; a poster shows Lil Wayne in Dirt Label fatigues. Next door lies a long room lined with tall windows and occupied by rows of tables where techies can start their company from a single desk; along one wall of this "incubation space" stands a phone booth, recycled from the street where it sat abandoned and useless. Like Maxwell Smart's "cone of silence," it serves as a privacy booth for cell phone callers.

Most impressive is a huge space where more than a dozen black women are busy sewing long quilted coats, gray on the outside and red on the inside. It's part of something called the Empowerment Plan, whereby the coats are given to shelters to distribute to street people. "These are homeless women who they hired to make these coats that can become sleeping bags," says Simon. "They're for the homeless." What about the women—do they use them? "No. Now they can afford to rent apartments," she says.

FAILURE OF THE TOP-DOWN

Just over a mile from Ponyride is Detroit's geographic focal point, a lozenge-shaped plaza called Campus Martius. From this hub, the arterial boulevards of the city radiate like spokes—Woodward Avenue to the north, Michigan Avenue to the northwest, Fort Street (from the days when Detroit actually was a fort) to the west, and via a slight twist, Gratiot Avenue to the northeast. Rectangular Cadillac Square, a corridor that leads to the Greek-revival elegance of the Wayne County Building, forms the southeastern spoke.

Though more of a central square than a central park, Campus Martius is nonetheless richly detailed with fountains, bistros, trees, café tables, a bandstand, and even a sandy "beach" that becomes an ice-skating rink in winter. And unlike a half-decade earlier, it bustles with people. The ground floors of surrounding buildings have added restaurants and cafés, and in some cases—at the adjacent Chase Tower, for example—additional outdoor public seating. In front of one building waits a giant chess set, its three-foot-tall pieces available for public play. If this park were all that visitors saw of Detroit, they would find it hard to reconcile its animated bustle with the corridors of dead buildings just blocks away.

Campus Martius is one of the few intelligent large-scale investments in Downtown Detroit, the result of $20 million anteed up in 2004. But it is successful precisely because it was built on a human scale with open access, in stark contrast to the parade of megaprojects installed in Detroit over the years in vain attempts to stem the tide of fleeing residents.

Not unlike the sweeping *Detroit Future City* proposals, since 1950 civic leaders simply hurled infrastructure investments into the vortex of the city's implosion, hoping they would somehow reverse that momentum and spark an urban revival.

These projects included the superhighways of the 1950s and 1960s. They were intended to make the city more auto friendly and easier to navigate, but actually resulted in the departure of 300,000 residents to the suburbs. Likewise for the construction of the Joe Louis Arena for the Detroit Red Wings (hockey), Comerica Park for the Tigers (baseball), and Ford Field for the Lions (football): all did little for the downtown beyond leveling historic neighborhoods and periodically swelling its streets with suburban fans.

The same mega-solution mentality manifested itself in projects like the elephantine Renaissance Center, headquarters for a General Motors that had already moved most of its plants and jobs elsewhere. The downtown's MGM Grand and Greektown Casino-Hotel were similarly constructed as fortresses—Norman towers erected in hostile territory. The Greektown casino complex actually encases brick-lined city streets in an air-conditioned bubble as surreal and antiseptic as a Disney World attraction.

None of these overblown projects proved catalytic for economic growth. Instead, it required the exhaustion of the city's top-down mentality to create an environment that finally attracted the current wave of entrepreneurial talent.

Campus Martius, the one success of these concepts, is actually not a top-down solution—not if the top is defined as the government or large corporations. Rather, it is an example of a private nonprofit group—in this case the Detroit 300 Conservancy—that designed and built the park with foundation grants (the conservancy now operates it under contract with the city). As Detroit's government began to pull back from civic obligations during its fiscal descent, more and more public institutions went this way, including the Detroit Institute of Arts, the Detroit Historical Museum, and the Detroit Zoo. All are now run by private nonprofits under contract with the municipal government.

Perhaps the best example of this transition from public mismanagement to private competence is the city's Eastern Market, located barely a mile from the Campus Martius hub. Originally founded in 1891, it remained vibrant as a retail marketplace for fruits and vegetables until the early 1980s, when then mayor Coleman A. Young bulldozed a nearby Polish neighborhood of more than a thousand homes for a central city GM factory. After that, Eastern Market became strictly wholesale, floundering for decades as the unwanted stepchild of various city agencies.

Finally, a three-year campaign backed by dollars from the Kellogg Foundation, the McGregor Fund, and the Kresge Foundation peeled the city's fingers from Eastern Market and turned it over to the Eastern Market Corporation in 2006. Today the market is a focal point for city life, its five massive "sheds" open on Saturdays and Tuesdays as public markets (it remains the city's wholesaler for meat, produce, and specialty foods). Resembling the iconic *Mercado Central* of Santiago, Chile, the peaked-roof sheds No. 2 through No. 6 (No. 1 was lost to highway I-75) sell a stunning array of produce, much of it grown locally in Michigan. They also vend artisanal wares like organic honey and baked goods.

BOTTOMED-OUT THRESHOLDS

While privatizing Detroit's control of public institutions has fostered new urban life, the more profound phenomenon of the New Pioneer has blossomed where the city has simply abandoned oversight. The vacuum left behind is where citizens can operate without restraint to pursue their ambitions for new businesses. Whereas the reduction of police and fire protection has resulted in more destruction, the absence of code enforcement has produced the opposite effect.

Capitol Park is a triangular plaza three blocks north of Campus Martius in the CBD (central business district). Just a few years ago, it was a bivouac for the homeless. Now cleaned up and replanted, it's become a favorite lunch spot for construction workers refurbishing office towers (mostly owned by billionaire Dan Gilbert) which bracket the park. On the twenty-third floor of one of these buildings (a brick high rise that eluded Gilbert and was purchased by a Chinese investment company) lies the headquarters of start-up GreenLancer.

With a twenty-first-century business model and a crew of employees in their twenties, GreenLancer typifies a millennial start-up. CEO Michael Sharber—its founder and the "old man" of the company at age thirty—says it could only have been started in the lean scene of Detroit.

Sharber calls GreenLancer a "plug-and-play solution" for contractors who want to install solar projects but can't afford to maintain engineers on staff. Using a mobile platform of smartphone or iPad, contractors send GreenLancer the specifications of their projects. GreenLancer then farms these out to professional engineers who freelance the projects. The cost for the contractors: about one third of what it would cost to maintain professional services on the payroll.

Sharber was actually born in Detroit, moving with his family to rural Michigan when he was seven. He had no intention of ever returning to Detroit when he launched GreenLancer in Colorado in 2009, but he found the start-up expenses too steep in the Rocky Mountain state, so he and a partner took their enterprise on the road—literally—operating from the back of their car as they camped out in national parks. Then he heard that Detroit was becoming a tech-savvy city with rock-bottom living expenses. He decided he would become a pioneer in that urban wilderness.

"We realized it was cheaper to live and work here than anywhere else, that we'd be able to do things we couldn't do anywhere else," he says. "Our dollar went much farther than it would being in Chicago, LA, or anywhere else."

Initially Sharber moved into a three-bedroom suite on the twenty-sixth floor of the Westin Book Cadillac Hotel, which he shared with his partner and a young attorney. The hotel has since been refurbished for $200 million, but at that time, the trio paid just $1,700 a month for their space. "Nobody was in the downtown back then," he says. "We had marble floors, granite countertops, and they would call me 'Mr. Sharber' every day when I came in. We had the pools and all the amenities. It was pretty sweet."

GreenLancer was initially set up in a downtown "incubator" with five other companies, but a few months later, Sharber moved the firm to Milwaukee Junction, a former industrial neighborhood two miles north. The company's new home was a huge brick loft behind the old Ford Piquette Avenue Plant, the factory where the Model T car was born in 1908. Sharber not only moved GreenLancer there, but he, his partner, and several employees lived in the loft while operating the company, oblivious to regulations—no permits, no business licenses, no taxes, no inspectors. The cost: five hundred dollars a month in rent.

"I had this entire company working out of that loft on Grand Boulevard next to I-75 behind the old Piquette plant," he says. "It was an old commercial building that you weren't supposed to be living in, but we set up in there and it was one of those 'turn a blind eye' kind of things for the landlord. It was beautiful, with twenty-foot-tall red brick walls and nine people working there. Everyone had keys and we worked from 6 AM to 11 PM." Some employees stayed there 24/7, sleeping in hammocks.

By 2013, GreenLancer had become so successful it could no longer operate under the radar. The company had won a high-profile award that year at the Solar Power International conference, and been interviewed by the BBC, CNBC, and Detroit's Fox affiliate. The media recognition was leveraged to secure one million dollars in start-up loans from Bizdom, a local venture capital firm set up by Detroit native and Quicken Loans CEO Dan Gilbert, but it meant that anonymity was over.

"Everything is under a microscope now," says Sharber about GreenLancer, which surpassed $1.5 million in revenue in 2014. "But starting out here was completely critical. If we hadn't done it in Detroit, we could have never have done it at all. Or it wouldn't be what it is today." Sharber himself has upgraded from the loft days, moving into a renovated 1917 schoolhouse near Eastern Market, where classrooms were turned into 1,700-square-foot luxury condos "with granite countertops, hardwood floors, and a Jacuzzi." Monthly rent: $1,700, including all utilities, internet access, and secure parking.

UNOFFICIALLY SANCTIONED

City officials in Detroit readily admit they don't have the resources to inspect or enforce regulations everywhere in the city, and especially where an underground economy has emerged in marginal areas. "You put your resources where they are the most needed," says city business development manager Mark Denson. "You don't have the resources to police and inspect those least viable parts of town that the 'creatives' find attractive."

Denson is a top official for the Detroit Economic Growth Corporation, the private-public partnership that, among other things, attracts new companies to Detroit. Working for the city, DEGC also provides staff to a half dozen of Detroit's public development entities like the Downtown Development Authority and the Economic Development Corporation.

The city's main concern with enforcing ordinances and regulations is public safety, says Denson, but it has not been blind to the emergence of a millennial workforce and its impact on the city's economy.

"There are parts of town [where] people are buying huge buildings for next to nothing and converting them illegally sort of, kind of, just under the radar," he says. "What happens is that these early adopters, these edge-living people, are highly educated, and they are creating these kinds of [business] opportunities that are as much about social responsibility as they are about making a profit. So, a cadre of people are building jobs, and the more people they attract like themselves, the more this place becomes a hotbed of employment, because the employers want to be near these kind of people."

The result, says Denson, is that the city does indeed look the other way, at least a little bit. "I do think that the city has developed a mind-set where you want to get out of the way and allow organic development to occur," he says. "I think that we have found a happy medium of allowing things to occur with minimal oversight from the city. So, yeah, you can build something, but eventually the city will come back and say, hey, you need to move that wall two feet to the left, or you need to build that fence to account for fire protection."

Ponyride's Cooley recalls how, when he first started Slows Bar Bq in 2005, the city was even more laissez-faire than it is today. Cooley originally applied for a change-of-use permit, something he felt he couldn't avoid because he was opening his restaurant on high-profile thoroughfare Michigan Avenue just outside the core downtown. That triggered an ordinance requiring he provide on-site parking for the restaurant's maximum seating by bulldozing an adjacent building. This in a city—including Michigan Avenue itself—that was perforated by the empty lots of demolished buildings. It took eight months to get a variance from the planning and zoning board; after that, Cooley simply didn't bring things to the attention of the city.

"They didn't hassle us on the demolition," says Cooley of his next step, for which he did not pull a permit. Cooley had learned the lesson of lean—if you simply act and keep quiet, there's usually little interference. These were also the wild years of maverick mayor Kwame Kilpatrick, who was later sentenced to decades of jail time for extorting payoffs and looting public funds. "One thing that worked out for us was that he [Kilpatrick] didn't overpolice you. He didn't go after the little guy. He let us do our thing," says Cooley.

The only conversation that Cooley ever had with Kilpatrick was the day the mayor drove past Slows during construction. "He stopped and asked what was going on. We had dropped the façade and had a bobcat in the pit. I was digging in the hole. He slowed down, stopped, and looked down the hole," says Cooley. "He just shook his head and drove on. I guess he knew he couldn't get any money out of us."

While such things are relative, Cooley says Detroit is already emerging from its regulation-free-for-all environment. "We are talking night and day from Kwame Kilpatrick," he says of later years. In 2014, for example, the Detroit Historic Commission issued Cooley a $1,000 citation for building the rear entrance to a historic building before they had issued a permit. With winter coming, along with expected approval, Cooley had the entrance constructed a few months early. Because it was actually built according to code and historic regulations, the fine was reduced to $500.

"The question is, how does government get out of the way and be supportive, but at the same time fulfill its mission of protecting the public?" asks city official Denson. "A lot of people who come to Detroit right now think 'blank slate,' 'blank canvas,' 'the frontier'—all those analogies. They're wrong . . . We can't assume people will do the responsible thing. That's why you have these regulations. That's why it's called civilization."

Having said that, Denson—a third-generation Detroiter who lives downtown—admits that he keeps a local, unsanctioned farm on speed dial. "I get my eggs there. It's a farm on Alexandrine [street] . . . you'd drive by and not see it, but he has chickens and crops . . ." Likewise, he says, "There is a whole apartment community in Corktown where two weeks ago I went to a bonfire—in the middle of the city. There was a stack of wood three feet tall, and there were literally goats running around. There were people in an Airstream selling food. Where were the regulations there? There were none—and they know who I am."

IT TAKES A VILLAGE

Because Detroit has so much vacant space, so few supermarkets, and so much surplus labor (in 2009 and 2010, unemployment levels exceeded those of the Great Depression), the practice of urban farming has taken root like nowhere else. According to FoodLab Detroit, a coalition of food entrepreneurs, as of 2015 there were 1,500 "community market" and school gardens in the city—and these did not include thousands of small, private gardens. All over the metropolis, like sod-busting pioneers of the Old West, citizens are using vacant spaces to plant crops; a city program that allows homeowners to buy adjacent lots for $100 to $500 each has accelerated the process.

One neighborhood that has become a virtual farming village is Brightmoor, located in the northwest quadrant of Detroit. Because it is so distant from the high-profile downtown and cultural cores, it is a largely unregulated area where locals have taken affairs into their own hands.

At the center of the Brightmoor community is Knuckle Head Farm, an appropriately named bed-and-breakfast with three acres of land reclaimed over the years in a neighborhood once overrun with drug houses. Its proprietor, a stout, handsome native of Holland named Riet Schumack, moved to the neighborhood with her husband in 2006 with the idea of doing some urban farming. There was certainly plenty of available space.

"When we moved in, in 2006, I have to say the worst [of the drug epidemic] was over," she says. "Most of the horror stories are from the eighties and nineties. That was when this place was beyond belief. There are probably fifteen empty lots just on this street, and the neighbors next door saw every house turned into a drug house and then burned."

Brightmoor had originally been a neighborhood of small, one-bedroom homes built for Ford workers drafted from the Appalachian regions of West Virginia and Tennessee in the early twentieth century. By the 1980s, with jobs drying up, the children and grandchildren of the original settlers began moving to the suburbs, and the housing became rentals for poor blacks. Then the crack epidemic broke out and swept through the neighborhood.

"That's when crime rates skyrocketed, and that's when whites started moving out unless they were poor and old," says Schumack. Residents who remained treated their homes like private Fort Apaches in hostile territory. "Those who stayed, barricaded and kept to themselves. And now the black population is moving out because the housing—whatever there was in rentals—burned down."

The burning of houses in Detroit—whether as an act of initiation for gang membership, a ploy to collect insurance, or the consequence of unsafe heating practices in homes without electricity—has been rampant for decades. Episodes of arson actually became a city tradition; for more than thirty years, the night before Halloween was known as "Devil's Night," with hundreds of homes going up in flames. The peak came in the mid-1980s, when an average of eight hundred houses were being torched the night before trick-or-treating.

Thanks to forty thousand to fifty thousand community volunteers who now patrol their streets on Devil's Night, the number of arsons has dropped to a few score. But the annual level has remained stubbornly high. According to the Detroit Fire Department, the average number of arsons throughout the 2000s has hovered at around five thousand per year. That has begun to fall, with just under four thousand arsons in 2014.

Not surprisingly, the charred houses became part of Detroit's landscape of blight. According to city records, two-thirds of the houses burned from 2010 to 2013 are still standing. Fire, however, is no longer the biggest worry of the Brightmoor community these days. Of greater concern are foreclosures and house strippers.

"When the housing market collapsed, a lot of people had [expensive] mortgages on their homes, so they lost them, and then a lot of people just didn't pay taxes. They just up and left. And people got old and died or moved to nursing homes," says Schumack. And when a house was abandoned, the strippers—or "scrappers," as they are known locally—denuded the house of metal piping and wiring. It is a practice that continues unabated today.

"As soon as a house is vacant even twenty-four hours, the scrappers come in. They make it unusable even for squatters. They will break open the walls to get the electric wires out, and they will take all the plumbing out, so there is nothing left. They will destroy an entire toilet just for the metal parts in it," says Schumack. "It's horrible."

The solution to deal with both scrappers and drug dealers has been a neighborhood vigil born of gardening. When drug dealers attempt to use an abandoned house, the neighborhood response is to start a garden in a nearby lot, creating an observable presence, and calling the police whenever suspicious activity takes place. Police eventually respond when residents start calling three and four times a day, day after day. As for keeping the scrappers at bay, the idea is to keep up appearances. When one Brightmoor house was left empty after the owner had a stroke, the garden club boarded up its windows and doors, kept the yard mowed, and patrolled it regularly.

In addition to the lots the Schumacks assembled for their own garden—and for the Brightmoor Youth Garden, where fifteen

to twenty kids grow food each season for the Farmington Farmers Market—they have purchased and rehabbed two houses in the
neighborhoods. Both are now rentals. The first house cost them just
$1,000, but then, says Shumack, "We spent $3,500 on permits and
we hadn't done anything yet. So guess what, the next house we didn't
ask for any permits, we just fixed it."

The same goes for a new wave of "young hippies"—as Schumack
calls them—who are moving into the neighborhood. "In the last
three or four years, ten households have moved in here, kids moving
into five-hundred-dollar houses that have been stripped," Schumack
says. "And they live without water or electricity sometimes for
months. They don't want to owe anybody any money. They want to
be self-sustaining and live simply. So they immediately start gardens and start growing things." They also live without certificates of
occupancy, using "buckets and composting" until plumbing can be
installed. Such is the hardscrabble life of the New Pioneer.

One thing that neighbors never do is call inspectors. That's the
last thing they want. "As long as people don't make a mess, we are
not going to tattle on anybody," says Schumack. "If people are really
making a mess, we try to work with them first before we tattle."
Occasionally there is a screwup, she says, such as when one house-
hold was raising eighteen baby goats. The goat's owners thought it
was so cute they invited a *New York Times* reporter to do a story on
the urban farm. When the reporter asked the mayor's office how this
was possible in a city where goats are illegal, the city had no choice
but to shut down the goat farm.

Such incidents have resulted in a "don't ask, don't tell" mentality
in the neighborhood.

ANARCHY AND ARCHIPELAGOS

Similar to Brightmoor, residents in other neighborhoods have banded
together and formed what amount to anarchist guilds, or loose asso-
ciations of pioneer vigilantes. In one of the "clear-cut" neighborhoods

near Eastern Market, for example, where in block after block only one or two houses remain standing, one street of intact buildings stands out. The street is home to a commune of Finnish artists, and every house is groomed. All the residents are also connected by cell phone. If there is suspicious activity on the street, an alert goes out, and anybody who is home emerges onto their porch, or starts strolling down the sidewalk. In their role as scarecrows, unoccupied houses are brightly painted like the others, with their yards maintained and filled with sculpture.

You can define anarchy in several ways, but all of them, like the raw frontier that eighteenth- and nineteenth-century pioneers faced, imply the absence of a controlling central government. The more pessimistic pundits see anarchy as a fast track to lawless turmoil. The more optimistic see anarchy as a passport to utopias where central authority is replaced by informal, self-governing networks based on common sense and consensual relationships. Detroit exhibits both.

On the one hand, it is a city of violent crime (five to six times the national average), where police resources are stretched wafer thin. On the other hand, it is a city of self-policing volunteers, propelled by the same spirit that fielded bucket brigades when a neighbor's house caught fire on the American prairie.

Throughout Detroit there is a feeling that the authorities have fled, and that it's up to the inhabitants left behind to establish their own mechanisms of order. There is a distinct feeling that a power vacuum exists and must be filled.

Not far from Slows Bar Bq on Michigan Avenue is the former home of the Detroit Tigers professional baseball team. It is now a fenced-off, empty field; in 2000 the Tigers moved to Comerica Park, a new stadium about a mile to the east on the edge of the central business district it hoped, but failed, to revive.

Vacant spaces surround the old field. These are not the result of decay or abandonment; these empty spaces were deliberately carved out to generate income. For nearly a century, anyone with property adjacent to Tiger Stadium could make more money renting parking spaces for the eighty home games played there each year than from renting retail or residential space all year.

Despite efforts to save the original stadium, it was finally demolished in 2009, ten years after the last game was played there. The city had no funds to maintain the structure, or even the baseball diamond when that was all that remained. But rather than go fallow, the field has been kept up by a quasi-legal volunteer organization known as the Navin Field Grounds Crew, composed of die-hard baseball fans and local residents of the ballpark's Corktown neighborhood.

"The field is still there and people keep it up and take care of it," says architect Mark Nickita, an urban planner and Detroit retail entrepreneur. "It's a grassroots effort by very strong baseball fans that break in sort of legally—not legally, really—and mow the lawn. They are like 'Friends of Tiger Stadium,' but it's not official. It's a bunch of people who love the field and know that it's sacred to baseball. The point is that the stadium is there, completely locked in and surrounded by a gate, and these people go in the summer months and keep it up and play on it and have little games. But it's all unofficial."

At the close of 2014, the city approved a $33 million plan by private developers to fill in the streets that surround the old field with a mixed-use, low-rise complex of retail stores, small apartments, and townhouses. The Police Athletic League would run the field. As of mid-2015, however, nothing had been done, so the baseball fanatics continued to maintain it, taking things into their own hands without permission—or the administrative fees, liability insurance, permit costs, business licenses, etc., that would make such an effort prohibitively expensive.

Directly north of the CBD lies Midtown, an area now lively with residents. This is the neighborhood where Whole Foods decided to place the only full-service supermarket in Detroit's city core. (The store itself, opened in 2013, was made with wood from Reclaimed Detroit.)

One reason so many people live in Midtown today is because small developers operated code free there for years—a situation now coming under some scrutiny—and were thus able to create affordable housing. Another reason is its proximity to Wayne State University, or more precisely its campus police force. Because so many students live in the neighborhood (the school has an enrollment of 28,000), campus security forces have extended their umbrella beyond the campus itself.

"This area is probably the safest place around, because this is all Wayne State, near the Wayne State campus," explains Scott Wright, a bartender at the neighborhood's Motor City Brewing Works. "If we called the Detroit Police Department it would take forever for anyone to get here. Wayne State has its own police department, so if I call Wayne State they'll be here at the drop of a dime. They're fast."

A similar private security force has improved safety in Gilbertown, a nickname for the CBD in deference to Quicken Loans CEO Dan Gilbert, who has moved 12,000 employees there since 2012. This area is now patrolled 24/7 by company security officers who also monitor three hundred surveillance cameras from a control center.

On both large and small scales, Detroit's recovery is based on a series of emerging nodules or clusters, self-sustaining and self-policing pioneer settlements that at some point will connect with collective webbing. As an urban planner, architect Nickita maintains maps of these emerging neighborhoods, streets, intersections, and corridors, groupings that he calls archipelagoes that feed off of each other.

"All of these little small-scale movements are happening in different locations and parts of the city," says Nickita. "It's really at different levels, but it's based on the common understanding of a series of small start-up companies or communities, retail oriented, or food oriented, or design oriented, or technology oriented. But there is a cohesive synergy. Detroit is currently in an all-hands-on-deck reboot."

The stretch of Michigan Avenue where Slows Bar Bq went into business in 2005, for example, has since sprouted a coffee bar (Astro Coffee) and a pub (Sugar House). Directly across the street, there is now another eatery (Mercury Burger & Bar), a bicycle shop, a furniture store, and a salon. All were empty when Slows first started smoking brisket.

RECYCLING A CITY

Not a block away from the Motor City Brewing Works in Midtown is the Green Garage, a former Model T showroom that is exemplary of another lean trend in Detroit—the city's cutting-edge obsession with recycling itself. In a nod to the concept of using the local vernacular, as well as to the practice of parsimoniously using local, available materials, the New Pioneers of Detroit are recycling the buried resources of the city.

Tom and Peggy Brennan—he an engineer, she a librarian—purchased the Green Garage in 2008 for what Tom calls "a deep exploration of sustainability in an urban area." At the time, it was an abandoned warehouse that had been stripped by scrappers. "There was nothing here, not even windows," says Tom. "There was a ceiling and concrete floors, but nothing left of the electrical, nothing left of the plumbing . . . It was on the national register of historic places as a Model T showroom, but it would have been torn down. That would have been the answer."

Instead, the Brennans meticulously rehabilitated the building, restoring its handsome brick façade, installing windows that had been boarded up, and removing a drop ceiling to reveal roof beams honed from the ancient forests of Michigan. And they did almost all of it using materials recycled from the building itself, and from the city of Detroit. Insulation piled on top of the drop ceiling was used in the walls; wood for flooring and benches was taken from oak, ash, and walnut trees knocked down in Detroit by major windstorms; cabinets and tables came from a Catholic school that had been demolished; steel windows and glass came from a shuttered power plant and an abandoned Cadillac factory. "Everything here would have been in a landfill," says Tom.

Because theirs was a prominent, deliberately high-profile project, the Brennans decided to work with the city rather than fly beneath the radar. And because they had the funding to be patient (the rebuild took three years and one million dollars), the Brennans worked to educate planning officials in order to be granted variances.

For example, instead of using asphalt for a pocket parking lot and an alleyway that connects the Green Garage to the Motor City Brewing Works, they used paver stones that allow rainwater to seep into the aquifer naturally. This was a big concession from the city; its ordinances require all lots to be paved with asphalt to create runoff for the municipal water purification plant, since important revenues are derived from processing this "sewer" water. But the Brennans were able to educate city officials about the value of natural drainage. Likewise, the requirement for emergency interior lighting was waived for light-amplifying "solar tubes" in the roof.

The building also uses heat pumps and solar panels, with piping under the floor, to save energy costs. Tom says the building is exemplary "green," using just a tenth of the energy typically consumed by a building its size. In terms of construction expense, however, little was saved—labor costs ate up the money that would have been spent on new, high-tech materials. "It cost about the same as it would have to knock this building down and construct a new, non-efficient building here," says Peggy. "It nets out to the same, but here you are shifting money from materials to labor, and we have a high unemployment rate in Detroit, so isn't that a good idea?"

The Green Garage now acts as an incubator for start-up companies involved on some level with sustainability. Like Ponyride, the Green Garage gives small enterprises the ability to gain traction before they are weighed down by the expenses of a traditional workspace.

New companies can start with as little as a single chair at a long table and evolve into cubicles or small offices at the back of the main space before being released into the wild.

There are also three small manufacturing companies in a side section of the building called "the makers' space." One builds steel-guitar pedals; another assembles furniture; the third is an old-fashioned printing shop. "We make things here," says Peggy, referring not just to the Green Garage but to the city as a whole. Like the word "opportunity," it is a leitmotif you hear over and over again in Detroit: We are a city that makes things.

Most of that "making" in the past has come in the form of massive factories, dinosaurs in today's landscape of tiny start-ups in the new Detroit technopolis. Things that are made today are made by hand, or in tiny shops, surprisingly similar to self-sufficient pioneer communities with their blacksmiths, craftspeople, and carpenters. It's these diminutive, pioneering ventures the Brennans hope to catalyze by providing a platform for the small.

"When cities are starting anew, the new sprouts come out organically in ways that are not supported through the zoning requirements and ordinances," says Tom, commiserating with the travails of start-ups. "The ordinances are so onerous that a start-up has no chance."

FoodLab Detroit is one "sustainable" enterprise for which Green Garage has provided an inexpensive platform. FoodLab is a nonprofit that helps small entrepreneurs in the food business, from urban gardeners to distributors to retail vendors. A good example of their work is a partnership called Detroit Kitchen Connect, spearheaded by FoodLab's codirector and "Chief Cultivator," Devita Davison.

One of the salient physical patterns of Detroit is the survival of its churches. Even in the most demolished neighborhoods, its churches stand, unscathed monuments to a faith-based past. They line central Woodward Avenue like a parade of immaculate soldiers, from the Historic Little Rock Baptist Church, to Temple Beth El, to the Cathedral Church of St. Paul. What Davison grasped was that some of these churches had large, industrial kitchen facilities that were sitting idle. So she connected capital-poor entrepreneurs with these capital resources.

"We realized that underutilized assets were lying dormant in our neighborhoods," says Davison. "So why don't we just activate them?" And that is just what she and FoodLab did, she explains, conjoining cooks with churches as a part of a broader vision to "connect low-income people to economic opportunities wherever they exist" and "assessing the assets available at the time and making the best of what you got."

One of Kitchen Connect's success stories is April Anderson, who was trying to launch a baking business from her home kitchen. "I was having to turn down orders because I didn't have enough space," she says. Now Anderson is the proud proprietor of Good Cakes and Bakes on Livernois Avenue, a large bakery she opened in 2014 to sell the goodies that she baked in the basement of the Ss. Peter and Paul Church. It has display cases of her popular red velvet cupcakes, sweet potato cakes, and pecan pies (not to mention the coconut, carrot, and German chocolate cakes). Her reputation became so widespread that it attracted a stopover from Bill Clinton when he spoke at a Michigan Democratic fundraiser in Detroit.

Another success story is Chloé Sabatier, a French woman who moved to Detroit to begin a bakery on a shoestring budget. Through FoodLab she was able to access the same kitchen as Anderson, where she began baking two hundred chocolate "molten" lava cakes a week for sale at Eastern Market.

"What happened to her was, when she was selling at Eastern Market, a gentleman came over to taste the cakes and ended up buying a dozen of them. He took them back to his offices at Air France, where he shared them with the executive team," says Davison. Today Sabatier's lava cakes are available for all first-class passengers on flights from Detroit to Paris, and Sabatier's business has taken off.

"These are women-owned businesses and minority-owned businesses," says Davison. "We lower the barriers to entry so that they can do what they do. We're giving them an opportunity to practice in a lean way."

The idea that Detroit can bootstrap its way to a new economy based on recycling itself is as pervasive in the city as the idea that its natives were born to build things. Back down the alleyway from FoodLab Detroit's incubator space at Green Garage, the Motor City Brewing Works bar lives by the same playbook.

Originally started as a local brewery in 1994, it added a kitchen in 1997. The bar today is a quilt work of wood, tiles, and windows clearly plucked from different demolished buildings and reassembled. "It's been pieced together throughout the years, adding to it little by little," says barkeep Scott Wright. Besides providing beer brewed on-site, all greens on the menu are grown at a community garden a few blocks away—which the bar/eatery provides with compost from the leavings of its brewing process.

During its first decade, says Wright, the city completely ignored the bar as it built out on the edge of a cratered parking lot. Then, a few years ago, the area began to prosper, with a cluster of retail stores opening next door—places like City Bird (gifts made by local artisans), Nest (housewares), Willys Detroit (clothing), and an outlet for Shinola, the high-end watchmaker based in Detroit. "At that point, code inspectors starting coming in, writing up all sorts of code violations," says Wright. "I think they were here just to collect some revenues." Fortunately, by then, the bar could afford the tab.

SALVAGING THE LOVELY BONES

In addition to his work as an architect and city planner, Mark Nickita recycles the culture of Detroit, and does so in the bellies of the monumental structures that remain. A native of the Motor City, Nickita lives with his family in suburban Birmingham, Michigan, where he was elected mayor. His offices remain in downtown Detroit, however, where he has created a string of small businesses that occupy and reprocess the city's impressive past.

In the downtown Guardian Building, a block south of Campus Martius, Nickita and his partners have three businesses: Stella Good Coffee, the Rowland Cafe, and Pure Detroit. Stella, with another branch in the Fisher Building in Midtown, occupies a small space in the lobby of the building. But both the Rowland Cafe and Pure Detroit occupy the building's grand atrium, a magnificent, fifty-foot-high arched space that once housed bank tellers when the building first opened in 1929 as the headquarters for Union Trust. The forty-story Art Deco landmark is considered one of the must-see attractions of Detroit.

The building is also known as the "Cathedral of Finance," and if it is indeed the church of business, then the atrium acts as the nave. The end of its colossal expanse is adorned with a gigantic mural by Ezra Winter entitled *Michigan*. In the mural's center stands an Athena-like divinity—presumably the goddess of capitalism—with rays of light emanating like spokes to all the important sectors of Michigan's economy: Lumbering, Agriculture, Manufacture, Commerce, Fishing, Mining, and Finance.

"A lower threshold [for starting a business] is clearly here in Detroit," says Nickita. "But it's not just what you can get as an entry-level cost. Yes, a storefront can be had for a lower price [than in Detroit's tony suburbs]. But what you get, in terms of a building, is so much more significant."

Occupying center stage of the Guardian's main space (along with some actual bank tellers at one end, in deference to its former incarnation) is Nickita's Rowland Cafe, with an open espresso bar, leather couches, and small black tables and chairs. Adjacent, behind glass walls that line the great room, is one of his four Pure Detroit stores.

Launched in 1998—the year that Nickita sees as the true bottom for Detroit's decline—the store's mission is to promote everything from, of, and about Detroit. "The idea is that it's a place for all things Detroit," he says. "We don't consider it a gift shop or tourist shop. It's a culture shop, promoting the culture of the city: food, drink, art, and architecture." In addition to books about Detroit, products made in Detroit (hot fudge, historic tiles), and T-shirts emblazoned with the city's name, the shop sells a popular line of women's purses woven from seat belts, and pant belts that use vintage seat belt buckles in place of standard buckles.

At one end of the store is the actual sign from the downtown bottling factory of local ginger ale maker Vernors, with a picture of the iconic Vernors gnome, Woody. "They tore the building down and someone saw the scraps in the pile and said, 'Hey, what are you doing with all these panels?' They said he could have them, and my partner bought them from that guy. This is the actual section of the wall from the factory."

The Guardian Building location for Pure Detroit was not the first one Nickita opened in 1998 but was store number three, opening in 2006 when the Guardian Building was restored. Store four was opened in 2014 at the old aquarium on Belle Isle, a large public island in the Detroit River that serves as the city's Central Park (and was in fact designed by the same landscape architect, Frederick Law Olmsted).

Further uptown, in an area known as New Center, Nickita has a second Stella Good Coffee location in the Fisher building. It was here that he assayed a pop-up furniture store that was, and remains, symbolic for a city digesting itself. Called simply Workshop, it was started with James Willer, the (then) head of Reclaim Detroit, a nonprofit that deconstructs rather than demolishes houses in the city.

The idea behind Workshop was to create unique modern furniture pieces from the lumber of dismantled old homes. Each table was imprinted with the location of the house torn down, as well as the date of construction.

"We created a couple of products, put it out there, and it was a big hit. It was a pop-up store, but we kept it open," says Nickita. "Now it's not only open but expanding, and we have agreements with furniture stores on a wholesale basis."

For Willer, Workshop was a practical outlet for his years of frustrating attempts to convince the city to recycle rather than demolish its vast stock of empty and abandoned housing. As far back as the early 2000s, Willer appealed to the city administration to divert funds earmarked for demolition. "All they had to do was change the word from demolition to deconstruction, but no one would," he laments.

Willer realized that a wealth of materials, especially lumber, was locked up in Detroit's eighty thousand abandoned houses. "Some people say that the wealth of the white pines in Michigan was more than all the gold harvested in California," he says. "You've got ten thousand board feet of raw lumber [in each house] times eighty thousand houses. Even at a low level of one dollar per board foot, that's close to a billion dollars of value in these houses, and that's at wholesale. If it's processed into something more valuable, it adds multiples of two, three, four . . ."

Finally, when a friend of Willer's secured a grant from Henry Ford College to train workers for construction jobs in Detroit, he convinced them to set up a nonprofit deconstruction company, Reclaim Detroit, to actually employ them.

Willer left Reclaim in 2012, again frustrated by its slow pace of harvesting just a half-dozen homes in two years—at a time when the city was starting to pay for thousands of teardowns annually. Indeed, by 2014, the city was tearing down four thousand houses a year, and paying $10,000 for each demolition. Since it cost $20,000 to deconstruct a house, and its lumber at face value is worth only $10,000, the stipend from the city was essential—but not forthcoming.

"Yes, it does cost more to deconstruct," says Willer. "But in demolition you are paying for the machines to do the work. In deconstruction you pay people to do the work."

For its part, the city doesn't have the patience to wait for the slow process of deconstruction, or for the time it will take to train enough workers to make an impact. So Willer has taken a private approach, using Workshop as a way to add value to the recycled remains of the city's carpet of century-old housing, once home to battalions of factory workers.

"People see [these houses] as part of our throwaway culture. We're opening the eyes to designers that this is beautiful lumber," he says. "We hand select each piece and turn it into a customized piece of furniture."

BIG FISH, LITTLE POND

It doesn't make sense to call the power to invest a billion dollars into a city a "lean" process, nor does it resemble the scrappy approach of a wilderness pioneer, but from the standpoint of billionaire Dan Gilbert, Detroit has been an investment into the wilds of urban decay with stunningly low thresholds.

Gilbert forged a multibillion-dollar empire out of selling mortgages online. His Quicken Loans was the first home-loan firm to go online in a big way, back in 1989. For him, timing proved key: He and his partners sold the company for $532 million in 1999, just before the dot.com collapse of 2000, and bought it back in 2002 for $64 million. A decade later, it was closing $70 billion a year in mortgage loans, and by 2013, the company's annual revenues were $3.6 billion.

In the build out of Quicken, Gilbert housed most of his employees in suburban Detroit. But when the company needed to expand, the lure of low-cost downtown buildings became irresistible—even with substantial upgrades, he could keep expenses to $150 a foot for quality commercial office space, compared to building it from scratch for $400 a square foot. So he began moving employees downtown in 2010, and started to buy buildings there in 2011. As of mid-2015, he had 12,000 employees downtown, including 6,500 new hires, and he owned seventy-five buildings, all within a one-mile radius.

Gilbert had another reason to move downtown, and to participate in the revival of Detroit: He was beginning to find it hard to attract millennial employees to his suburban location. They wanted to live in exciting, edgy cities like New York and Chicago—the kind of place that downtown Detroit was becoming.

"More than anything else, Dan Gilbert is saving Detroit to help his business," wrote the *Wall Street Journal* in 2014, noting that Gilbert was running out of young recruits when he decided to relocate to the city's CBD. This is not to say that Gilbert has not contributed a major boost to downtown Detroit's revival. Indeed, in 2010, 78,000 people worked there, and by 2016 that number was expected to reach 100,000, thanks largely to Quicken's CEO. But in the eternal debate of chicken vs. egg, and in the context of Lean Urbanism and the city's New Pioneers, Gilbert arrived *after* the initial wave of risk-oblivious millennial pilgrims had landed and begun to forge a new city.

"Gilbert's movement of inviting people to come, and having them intern [his companies employ 1,200 interns a year] worked well to grow the downtown population," says architect Nickita. "But I think a lot of the people doing the entrepreneurial stuff were doing it before he stepped up his investment cycle . . . He came in with a vengeance, but he wasn't here first."

What distinguishes Gilbert from other top-down mega-investors in Detroit—men like Henry Ford II with his Renaissance Center, or Michael Ilitch Sr. (founder of Little Caesars) with his Comerica Park and Greektown Casino—is that Gilbert understood that the future belonged to the millennials, the workforce of today's and tomorrow's technology revolution, the very people pioneering Detroit's urban frontier.

That vision of Detroit becoming a vital center in the high-tech revolution is not far off the mark, according to the Brookings Institution. In several 2015 reports, Brookings identified Detroit as one of the hotbeds for "advanced industries" that will rely heavily on software development. In one "paradigm" report that ranked US cities in terms of their commitment to R&D and STEM (science, technology, engineering, and math) workers, Detroit came in fourth—bested only by San Jose, Seattle, and Wichita. The reason? "Underneath the prevailing narrative of Detroit as a Rust Belt ghost town is a busy metro area marrying its industrial past to a digital future," according to the assessment.

"Detroit was the epicenter of the American Industrial Revolution," says GreenLancer's millennial CEO Sharber. "Now it's at the center of the whole transformation from the industrial era to high technology."

In another 2015 report comparing Detroit to Silicon Valley, Brookings noted that more than 32,000 professionals in the metro area were employed in the computer design sector alone; it also noted that GM—still one of Detroit's biggest employers—had filed for 592 software patents between 2010 and 2015. The trend: That all manufactured devices, including cars, will become increasingly linked to software programming, in both the manufacturing process and the end-user experience. And for that work, you need a workforce of educated millennials, just the type of people who've been attracted to Detroit's lean, bohemian scene, where the city puts two fixer-up houses up for auction each day at $1,000 each. It doesn't get any more roll-up-your-sleeves pioneering than that.

Some of this trend shows up in the demographics of Greater Downtown Detroit, a 7.2-square-mile area that includes the Central Business District and the adjacent neighborhoods of Midtown, Woodbridge, Corktown, Lafayette Park, and Rivertown. Combined, these districts and their 36,500 residents contain virtually all the academic, cultural, business, sports, and medical centers in the city.

Between 2000 and 2010, the population in this core declined, but at half the precipitous rate for the rest of Detroit—a drop of 13 percent compared to 25 percent citywide. Looking more deeply into the numbers, part of Greater Downtown actually increased in population during that time—namely the CBD, which grew by 24 percent, 29 percent, and 9 percent, depending on the sub-neighborhood.

Just as important are the characteristics of that growth. As a share of population in the Greater Downtown, two groups grew: residents between the ages of 18 and 24, and those over 55—the millennials and the empty nesters. The 25-to-34-year-old group held fairly steady, while the middle-aged segment (35 to 54) shrank, relatively speaking.

Greater Downtown is also where young professionals are choosing to live. Whereas only 1 percent of the total population of Detroit is between the ages of 25 and 34 and college-educated (as of 2010), that figure jumps to 8 percent in the Greater Downtown, and to 24 percent in the core CBD. It is here—where new business growth and adaptive reuse are the fruit of the New Pioneer efforts—that residential occupancy now stands at 98 percent.

This anomaly has not been lost on employers such as Microsoft, Twitter, and CompuServe, all of which currently have operations in downtown Detroit. These would-be employers are banking that millennials will remain attracted by both the culturally authentic experience of Detroit and its amazingly low cost of living, a key low threshold for entry. According to *Forbes*, earning just $43,000 in Detroit is the equivalent of a $100,000 salary in New York or a $142,000 paycheck in San Francisco. Everything costs less in Detroit, especially housing. Combine that with the still-pervasive absence of regulatory enforcement everywhere except downtown, and you set the stage for the New Pioneers to arrive, thrive, and rebuild one of America's great cities.

chapter two

THE COTTON DISTRICT AND SEASIDE: THE TIME MACHINES

The Power of Slow to Build Organic Value

The Cotton District in Starkville, Mississippi, and the town of Seaside in Walton County, Florida, share remarkable similarities. Both are small, dense, and beautifully crafted urban communities, exemplary of the New Urbanism mixed-use holy grail of walkability. Both were also created by visionary New Pioneers who developed these communities over several decades, with almost no initial capital—but with no initial zoning or building codes. Neither could be built today, but both illustrate the incredible power of lone pioneers when they are untethered from regulatory constraints.

In both cases, the opportunity for New Pioneers was provided by the low cost of land and the indifference of local government. The Cotton District was an urban slum. The properties were cheap, and city officials weren't concerned with code compliance. The land for Seaside was more desirable, but still relatively inexpensive due to its remote location. Its rural locale also left it a code-free zone ignored by the county government.

Each of the communities created wealth in a gradual way that did not require a substantial initial investment or overbearing debt. As each structure came online, it made previous structures (and the land) more valuable, providing a basis for the capital needed to grow. In the case of rental housing or sales, it also created cash flow.

Operating off the grid, both the Cotton District and Seaside were able to develop communities not unlike early settlements in America, where new towns were constructed by small builders, where buildings were designed to a human scale, and where homes were built not to flip but to occupy. The result was a craftsmanship and sense of aesthetics that created places where people wanted to live. These are the kinds of communities buildable by New Pioneers from the raw resources of the frontier, both literally and figuratively. They also are tales of the power of one, unbound.

Hand Crafted: The Cotton District has the feeling of an old European city, only in the middle of rustic, permit-lax Mississippi.

Lean Start-ups: New retailers in Seaside enjoy lower thresholds to entry, joining the community's Central Square in Airstream trailers.

THE COTTON DISTRICT:
A WORLD OF ITS OWN

When Dan Camp received the Arthur Ross Award for Community Design in 2000, one of the celebrities at the New York City event was actress and spokeswoman for the arts Kitty Carlisle. When an image of his "temple" house came up, she asked Camp what the building was used for. "I said, 'Oh Kitty, that is just typical student housing in the backwaters of Mississippi,'" says Camp in his deep Southern baritone. "You should have seen her jaw drop."

Not a surprising reaction. Then, as now, the buildings of the Cotton District are unexpected for a college town in the rural South. The 150 houses that comprise this Hobbit shire on the edge of the Mississippi cotton belt create the impression of a centuries-old town, with the odd temple—as a small home—thrown in. The streets are narrow and tree lined. Many of the houses come up to the street and are close to one another.

There is substantial variety in the style of buildings: Greek Revival, Federalist, Georgian, Italianate, and some just whimsical, like a row of Bahamian-style "Key West" houses, or a small replica of the Parthenon, or a front-door overhang that looks like the teardrop of a Russian dome. The buildings vary in size as well, from columned "great" houses that contain multiple residences to tiny cottages. There are brick alleyways, miniature courtyards, surprise fountains, iron filigree, and handsome details in every structure: dormers, arches, glass transoms, Palladian windows, porches, French glass doors, lanterns, balconies, weather vanes.

While specific styles vary, all fit within the vernacular of classic Southern cityscapes found in places like Charleston, Savannah, Vicksburg, and New Orleans. The sense of time is overwhelmingly nineteenth century. And everything, even the occasional "great" house, is built small. It's like a vintage Southern neighborhood constructed at three-quarter scale—in perfect proportion, mind you—creating a sensation of Old World charm.

Most visitors to the enclave assume it's been restored from a bygone era, like some sort of Dixie Jamestown. It is, in fact, now called the Historic Cotton District. But as Camp—the man who started calling it that—well knows: "It's anything but historic." Most of the buildings were erected over the last few decades; the very first houses broke ground forty-five years ago. That's when Camp, a young college instructor at the time, had his flash of insight.

BIRTH OF A NOTION

Dan Camp was a graduate of Mississippi State University when he got the inspiration for his village. He had no idea it would grow into a model for both New Urbanism and Lean Urbanism. Back then, neither phrase had been coined.

"The most miraculous thing is the time frame when he started this, a good ten years before New Urbanism started," says Memphis architect Stephen Skinner, a former student resident of the district. "He kind of beat them to the punch."

Camp's degree was in industrial education, which meant he was qualified to teach shop and mechanical drawing and little else. One thing he did know, first employed as a high school shop instructor in Vicksburg, was that his housing situation there was ideal. He lived in a small rented townhouse. It was in a compact neighborhood where he could walk to stores and to the high school where he worked. It was an urban environment different from any he'd experienced.

"I was introduced to a town where the houses were very close to the street. It was tight and packed, really fascinating," says Camp. "And the walkability of Vicksburg was incredible. It put me on a different level of looking at things. I didn't need a car. Plus I was living next to the nursing college!"

When Camp subsequently accepted a job teaching shop at his alma mater, Mississippi State, he got his inspiration while taking summer classes for a master's degree at North Carolina State in Raleigh. Rooming in alumni housing, he discovered the nearby birthplace of Andrew Johnson. It was a small, one-room shack with a loft.

"I was staying across the street. Outside my window was this gabled roof, a typical North Carolina cottage. It was Andrew Johnson's birthplace, and being bored at the time, I paid twenty-five cents to go through it. And I thought, what a great idea to build small cottages like this for college students," says Camp. "Then I found Chapel Hill and thought I'd died and gone to heaven."

Chapel Hill, more specifically the University of North Carolina at Chapel Hill, was a liberal arts college at the height of the '60s youth revolution. The campus seemed to blend with the city streets that enveloped it. "At the time they had all these street artists, and they had the flower girls on the streets, and they were selling goods and wares. It made it a very exciting place. Right across from the campus you had all this activity going on."

Mississippi State University wasn't across from anything except for farms, woods, and a nasty shantytown then known as the Mill District. The district had once been a thriving neighborhood that housed workers from the Sanders Cotton Mill on the western edge of MSU. But the mill was long shuttered, and the neighborhood merely a drive-by embarrassment lodged between the university and the city of Starkville.

ONE MAN'S GHETTO

Anyone familiar with Mississippi knows the profound influence cotton has had on the history of the state. With its abundance of rich land and slave labor, the Deep South became a powerhouse of cotton cultivation after Eli Whitney invented his gin; Mississippi was its epicenter.

By the early 1830s, "King Cotton" exceeded all other US exports combined, and the state that produced the most was Mississippi— more than a half million pounds a year by the start of the Civil War.

Even after the war, and well into the twentieth century, cotton culti-vation remained indispensible to Mississippi's economy.

When electrical power transformed the US in the early 1900s, textile mills formerly dependent on hydropower in the Northeast moved closer to the sources of production. Mills sprang up across the Cotton Belt. One of the most powerful families in the business was the Sanders family—James and his son Robert, who operated a conglomerate of Mississippi cotton mills from 1911 to 1953.

One of the most successful of the Sanders mills was located between the business district of Starkville (population at the time: 3,000) and Mississippi A&M College, which later became Mississippi State. The mill was originally built in 1901, and purchased by the Sanders family in 1916. By 1929, with a workforce of 350, it was producing 1.5 million yards of "Starkville Chambray" for dress- and shirtmakers.

During the heyday of the 1920s, Sanders Mill District was in its own way a model of successful urbanism, a community where work, shopping, cultural life, and residential accommodations existed side by side. There was a church, a wagon shop, a blacksmith shop, a barbershop, a meat market, and a grocery. In 1925, a grade school was added, and in 1933, the Blue Goose Restaurant completed the array of amenities. It was a working-class community with middle-class aspirations, adding paved streets, sidewalks, electricity, city water, and indoor plumbing as time passed. The years of WWII were especially prosperous, as US Army demand for cloth kept the mill operating at capacity around the clock.

After the war, everything began to change. Demand dropped, the factory scaled down, and with the death of Robert Sanders in 1954, Sanders Industries sold the Starkville mill and the village houses. The new owners struggled to keep the mill open, further downscaling until finally closing it in 1962. In 1965, Mississippi State University purchased the mill and made it part of the campus; ten years later it was added to the National Registry of Historic Places. Today it is a conference center for the university.

By the time Dan Camp returned to MSU as an instructor in the late 1960s, the district had fallen into disrepair. But he saw an opportunity to buy very inexpensive property on the edge of campus and build small, high-quality housing that he could rent to students.

"This was a destitute, dilapidated area, and when I came over here, everyone said I was a damn fool," Camp recalls. But he had come across the works of economist John Kenneth Galbraith, and was convinced he could create wealth gradually, by building rental properties and retaining them as leverage for bank loans to build additional rental properties.

"I was interested in making money. I was not interested in getting to be known for what we did. I had finished reading John Kenneth Galbraith's book about money. That was a thick son of a bitch, but I read it, and it has helped make me extremely wealthy today," says Camp, a tall, bearded man who looks like a cross between director John Huston and Gandalf the Wizard from *The Lord of the Rings*. "The other thing I did was to follow my mother's advice. She would say, 'Never have a partner, and never sell anything.'"

Camp listened. He's remained stubbornly independent of the opinions of others, let alone partnering with them. As for selling, Camp has done precious little, retaining ownership of more than 100 buildings while his sons Robert and Bonn have built, and own, another two dozen.

Of great importance is how the houses were built successively over four decades, generating the gradual money the Cotton District needed to grow organically. The equity of existing housing provided capital for future projects, while rents provided cash flow. Camp is contemptuous of the modus operandi of most developers to build and sell, or to upgrade and flip, instead of choosing a gradual, incremental approach to growth and development.

Camp began with a row of townhouses, using a design based on a streetscape he saw in Alexandria, Virginia. He built eight units on a side street that was literally a stone's throw from the campus. After that, he never looked back.

"It took a little while to get the first eight units going, but then I went up to the corner, bought another piece of property there, and built a duplex," says Camp. At the time, the city of Starkville, desperate to clean up the mess of the Mill District—which Camp later redubbed as the "better sounding" Cotton District—designated the area as an Urban Renewal zone in 1967. This sparked redevelopment of properties along the arterial University Drive between the city and the campus, which became convenience stores, apartment complexes, gas stations, and sandwich shops. But most of the small properties on the winding side streets were ignored. And they were for sale at rock-bottom prices.

"What would happen is that all the people that the Urban Renewal did not buy from came to me and said, 'We'd like you to buy this.' So I would accumulate property because of them soliciting me, not me soliciting them," says Camp. "People would say, 'How can you stand to buy all that trash over there?' But I had good bank credit, so I was able to accumulate enough stuff to build what I wanted." With the Cotton Mill worker's ghetto as his raw frontier, Camp became its trailblazing pioneer.

THE DOING OF THINGS

Essential to the development of the Cotton District has been Camp's ability to construct houses with the help of a small cadre of apprentices he has trained over the years. This is a fundamental tenet of the New Pioneer—the idea that people can actually be trusted to build homes themselves, and can learn to do so as apprentices, just as they did for millennia prior to the advent of professional, licensed builders.

Camp had always been fascinated by the act and process of building. If you go into the men's room at Commodore Bob's restaurant on the district's commercial Rue du Grand Fromage ("Street of the Big Cheese," named after Camp), you can see a picture of the boat he built as a teenager.

"I started the boat when I was thirteen, and it took me until I was seventeen to finish it. It was a twelve-foot, flat-bottom cabin cruiser with an inboard engine," he says. "I had zero, absolutely zero, adult supervision. So I learned about bending plywood, and about brass screws and about waterproofing. I learned about frames, and I learned about the holding powers of materials. I had to figure out everything myself."

That sense of self-reliance carried Camp to the building of his first house, just before he started on the Cotton District—a small Cape Cod domicile that cost him $16,000 to construct, using the capital he had accumulated over several years of savings and successfully playing the stock market. That amount was less than the appraised value of the house, which he then mortgaged for the cash he needed to start the first Cotton District townhouses.

After that, Camp became a self-educated student of architecture, studying the vernacular of Southern cities and deciphering how to create the elements in his own workshop.

"I went to Savannah and I went to New Orleans. I would go and study these places. And I had Mrs. Toledano's series of New Orleans books [*A Pattern Book of New Orleans Architecture*, by Roulhac B. Toledano] to look at. I would study the proportions of columns, or the details of 1820s, '30s, and '40s dormers. These dormers now represent some of the finest details on our 'Purple' cottages. We would build them on the ground like furniture and swing them up into place with a boom crane. We would do all kinds of things like that, and still do things like that today, like making molds for concrete."

Camp created one set of molds for making the curbed arches for Palladian windows; others he used to cast the bases for columns, or for bullnose-edged "stone" stairs. For other elements, he employed the lean concept of recycling native materials—in this case components from older structures being razed by area developers. In one instance, he bought all the columns and windows from the soon-to-be-demolished Savery House in Tupelo, famous because Elvis once stayed there. In such cases, says Camp, the available elements would dictate the design of a new house.

Today, Camp's workshop is tucked into the bend of a brick drive that runs behind his family's Charleston-style four-story brick home—which he also built, of course. The wooden workshop is a weathered one-story, tin-roof shed with large double-hung windows. It looks like it's straight out of the 1800s, though it's just a few decades old. The outside walls are buttressed by sheaves of unfinished doors and windows; the yard is stacked loosely with planks and beams, a sawhorse, and latticework.

The inside smells of fresh-cut timber. There are saws and benches and drills, and shelves loaded with frames and dark lumber. It is a craftsman's shop, filled with half-finished projects—decorative brackets for wraparound porches, burnished sections of bannisters, assorted molds, and millwork. If it weren't for this shop, much of what Camp constructed would not have been possible. The cost alone would have been prohibitive.

With a garage door built into one side of the shed, the shop has been able to produce larger elements for the houses as well. "We have done all sorts of things in here," says Camp. "We have built a self-supporting curved staircase in here. We have it in one of the rental cottages. It has the old bent rail . . . if we are presented with a challenge, we will attempt it. We are not afraid. Of course, it helps that we have a wonderful guy [one of his apprentices] who is an artisan and a millworker."

"Most people can't afford to build like this, so they compromise their design, and buy what they can off the shelf," says Memphis architect Skinner. "Dan can build it exactly to what the proportions demand or require, and doesn't have to settle for what the local supplier has to offer. Very few in the industry can do that."

The training of skilled workers is a Camp hallmark, hearkening to his days as a shop instructor. He teaches basic building skills to everybody who works for him—something he says is missing in architecture curricula. Neil Strickland, for example, joined Camp as intern from Harvard, where he had earned a degree in Environmental Science and Public Policy. When he arrived in Starkville, his first assignment was to build a house. Literally. Which he did over ten months with a carpenter and fellow laborers. Today, Strickland works for Camp as a project manager.

Most of Camp's workers, however, are recruited locally. Camp assembles the team every weekday morning at 7 AM. They are a motley crew, a dozen, mostly black, middle-aged men. They are dressed in paint-splattered overalls and sweatshirts, dungarees, and wool coats and caps. They work as painters, carpenters, stonemasons, and the maintenance crew. All of them have worked for Camp for years— Carl and Jimmy for better than a decade, Eddie and "Bone" for twenty years, Abraham Lincoln Prader for forty-seven years. Collectively they know all the ways and means of building houses.

"I call this the distinguished gentleman's group, this morning bunch," says Camp. "Abraham Lincoln there, he can take a divided-light window smashed by a student and reconstitute it to look as though it had never been destroyed . . . I have trained these people. Remember, my background was shop, teaching people how to do things."

Each morning Camp goes over the day's marching orders, figuring out what projects were completed the day before and what still needs to be done. He grills the crew over intensely specific details and then issues the directives.

"Carl, did you finish the work on the cottage at the end of Lumus Street?"

"No sir, we were still painting the blue buildings."

"Well, here's what you need to do. You need half a dozen two-foot studs to brace the stairwell, and some treated plywood from the shop to replace those broken steps. I want something stronger than that damn pine. It just rots out."

"All right then, I'll see Abraham about those steps," says Carl, who then heads off to his day's assignments.

"And take AJ [a recent hire] with you. I want him to see how you do that."

BARRIERS TO ENTRY

One of the common prerequisites for the advent of the New Pioneer is the previous abandonment or neglect of an urban neighborhood. This creates a metropolitan wilderness equivalent to virgin forest or prairie, a place where you can build without interference. This was clearly the case of the Cotton District, a neighborhood that was so degraded the city consigned it for Urban Renewal, i.e., urban clearance.

This proved a boon for Camp. Whereas building codes in the more affluent residential and commercial sections of the city were enforced, city officials didn't care about codes in the Cotton District. They were so pleased that anybody would build new housing in the area, they gave Camp what amounted to carte blanche. After establishing himself as a credible builder, Camp would often get quick approvals based only on a sketch of what a building would look like. He was also given the okay to build on tiny lots, once for mill workers' housing and smaller than those permitted today.

"In those days, they'd approve it as long as you'd stay in that part of town," says Camp. "It was kind of a good-old-boy thing. We'll approve you doing this over there, but just don't get the wild idea that anybody else wants you."

Camp still needed the help of some experts. In his case it came down to the soil, and whether it could support a given structure. "I had a friend who was a concrete expert from the university, in civil engineering. For my own house he came to me and said, 'Your soil is shit. You're going to have to put pilings down, and you're going to have to put two in each corner.' And would you like to know how I got the pilings dug? I had the city electric boring truck come out and punch them in for me. There was no one around here who had a boring facility—this is thirty-some years ago. But I had a good rapport with the department head and various people in the city, and they would come out and accommodate things like that. They saw what I was doing, and I think it was a matter of them being supportive."

As the years passed, regulations began to tighten up. Camp began presenting city planners—and the aldermen who could overturn their decisions—with more sophisticated presentations. By the time he got to a street of houses known as Planter's Row, he had graduated from sketches to scale models.

One of the planning board members at the time was James F. Barker, who later became president of Clemson University. When Camp showed him the model for Planter's Row—two lines of houses facing each other across a brick roadway, with parking in the alleys behind the houses—he was so impressed he led a drive to scrap the town's ten-acre requirement for a planned unit development.

"His point was that we don't have ten acres of land in Starkville that's open [for development] so why do we need such restrictions? So they eliminated that requirement, and I did it as a planned unit development [PUD]," says Camp. "With a PUD you could do your own setbacks and put parking where you wanted, etc. So we did Starkville's first PUD with Planter's Row, twenty-eight units on a little over an acre. We don't believe in big things around here."

That blank check was one of the last for Camp, however, especially when he started to develop commercial buildings at the edge of the Cotton District along the main artery of University Drive. By the time he got approval for the buildings on what he wistfully agreed to call the Rue du Grand Fromage—which included several food establishments—he was subject to the codes.

"It used to be that he would just hand them a drawing on a napkin and they would say okay," says project manager Strickland. "Now they [the city planners] feel legally liable. If you let him do that, then you have to let everybody do it. Otherwise they'd be open to lawsuits from other developers."

"There's no question that we did things we can't do today," says Camp. "It was not like it was on the sly, but some of the things *did* come on the sly. Such as a building I call the Hermitage, where I put six [units] and a cottage on a sixty-by-fifty [-foot] space, with a beautiful little fish-scale courtyard in it." Such density would not be permitted today, with Starkville codes heavily influenced by suburban sensibilities. "But the thing was, back then it was a slum and they were ready to get rid of slums. Nobody paid any attention to it, because it wasn't on the main entrance to the university."

Camp now practices the lean urban tactic of working around the codes, sometimes by changing the language used and other times with creative interpretations. For the Rue du Grand Fromage—a narrow street straddled by an archway, with apartments above—the code required a square footage of green space that would have made parking in the alleyway impossible. So Camp built trellises over the parking lane, and thickly planted them, to satisfy the provision.

For a pool house adjacent to his home—essentially a small, private spa with an oversized hot tub—Camp became even more creative with language. To call it a house would require the satisfaction of numerous time- and money-consuming requirements. So instead, he pulled a permit for a pool, and called the house a "pool cover," for which the code was much leaner.

Being able to understand and find loopholes in local code is something that Camp assigns to his son Bonn, who along with brother Robert is carrying on the family's development of the Cotton District. Bonn has become an expert in the International Building Code, as well as acquiring a variety of contracting licenses.

"He [Bonn] is very astute as to what the code is. That's what we argue about, what is permitted and what is not. We don't argue about money or girls or things like that. It's over codes and such, and he'll go to the International Building Code and say 'Dad, you're wrong, you can't place windows like that.' And I'll say, 'I'm only telling you what the fire chief told me I could do.'"

The use of officials to patch or grant variances to code is, of course, the last refuge to escape regulations that restrain. This relies

on relationships with city officials and the ability to convince regulators to make exceptions. A good example is a new regulation on
the books in Starkville commonly known as the Tree Ordinance. It
states that all new buildings in the city must have a five-foot planted
border around all four sides. Unfortunately this makes it impossible
to bring buildings up to the street and put parking in the rear, a
hallmark of the Cotton District as well as classic European cities.

"They put this landscape ordinance in place that doesn't really go
with our urban concept," says Bonn, who also designs new district
structures. "I was trying to tell them—we had to go in front of a
'street warden,' a position I hadn't even heard of—that it makes no
sense. Go do this around a gas station on Highway Twelve, or a Taco
Bell, but not around what we're trying to do."

Unlike his father, Bonn is also faced with engineering regulations not previously enforced. "Because you have to have a professional to stamp your site plan, you have to pay someone five to
fifteen thousand dollars to come do soil testing for you. Then you
have to pay an engineer to draw the foundation before you get it
stamped," Bonn says. "This is the problem with the whole development [field] right now, that the city is trying to create jobs for
so many professionals. By the time you get through all of the professionals, you're broke."

Like his father, Bonn works to develop relationships with city
officials who have the power to grant exemptions. Several city officials actually live in the Cotton District, which doesn't hurt. The new
Starkville city planner lives in one of the houses, for example. "The
stairs [to his house] are totally against code, but he's happy to live
there," says Strickland.

That is something not taught in architecture school, Bonn notes:
"They don't understand the fact that you have to go to the city and
have relationships with them."

Even with the most affable municipal connections, however,
enough has changed that re-creating the Cotton District today

would be tantamount to impossible. "Dan would not be able to start out now if he tried to," says project manager Strickland. "The codes have changed too much, even in rural Mississippi." Beyond codes, the incremental nature of his development would not be tolerated. "They would not let a Cotton District evolve anymore. It would be too unfinished . . . People want the apex condition from the start."

END GAME

The final "apex" structures are what Camp and family are now focusing on—public spaces where the district meets the main University Drive. On one corner, they have built a large multiuse building (retail on the ground floor with rental units above) with an elegant solution to the wheelchair access code—a sloping, circular walkway wrapping around an ornate fountain out front. Across a side street is a restaurant/bar called BIN 612 and a cigar lounge, and on the other side of University Drive are the buildings of the Rue du Grand Fromage—a small complex containing a taco bar and a juice bar fronting University, with a barbecue sports bar, restaurant, and hair stylist tucked down the Rue in other small spaces.

Next up, says Camp, is "a greasy hamburger place with beer"—actually a microbrewery—followed by a twelve-unit Georgian-style building that may or may not become a hotel, depending on whether anyone in the family wants the bother of running it.

On weekend nights, this cluster of public buildings is a focal point for social life, jammed with hundreds of students and millennials who congregate here. It's part of what makes the district attractive to its student residents. In addition to the proximity of MSU, the cluster of eating and drinking establishments means that food and entertainment are also walkable. It's what Strickland refers to as the DUI factor—that students who live in the district can walk home after having a drink. (The first student bar to go up was called, appropriately enough, the STAGgerIN Sports Grill.)

The commercial spaces of this nexus also deliberately provide low thresholds to entry for young entrepreneurs. The spaces are small, but so are the rents, offering a chance for a new business to get started.

"The whole point is to create small affordable spaces for entrepreneurship, especially student entrepreneurship," says Camp. "Whenever you sit around and talk about ideas and wish you could do this or that, you go out and start to investigate. And the first thing you find is that you have to pay two thousand dollars a month for a place to do anything. My thought was, let's create these small spaces where people can go in and get traction."

The small spaces that Camp has created are 300 to 500 square feet, with monthly rents of $400 to $500. Among the most recent takers: a juice bar that fronts University Drive (with student housing above) started in the fall of 2014 by Jessica Cheek, twenty-five, an MSU grad who lived in the Cotton District as a student.

"I loved living here," says Cheek. "It's just so people-friendly with so many awesome things to look at. And when you walk outside in the morning, you see ten other people walking their dogs at the same time." Cheek was a business major who had become an avid juicer, and thought, "Why don't I just open up shop so it's easy for people to get something on the go, instead of having to buy a juicer and buy all this equipment? That's how it happened."

In the meantime, the area as a whole has become infected with redevelopment, roughly surrounding Camp's properties. One is a multiunit property on the edge of the district that a developer bought after bidding far more than Camp was willing to invest. "They paid $450,000 for that little lot and they are going to put twenty-nine units in there," he says. "I immediately came back and added 20 percent to my financial statement."

Perhaps the ultimate symbol of the Cotton District's influence and coming of age is the fate of the old Sanders cotton mill that frames its southern edge. It has now been redeveloped for $40 million to become a hotel and conference center.

Camp himself is amused by the fact that the university is making a handsome profit on the redevelopment project, based on his Cotton District's success—despite the fact his alma mater has given him little recognition for what he's accomplished. "That's fine with me. It just makes my properties more valuable."

SEASIDE: IT TAKES A VILLAGE

Seaside is a small town on the Gulf Coast of the Florida panhandle. Like Mississippi's Cotton District, Seaside is a thoroughly delightful place to spend time. Both communities are built on a diminutive scale, with fantastic attention to architectural detail. Both create unique urban spaces, with hidden walkways, twisting brick paths, intimate courtyards, and interesting public areas. While the two communities developed independently, they both created New Urbanism models of compact, diverse, and highly walkable worlds.

Both communities were also created in the milieu of Lean Urbanism, where codes and regulatory restrictions are absent or ignored. This creates the equivalent of raw wilderness, with a consequent release of pioneering innovation and creativity. Both were also started in a lean manner financially, with very little initial capital, trading the commodity of time for the commodity of cash. Consequently, both developed over decades, using the value of what was already built to fund what was yet to be built.

The lean parallels continue from there. The Cotton District and Seaside were the brainchildren of single visionary pioneers, albeit with the aid of key advisors, especially in the case of Seaside. Both eschewed gizmo green, and instead used traditional, original green methods to solve environmental problems. Both were built on a small scale, using form-based codes that pushed houses to the street and hid parking behind. Both used the vernacular style of the old South to give their communities dignity and beauty. Both trained small cadres of apprentice workers to execute artistic details with authentic craftsmanship. And both lowered the thresholds for new, entrepreneurial businesses that were incubated in the community.

The history of Seaside does not need extensive detailing here. Started in 1970 by Robert Davis and a small group of maverick architects and planners, it is considered today to be the quintessential model of New Urbanism: a compressed community, entirely walkable and self-sufficient, with a dense core of retail and entertainment. In the case of Seaside, there is, in addition, easy access to immense natural beauty via a white-powdered beach and a tree-buffered lake. Unlike the Cotton District, however, Seaside had no extant stock of denigrated housing; Seaside's creation on remote coastal scrubland was more like carving a settlement out of true, native frontier.

Like the Cotton District, Seaside is also architecturally beautiful, attributed in part to the stunning roster of now-famous architects who cut their teeth here. The array of talent is impressive: Walter Chatham, Steven Holl, Léon Krier, Robert Orr, Samuel Mockbee, and Alexander Gorlin, to name a few. Regardless of any particular design, the attractiveness of Seaside also has to do with the simple fact that different architects designed and built different houses. This created the feel of handcrafted individual structures within a "planned" community. And while the houses in the Cotton District were designed by one man and his two sons, in a way they were really designed by different architects as well: their styling, proportion, and details were decanted from a variety of classic models found in old Southern cities (in Seaside, by comparison, variations of the Old Florida vernacular style predominate).

Just as importantly, the New Pioneers behind these communities built them over time. By constructing the individual buildings in succession, each one fit integrally into the context of the previous structures and existing streetscapes.

The successional nature of both the Cotton District and Seaside was critical to their success and represents a paramount lean attribute: Slow development enabled these communities to be born, grow, and mature with gradual money. Their multidecade time scale was, of course, the dream of any urban planner—to work within a generational framework. But just as importantly, the drawn-out time scale lowered the threshold to entry for the young, visionary pioneers who developed them.

THE ECONOMICS OF SLOW

Ask Robert Davis why he created Seaside, and he will tell you that it was to re-create the summer vacations of his childhood, when his parents would take him and his siblings down to the Alabama coast to stay in seaside cottages. It was a place where the world was palpable, where you walked and ran and swam and got covered in sand and salty water. Today's kids, he fears, experience the world "in straitjackets, in the backseats of cars, experiencing the world as a moving picture, through a window about the size of a TV."

When Davis started Seaside, all that he had was cheap land. The cheapest, actually: eighty acres on a half mile of beach on the Gulf Coast of the Florida Panhandle that he inherited from his grandfather. It was in the middle of nowhere, on County Road 30A, about halfway between Pensacola and Panama City. So he used the land, bit by bit, to pay for and advance the project. Davis would sell a plot at a time, and allow the building on that plot to increase the value of the next.

"The way Seaside started was that Davis sold one waterfront lot," says architect and urban planner Andrés Duany, who designed Seaside with the developer. "He had the land free and clear, so he separated one lot and sold it. Then he did successional stuff. The sewage was successional. The planting was successional. And the housing was intrinsically successional because he did one at a time. So it evolved organically as [the builders and buildings] learned from each other. And the value went up, because each house guaranteed the value of the town, making it even better."

Both Duany and Davis admit that the initial motivation to move slowly was economic; Davis had done some earlier developments in Miami, where he was nearly ruined by being overleveraged with banks. "When the time came to do Seaside, what drove Robert was actually to not be in debt. That was very important. Otherwise he couldn't sleep," says Duany. "Many of the decisions of Seaside, especially the successional ones, were because he had to generate the cash along the way to do it."

Even the team of young architects and planners that Davis assembled, a half-dozen recent college graduates including Duany, initially worked for free, later being rewarded with plots of land. Even when cash flow eventually provided salaries for the carpenters, electricians, plumbers, etc., these workers were still offered plots at low prices that later escalated astronomically.

Regardless of its cause, the slow build out of Seaside provided object lessons in how to carve a community out of raw wilderness without the overarching resources of today's large-scale corporate developers who create entire subdivisions at one throw.

"I think the real lessons that we learned in Seaside were almost by accident," says Davis. "Because we didn't have enough money to build the whole thing out, we learned that it was best *not* building the whole thing out, which actually improved the marketing performance. At any given time, there were only a few lots available." And after those lots were built, the next ones would come on market at a higher price, ultimately providing the capital resources for the commercial buildings and public spaces.

BUILD IT AND THEY WILL COME

A tremendous advantage for the lean, emerging Cotton District was the proximity of Mississippi State University, with its multitude of educational and cultural options within walking distance. From class lectures to theater performances to sporting events, there was always something to do, and there were resources like a library, bookstore, cafeteria, and food court. In Seaside, there was literally nothing to do besides beachcomb, and nowhere to eat.

Davis approached this with the same lean, slow approach he took for the housing: start small and slowly grow larger and more complex.

"We started with a shrimp shack," says Davis. "It was a kind of a roadside attraction, since there was nothing for miles in either direction. We served boiled shrimp and cold beer. And when people stopped and asked what we were up to, I used it as an opportunity to tell the story of Seaside. Because that's all we had to sell at that point, the story of the community that we were going to build."

The original Shrimp Shack was a tiny, peach-colored building, maybe 100 square feet, with just enough room to boil shrimp and keep beer on ice. It is now built into Pickle's Beachside Grill as a serving window; like many of the original structures at Seaside, it was recycled. "Everything at Seaside gets reborn and used for many functions," says Robert's wife, Daryl, who led the effort to incubate retail at Seaside. "It starts out as one thing and transforms into another."

Case in point: Not far from Pickle's is an entrance to the sea that is flanked by two of Seaside's "Cinderella cottages," local shacks that Davis rescued from demolition. One of them is the current incarnation of the Shrimp Shack. The other is now part of the multilevel Bud & Alley's restaurant, which was enlarged over the years by adding on other rescued Old Florida structures.

"The big restaurant [Bud & Alley's] was done in seven different phases. It's a cobbling together of different buildings," says Douglas Duany, the landscape architect and Notre Dame professor (and brother of Andrés) who planted Seaside with native species. "Everything here was done in stages. It never happens that way today. It's a strategy based on poverty."

Named after Seaside's first dog and cat residents, Bud & Alley's is emblematic of how commercial proprietors in Seaside were incubated in partnership with Davis.

"After the Shrimp Shack, Davis found these guys down on the beach who were surfers, and they made really good hamburgers," recalls Andrés Duany. "So he said, 'Come up the hill and I will help you get into business.'" The two surfers had some restaurant experience; they both worked as waiters at a French restaurant in Destin, twenty-five miles away, where the Davises ate. One of their fathers, in fact, managed the restaurant. But Robert lowered the threshold dramatically, starting them with virtually no rent and helping train them by bringing in a chef from Birmingham.

The Davises did this with most of their retailers, germinating and nurturing them. Daryl herself spearheaded the merchant side by setting up a Saturday vegetable stand, and then inviting people to sell things along with her. She began with a half-dozen tables set up by the Shrimp Shack, and then added umbrellas, and then added lockers so that merchandise didn't have to be transported daily.

"In those early days I was joined by an organic baker, a potter, a photographer and framer, a bookseller, a jewelry maker, and others," says Daryl. "This was a pivotal point in the beginning of community making and later retail development." She herself became expert in the selling of cotton dresses and shirts, for which there was considerable demand; this combination of a few groceries and cotton clothing, along with housewares, later grew into a general store called Perspicasity.

Meanwhile, Daryl was incubating other retailers, like the owners of Sundog Books, which is now a large bookstore on Seaside's Central Square. Daryl found them in a strip shopping center in Destin where the rents were too high and started them in a small 100-square-foot shop in Seaside. That was more than a decade ago. As business grew, they expanded to 250 square feet, then 500, then to their present, thriving 1,300-square-foot shop.

Likewise, the town's beloved Modica Market was lured to Seaside and incubated by the Davises. Charles Modica and his wife, Sarah, ran a grocery store in Bessemer, Alabama, when they happened to stop into Seaside on a trip to Panama City. The Davises ultimately persuaded them to move to Seaside, and to start small with a panini and ice cream shop, which became very successful.

But Robert wanted a gourmet market, so he convinced the Modicas to start one by flying them to New York to see Dean & DeLuca's, Balducci's, and Zabar's gourmet shops. "He showed them what people were buying in New York, what kind of olive oil and what kind of mustard," says Daryl. "They couldn't believe anyone would pay that much for olive oil and mustard!"

But they did, and Modica Market became a great financial success. It also became a social focal point for the community, thanks in part to the embracing personality of Charles Modica (who sported a Hemingway-like white beard) and his personable wife. "They were ambassadors for the community. As soon as you came back to Seaside, you went and said hello and found out what was going on," says Daryl.

"Charles Modica looked like you'd called central casting and said, 'Send me a wonderful grocer,'" says Andrés Duany. "And he came complete with the smile and the smock. So Robert put him in business because Robert himself needed olive oil and better food."

Modica Market was an example of lean retail, incubated initially in a low-cost small space that later expanded. But it also illustrates how businesses that are born lean and grow over time tend to be more intertwined with the community than businesses that are dropped in from above, fully formed, and staffed by professionals—a hallmark of gentrification. Lean individuates retail, far more than chain retail, providing what Daryl calls "a textured environment to the community."

"The whole small way they started their retail was huge," says Diane Dorney, who now runs the educational Seaside Institute. "They didn't try to make things big, they started by putting up shacks and selling things out of them. It was all about how you can grow a town versus dropping one down like a spaceship, opened up with all the leases and everything in place."

The lean path to retailing is also an illustration of lean education at Seaside, where budding retailers were instructed on how to do things that normally require the assistance of professionals. "Along the way," says Daryl, "we taught them skills, like cash-flow management for seasonal businesses and visual merchandising, with seminars on the science of buying. We did seminars to instill in them tools, even how to sell."

To generate a growing sense of community, and to provide something to do, Davis and his wife began creating weekend events. In the spirit of low-threshold lean, these social occasions cost very little beyond the time and space required to sponsor them—things like volleyball tournaments, sailboat regattas along the beach, sandcastle-building contests, dancing under the stars, Halloween balls, piano recitals overlooking the gulf at sunset, and outdoor movies.

Despite its arrival as a now super-affluent community with high property values that prohibit entry-level homeowners, Seaside continues its tradition of low-threshold events, along with the incubation of retail. The so-called Central Square is actually a huge half circle of grass resting on County Road 30A with a shop-lined street around its perimeter and a stage at its hub. This open space still hosts, for example, the annual October dachshund races, followed by a doggie costume contest. "I love these sorts of things because they are practically free to put on," says Davis. "And people love them." What's not to love watching dashing dachshunds named Smokey, Roxy, Dash, and Beau, followed by dogs dressed up like clowns, pirates, or a plate of spaghetti with dangling meatballs?

As for lean retail, the wide sidewalk that forms the base of Central Square along County Road 30A is home to a half-dozen "silver bullet" Airstream trailers. Each houses a start-up eatery, from Wild Bill's Beach Dogs (frankfurters) to an Italian Ice snow cone vendor. The most recent is an Asian food vendor called "Sóng."

"What you have done is taken raw food trucks and put umbrellas and heaters and lighting out front so that they look like Parisian cafés. Which is actually lean. It's about recycling basic elements," says Douglas Duany.

"The snow cone business is the most astounding," says Davis. "He sells frozen water with a little syrup on it. And the profits are enormous. Kids line up at night. His annual dollars per square foot in sales is in the ten thousand dollar range, which is more than any other. But his square footage is very small."

THE VIRTUES OF SMALL

Like the Seaside retailers who began in small spaces and gradually grew larger, the building of homes in Seaside proceeded incrementally, one piece at a time. It was almost as if the community began as a sketch, slowly coloring itself in.

"After year two you could actually begin to feel what the first streets were going to be like, because they were starting to get lined by houses," says Davis. "And then we reinforced that by planting the trees and building the picket fences—whether we'd sold the lot or not." It was a kind of façade building, and another way to improve value by giving future residents an idea of what the community would become. "The picket fences cost us a few hundred dollars per lot back then. As soon as someone bought it, we'd hang a sign saying 'John and Mary Smith from Dauphin, Alabama,' along with the names of their kids and maybe the names of their dogs and cats. And because the South is such a small place, somebody knew somebody who knew John and Mary Smith. It was a way of marketing."

"Vacant plots, empty storefronts, and underutilized courtyards waiting for development or the next tenant are usually perceived as having a negative impact on their surroundings," writes Dhiru A. Thandani in his book *Visions of Seaside*. "From its start, Seaside has tried to stay one step ahead of this perception by reusing and relocating structures, or building small temporary buildings to fill empty spaces."

In this vein, and in conjunction with the guerilla marketing technique of picket-fence building, Davis also permitted new residents to build just their front porches, and to stay in tents behind the front-porch façades. This was especially relevant for workers who were sold lots inexpensively in the early days of Seaside, lots that provided not only homes but "investments that gave teachers and electricians and carpenters the resources to put their kids through college," says Davis.

Low-cost lots were lean, low-threshold entry points for the apprentices who became the builders of Seaside. This was another way that Davis was able to create Seaside as a traditional-looking town of classic nineteenth-century Florida architecture. Like Dan Camp, Davis had to build a team of what amounted to local artisans and craftspeople to construct houses with the detailed woodwork exemplary of the bygone era of pioneer Florida home building.

"These are skills lost to modern builders in general, let alone to the carpenters of the Panhandle," says Davis. "We could hardly find guys who could hammer in a straight nail to begin with. Our people had to be cultivated for what was a craftsman-like approach to small housing done in a classical way."

In a sad psalm to the lost days of American pioneers, the people of the Panhandle themselves had forgotten the skills necessary to build. They had become beholden to large-scale developers who could field staffs of professionals, experts who knew the magic formulas for home construction.

LEAN GREEN

A critical parallel between Seaside and the Cotton District was the absence of zoning or permit restrictions. In the Cotton District, Dan Camp was given what amounted to free rein because the city was desperate to clean up the area. Seaside, located in rural Walton County, simply had no regulations drafted by the local government (such zoning codes and regulations are now in place, of course).

Because it was in a code-free zone, Seaside could do things that today would be impossible. In many cases, this led to unique, low-tech green solutions for the community.

The most prominent of these is the drainage solution to flooding during a heavy rain. The semi-circular Central Square of Seaside, with its central stone stage, is actually shaped like a large drainage bowl. The elevated stage sits at the bottom of a shallow, grassy bowl. Most of the time, the sloping sides of the bowl are dry and provide a gentle incline for residents to sit and watch the stage. When excess rain deluges Seaside, however, the bowl fills with water. The children of Seaside love this occasional event, creating as it does a giant splash pool.

"A lot of the decisions were based on wanting to build as little as possible at the time," says Diane Dorney of the Seaside Institute. "The amphitheater, for example, is where all the water collects. It's just water retention that has become this wonderful public place. Or the streets. They made them of brick and sand for economic reasons, but that also permitted natural drainage." In addition, it added a charming touch.

This sort of simple, low-tech solution would not be permitted today, and the town would have been required to build an expensive drainage system of pipes and culverts, with paved streets lined by sewer drains. But the amphitheater and the sandy streets are symbolic of how Seaside approached green alternatives in a way that employed traditional and natural solutions.

Seaside's slow and natural modus operandi is also evident in its landscaping. Employing the lean philosophy of recycling local materials, all of Seaside was planted with native flora by landscape architect Douglas Duany. The result is xeriscaping, with hardy indigenous plantings that require no irrigation and little maintenance. Typical developments today create instant landscapes with nonnative plantings that require sprinkler systems installed in tandem. Natural landscapes that can exist with average local rainfall take decades to grow into place—decades that the slow pace of Seaside permitted. The low cost likewise made it a lean approach.

Seaside is also "green" thanks to its passive use of natural conditions. Most of the streets are perpendicular to the shoreline, which helps carry prevailing breezes deeper into the village. The sea-grass bluffs on the shoreline, typically leveled by developers to prepare building sites, were left in place, providing a natural barrier to ocean surges during major storms.

The use of classic pioneer Florida architecture also helped, thanks to its passive cooling solutions and original green techniques: overhangs that allow windows to remain open even when it rains, alignment of the houses and their windows to maximize ocean breezes, elevating houses to permit cooling underneath (and further natural drainage), the use of tin roofs to reflect the sunlight, and the extensive use of porches as additional "rooms" of the home.

Even the small scale of the homes is an ecological posture, minimizing the carbon footprint of the buildings via reduced requirements for heating and cooling. The streets they line are, again, covered with gravel rather than asphalt, helping to naturally filter the rainwater. And, of course, the ability of residents to eschew the car in favor of the foot, the essence of New Urbanism, is ecological and sustainable by its very nature.

IN THE LONG RUN

Although Seaside has now entered what can only be called a mature stage, it continues to evolve in small and subtle ways.

In 2008, for example, one of the Airstream-housed retailers— Raw & Juicy—helped launch a Saturday farmers market. In typical incremental style, it began as three vendors with stands next to the Raw & Juicy Organic Juice Bar and Café. By 2010, the Seaside Farmers Market was the only year-round market in the Florida Panhandle, featuring the produce of numerous small farmers and local artisans. Several of Seaside's permanent vendors used the market to incubate their businesses, later opening up storefronts, while others have become regional suppliers to restaurants and retailers.

Using the public spaces at the center of the town, Davis has also created an academic village for visiting artists—including the use of recycled Katrina Cottages (originally built to house displaced victims of Hurricane Katrina) as a low-cost solution to accommodate these visiting artists or for students who come to study Seaside.

In terms of entry-level housing, however, Seaside has become the victim of its own success. Like all urban regeneration that emerges from a lean New Pioneer scenario, in the end, property values rise. This is an almost inevitable outcome along the path to prosperity that Lean Urbanism provides, and it is a not necessarily a bad thing: it is how wealth is created from low-threshold entry points for people—especially young people—who have energy and innovative ideas but not the capital needed to penetrate a hyper-regulated environment.

In this context, it is the successional nature of Seaside that is most exemplary of lean principles. It is a foundation for both the intricate, organic nature of the build out and for the economic model that made it possible despite lean beginnings. It is a concept that Davis calls "patient capital."

"The takeaway from 'patient capital' is that real estate until fairly recently, maybe the 1960s or 1970s, was the most boring investment, the slowest-growing asset class. It was something that was safe but illiquid," says Davis. "Investors would put their money into it and assume it was a twenty-year investment. You would get it back eventually. And because, as Will Rogers used to say, 'They're not making any of more of it,' the property should be worth more."

The monkey wrench in this paradigm was the suburbanization of America after World War II, accelerated by the interstate highway system. "We suddenly had lots of accessible land, and what we basically started doing was converting farms into subdivisions," says Davis. Plentiful land also created a class of real estate developers who made their money by building and flipping, earning even more by developing large tracts with cookie-cutter architecture that was cheap to produce if you kept it all the same.

Big developments also required big capital, which implied lots of leveraging via bank loans—along with the ensuing risk. Seaside, being debt free and not over-leveraged, did not suffer a collapse during the big real estate downturns over the last thirty years. Instead, things just slowed down for a while before moving forward again.

"Part of Seaside's message, which hasn't gotten across effectively, is this whole financial idea about patient capital—and turning real estate back into a safe, boring asset class," says Davis. "That's what you see here. I mean, it's exciting in terms of what you see on the ground—it's a fun place—but it was done so slowly that it was never much at risk. I never had much of a financial thrill, as did [some of the area's 'overnight' developer-moguls] who then lost it.

"The other part of the message is that if you do it slowly and carefully, and you do it as urbanism, you're building a place that's more and more urbane every year, and gets better and better every year," says Davis. "And because of that, the values go up every year."

And thus beauty and wealth are created by the New Pioneers of Lean Urbanism, which in these communities represent both a return to the way in which America was originally built, and a path toward a future where the young, the small, the new, and the undercapitalized can create value for themselves and their new world.

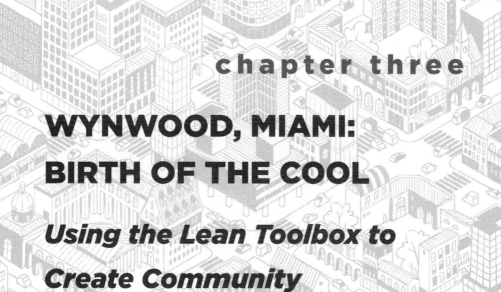

chapter three

WYNWOOD, MIAMI: BIRTH OF THE COOL

Using the Lean Toolbox to Create Community

In 2005, Miami's Wynwood neighborhood was a run-down collection of single-story warehouses: eighty square blocks worth of storage and light manufacturing laced with cracked sidewalks, barbed wire, and homeless shelters. That year Wynwood was discovered by Tony Goldman, the visionary urbanist famed for transforming SoHo in New York and Miami Beach's Art Deco district. Ten years later, Wynwood had become the most interesting place in Miami, an edgy enclave of galleries, bars, art spaces, studios, restaurants, boutiques, cafés, shops, museum collections, and a performance theater. Everywhere there were murals, a mad kaleidoscope of painted images covering virtually every surface in the neighborhood.

How Wynwood jumped from desolation to destination is a lesson in Lean Urbanism and the power of the New Pioneer: an inner-city neighborhood transformed with little capital but lots of artistic innovation. It looked to the world as though Goldman had created the phenomenon of Wynwood with nothing but buckets of paint—white on the inside for galleries and studios, a rainbow of colors on the outside for pedestrians. But while he was lauded as a magician of urban transformation on the cheap, a cadre of New Pioneers had already invaded the grimy industrial ghetto and brought it to life.

Years before Goldman and other developers invested in Wynwood, these New Pioneers—visual and performance artists operating under the radar—had created a beachhead of galleries, studios, and artist-run spaces in what had been a marginalized district rife with drug dealers and petty crime. It was their cachet that attracted the developers. Today everybody wants to own a piece of the trendiest neighborhood in town, which has driven prices so high that the Goldmans are subsidizing low-threshold platforms for small businesses—art galleries included—to make sure the neighborhood retains its edgy essence. The New Pioneers, meanwhile, have moved on.

Creating Value: The blank warehouses of Wynwood became canvases for massive murals, drawing visitors from around the globe.

THE NIGHT IS YOUNG

On a typical weekend evening in Miami's Wynwood neighborhood, circa 2015, the tourists roam the streets and alleyways, cameras in hand. They are chatting in myriad languages, pointing at the walls, strolling the celebrated streets of Miami's überhip arts district. The sun is setting and the lights are coming on in Wood Tavern, Wynwood Kitchen & Bar, and Panther Coffee.

The tourists are not here for the beer and the lattes, however, though all the food and drink venues will fill up before it gets dark. For starters, they are not your typical tourists, not the overweight refugees from the Northeast, Midwest, and Europe looking to don baggy shirts and cop a quick tan before the evening's libations. These are culture tourists, here to eyeball inventive strokes and shapes by scores of artists who have used the buildings as their blank slates.

They are mostly young and slender globetrotting millennials, here to see what amounts to the world's largest display of public art.

For block after block, the artwork is unrelenting. Every building is covered with paintings, including truck-sized garage doors and cargo bays, for this was once an industrial hub of manufacturing plants, import-export businesses, and auto-body shops. The warehouses these enterprises built and inhabited—and still do in diminishing numbers as the neighborhood fragments headlong into the future—provide the windowless walls–turned–canvases for artists both famous and unknown.

The imagery is literally fantastic: A great twisting Jack and the Beanstalk vine ensnared by octopus tentacles lines one alleyway; opposite is a grid of meditating Buddhas, each a raspberry dollop on a yellow background. Down the street, a random pattern of oversized green and black shirt buttons covers the wall; next to this, under the words "Yo, Brooklyn in the House," a mural of a jazz singer wails into a giant microphone. Next comes the huge face of a smiling woman, her skin mottled by psychedelic layers of paint. On the other side of the street the image of a duck-like creature with a long cigarette holder holds court, adjacent to a Roy Lichtenstein–wannabe woman covered with a hairnet and a "primitive art" painting of two black men deep in conversation.

And so it goes, block after block: surrealist visions of gigantic insects with metallic body parts, or walls covered with charging bulls, or the length of a building adorned with a languorous woman in repose, or a series of monstrous crocodiles, or a family of chubby blue aliens adorned with bikinis and rainbow Mohawk hairdos.

Even the sidewalks are covered, spray-painted with stenciled words and icons. IN THE END LOVE WILL BE WHAT SAVES US ALL, says one. LOVE KILLS, SEX HEALS, and HATE IS HEAVY SO LET IT GO, admonish two more. One image of a black cat with bats and stars hovering above announces: YOU ARE THE ONLY MAGIC IN THE CITY, referring to Miami's moniker as the Magic City.

These sidewalk scrawls are mere whispers, however, compared to the bright and intricate murals. Birds, bugs, fish, rodents, flowers, children, faces, hands, heads, eyeballs, monsters, and all colors known to man—it is an array that ranges from amateurish splatters of paint and gang-like graffiti to abstract patterns and truly sophisticated images created by world-renowned artists.

The sizes are as varied as the subject matter, from an entire building wrapped in a deep-green Rousseau-like jungle to a doorway painting of a chimpanzee, its eyes hypnotic circles, with the inscribed command: GOOGLE MY WIKI. Even the local middle school on the edge of the district is festooned with massive murals of stylized women, chrome canines, sea creatures, and enormous human visages.

And all of it emanates from the place where the finest of the wall art resides, the ground zero from which this visual explosion radiated: the Wynwood Walls.

PUBLIC ART AS A DESTINATION

When Tony Goldman discovered Wynwood in 2005, he was already famous for having "flipped" the historic districts of Soho in New York City and South Beach in Greater Miami. Both neighborhoods had been marginalized and effectively abandoned, yet both had dense collections of signature architecture. In Soho, there was an army of iron-façade mid-rises built in the late 1800s. In South Beach, there was an eight-hundred-building Art Deco cluster built in the 1930s.

"Wynwood was desolate at the time," says Jessica Goldman Srebnick, Tony's daughter and apprentice who is now CEO of Goldman Properties (Tony passed away in 2012). "The beauty of what my father did was to see what a neighborhood could be instead of what it was."

What it "was" consisted of a city district strategically located between downtown Miami, Miami Beach, and Miami International Airport, adjacent to I-95, with zero street life, and nothing worthy of architectural preservation. It was a treeless boxed set of one-story cement-block warehouses filled with machine shops, light manufacturing plants, and import-export businesses serving the Caribbean, and South and Central America. Largely nondescript, the neighborhood was tagged with graffiti and, in Caribbean style, tattooed with the images of what went on inside: sneakers and shoes painted on the warehouse for footwear imports, a small engine painted on the building where compressors were rebuilt.

"We were looking for the DNA of the neighborhood," says Jessica. "Because there were no windows, these buildings made for spectacular canvases. What my dad recognized was that it was a canvas waiting to be painted on." There was also, Jessica notes, "a foundation for art and culture and creativity that had started to percolate and just needed a little help to get it to the next level." Scattered across the neighborhood were a handful of galleries and studios, many occupied by artists driven, ironically enough, from Miami Beach by the Goldman revival there. Unheralded, these were the New Pioneers who had already created an arts beachhead that the Goldmans enhanced and expanded.

SPACE, THE FINAL FRONTIER

While Tony Goldman gets much of the credit for igniting Wynwood—the main stretch of NW 2nd Avenue is now called Tony Goldman Way—he was not among the avant-garde who gave the neighborhood its initial imprimatur as an arts district. That accolade goes to a handful of collectors and exhibitors who came to the district for its large, inexpensive spaces, followed by a cadre of artists and gallery owners.

In the mid- and late 1990s, warehouses could be bought in Wynwood for less than $10 a square foot—a low price, even for the times (by 2015, the same properties were selling for $500 to $600 a square foot). Among the first collectors lured by these rock-bottom values were Mera and Don Rubell, New Yorkers who began assembling their art collection in the mid-1960s. Don was a doctor and the brother of Steve Rubell, cofounder of New York's infamous Studio 54. Together with their children Jason and Jennifer, the Rubells began purchasing inexpensive hotel properties on Miami Beach (following the Goldman lead) as well as a 45,000-square-foot warehouse in Wynwood on 29th Street, a main artery on the northern edge of the district.

A former DEA storage place for confiscated properties, the warehouse had twenty-three-foot-high ceilings. The Rubells opened it, and their collection, to the public in 1994; the family built an adjacent home and moved there in 2003. It was a fortress and a compound; since then the family has moved on, but the display remains open as a self-styled museum of contemporary art, with a collection that now boasts some 6,800 works by more than 800 artists.

The Rubells were followed by another Miami art collector, developer Marty Margulies. He purchased 45,000 square feet of his own warehouse space, a cluster of attached buildings on the western edge of the district by I-95. Knocking down the interior walls, Margulies created a huge walk through museum for enormous, oversized sculpture, painting, and installations, as well as an immense compilation of photography. Called simply the Warehouse, it's been open to the public since 1999.

Individual artists also fled to Wynwood from Miami Beach's Lincoln Road art scene, driven out by rising rents. One of these New Pioneers was photographer Tim Walker, who bought a warehouse in Wynwood for eight dollars a square foot in 1995; he used it as his studio while he lived in a sailboat docked on the Miami River. "It was cheap real estate and it was a great location, the two things I needed," says Walker. "At the time there was nothing here, no galleries and no artists that I was aware of, just warehousing that serviced the Caribbean islands and Central America."

Walker says that, unlike Soho or South Beach, Wynwood was never inhabited by a large number of artists. While some did live illegally in their industrial studio space, there were very few second-story buildings suitable for turning into lofts. Instead, what made

Wynwood an "arts district" were galleries and artist collectives, also attracted by the large, inexpensive spaces that lured the big collectors.

Among these pioneers was Locust Projects, an artist-run nonprofit "dedicated to providing contemporary visual artists the freedom to experiment with new ideas," as they declared at the time. "There was nothing there when we started, just broken streets and the homeless," says Elizabeth Withstandley, one of a trio of Miami artists who founded the exhibition group. "It was a real urban frontier, forgotten by time—and the rest of Miami." Locust leased cheap space across from a Salvation Army compound on 23rd Street. Back then (they arrived in 1998), it was a daring probe into a lifeless precinct of urban wilderness. Oblivious to the risks, they started holding illegal late-night gatherings of hipsters for pop-up displays of sculpture, paintings, or installations.

By 2015, the original location for Locust had been bulldozed for a new charter middle school, and the organization—now funded by numerous foundation grants—had moved to Miami's tony Design District. But at the turn of the millennium, their presence was seminal for Wynwood's rebirth.

"Our first encounter with Wynwood was in 2000, when we had an exhibition at Locust Projects," recalls installation artist Roberto Behar, who rented a studio nearby. "Locust was the first nonprofit artist venue in the district, and the first time that people not from the neighborhood actually came around. Because of Locust, a number of artists got introduced to the neighborhood and started renting space for very little money, together with a number of important galleries."

INTO THE CRACK ZONE

The first regular art gallery to establish itself in Wynwood was the Dorsch Gallery, which opened in 2000 on 24th Street, one block north of Locust Projects. Unlike the commercial chockablock warehouse street where Locust operated, 24th was even more off the beaten path. It was a dimly lit street with a mix of storage and residential buildings—a leftover from when the neighborhood was created in the 1930s, when small homes were interspaced on side streets so that warehouse workers would have a place to live.

Gallery owner Brook Dorsch, a true New Pioneer who lived illegally in the back of his showroom, found himself in the darkest heart of the district, in the thick of crack houses and what he calls "opportunistic" petty criminals, the smash-and-grab variety. "They weren't the sort of people who would assault you in daylight," he says. "It was more about making sure you didn't leave anything valuable in your car."

As a former gallery owner in posh Coral Gables a few miles south, Dorsch had previous experience with municipal bureaucrats and knew how to play the rules and regulations game. He had managed to live in his first gallery thanks to a friend in city government who found a loophole whereby owners could apply for a certificate of use for "an art gallery with incidental caretaker's quarters." Even so, the application process for that exemption took almost a year, an experience that helped convince him to operate under the radar in Wynwood.

Consequently, when Dorsch first bought his 7,000-square-foot warehouse (prices had climbed to seventeen dollars a square foot by then), he simply went ahead with his gallery shows, as well as his covert living space, without pulling any permits or satisfying any zoning regulations. While he did make an initial visit to city hall, he says, "they gave me all kinds of nastiness about why I couldn't do a gallery there. They basically said, 'We won't permit anything, so get out of here.'" Dorsch decided to ignore the city's admonitions.

He was, however, slapped with an immediate $500 fine for dumping. That was thanks to the previous owner of the building, who had jettisoned bundles of paperwork and worthless checks onto nearby streets—with the building's address on it. "I explained to the court that I wasn't the owner of the building at the time it was dumped . . . They said, 'It doesn't matter, you own the building now, it has your address on it, so you get the fine.'"

Ultimately, Dorsch was able to get the fine reduced to fifty dollars, but it was another lesson in the illogic of regulations. Fortunately, since Wynwood was off the radar of city inspectors at the time, he went ahead with renovations without permits, gutting his warehouse and installing the electrical and plumbing himself, and then holding nighttime art openings without any interference.

Thrown into the warehouse deal was an adjacent residence, a small house occupied at the time of purchase by a crack dealer. Dorsch had considered living there, but the crack-dealing tenant refused to leave. Fortunately the miscreant was arrested a few months later; unfortunately the house was structurally unsound, damaged by a collection of eight hundred tires jammed inside the home.

"You know when you change your tires how you have to pay an environmental fee to get rid of the old ones? He [the crack dealer] was bypassing the system by collecting the money to get rid of tires, but not getting rid of them," says Dorsch. "He stuffed them in the house, so much so that the weight of the floor-to-ceiling tires cracked the subfloor, and the whole house was caving in on itself."

Unable to live in the house as planned, Dorsch instead walled off part of his warehouse gallery for an apartment. He lived there illegally for eight years. It was something he had to keep hidden when he eventually applied for a certificate of occupancy for the gallery, years after all his non-permitted refurbishing was complete.

"We were going for our [certificate of occupancy] for the gallery, so we called the apartment 'storage,'" says Dorsch. "It was an eight-month process for all the inspections, but I was showing this one artist who had paintings that were huge, four feet by eight feet. I still worked a full-time job when I was doing this, so when an inspector came, he had to make an appointment. So I knew he was going to come, and basically on that morning took my mattress, pushed it against the wall, took out the stove, took out anything else that would have looked like I was living there, and covered up everything with the paintings, even the closets where I had my clothes."

After that, Dorsch says he merely had to deal with a fire inspector who would come by every year or so, "always determined to find something." While Dorsch complied with safety requirements—placement of fire extinguishers and exit signs—he said the "nitty gritty" of every code requirement was impossible to meet. Push-out doors were required for emergency exits, for example, but were easy to break into. "So I had dead bolts on them," says Dorsch. "When the inspector would come I would remove the dead bolts and plug up the holes with tape so it looked like they didn't exist. But as soon as he would leave, I would have to put them in again because otherwise it exposed us to people breaking in."

Dorsch did not get away with everything. Without a permit, he insulated the ceiling of the gallery with a fire-retardant foam material. The fire department inspector insisted that he take it down because it had been not been attached with a code-approved adhesive. "We held blowtorches up to it and it would not burn. He [the inspector] did not care. If it wasn't applied right, it was in violation. He basically said to rip it out, even though it cost me twenty thousand dollars," says Dorsch. "And this is an art gallery, with nothing to burn except a couple of paintings—and it's a cement roof." After a two-year fight, Dorsch discovered a work-around, where he only had to cover the insulation with drywall, which became a legal "fire block."

BUILDING BLOCKS

While Dorsch and his fellow gallerists were holding off-the-grid art events, Wynwood was ignored by Miami's real estate community. Far quicker money could be made in the condo boom, now starting its long ride to the bubble burst of 2008. One exception was a Miami Beach real estate owner (of apartment buildings) who saw Wynwood purely for its space appeal, and started investing in the early 2000s.

"When I got here I could buy these buildings at forty dollars a square foot," says David Lombardi, who by 2015 would sell his Miami

Beach properties to purchase forty buildings in the district. "I was able to buy them for less than the cost of building them." Because Wynwood was so well situated, Lombardi thought he would rent warehouses for storage space to anybody from government agencies downtown to hoteliers on the beach. Then he discovered Dorsch and Locust.

"When I got here there were two galleries, but you would never know they were galleries. They didn't have signage, they didn't market themselves, one didn't even sell art," says Lombardi. "When I started buying my buildings I didn't know they existed." Then a newspaper article about Locust and Dorsch got Lombardi to attend a night opening at Dorsch's gallery.

"That was a street that was very dark. Windows blocked up, barbed wire, mean dogs behind fences, and a half-dozen body shops," says Lombardi. "We were walking through that and we walked into this guy's warehouse. And it was a crisp white space with colorful art on the walls and fifty young people looking at art, on a Saturday night, drinking wine and talking about art. I said to my wife: this is what we have to do with these spaces."

Lombardi began buying and renting warehouses for art galleries. He also bought the only three-story warehouse in Wynwood, the 1928 Seminole Building on 25th Street, which he converted to eight 2,000-square-foot live/work lofts that he rented to artists, despite the area's commercial zoning. "You have to understand, this area was economically marginalized," says Lombardi. "The head of the zoning commission at the time said to me, 'We know what you're doing, but we really like it. We know it's not zoned for this, but we are going to ignore it.'"

Both Lombardi and Dorsch remember those early days of "light" regulation as the Wild West days of Wynwood, when you acted first and asked for permission later. Dorsch recalls petitioning the city to make his street "one-way"—it was so narrow it would gridlock with traffic on the Second Saturday Art Walk nights that he and the other gallery owners started. When the city ignored him, he bolted up "official" one-way street signs he bought through the mail.

Lombardi also went guerilla with a broken phone booth in front of a small apartment building he owned on the edge of Wynwood. He complained to the city that the booth was being used as a drug dealer's headquarters. When the city ignored him, he unbolted the phone booth in the middle of the night, cut the dead wires, and dragged it away. For good measure, he moved the bus stop sign, also right in front of his little building, to a new spot down the street. "The next day the bus driver just pulled over at the new stop, and didn't blink an eye," says Lombardi. "He thought the city had moved it."

Despite the success of Lombardi's Seminole loft project, bankers were slow to realize the potential of the area, and it took him three years to get a bank to finance another mid-rise project called the Wynwood Lofts. It followed the high-ceiling factory design of the Seminole Building, and when it was finished in 2005, its thirty-six units sold out immediately.

By that time, Wynwood was becoming known as an arts district, thanks in part to marketing by the early pioneers. In 2003, when there were about fifteen galleries, Dorsch, Lombardi, and their colleagues formed an official Arts District organization, printing maps of gallery locations and launching the Second Saturday Art Walk, a night event when all the galleries would be open.

Second Saturday became a cult hit and introduced thousands of new people to the Wynwood art scene. Art Basel, which started its huge and prestigious annual show at the Miami Beach Convention Center the year before, gave the district an extra boost by housing its satellite events there. And then Goldman arrived.

THE ONCE AND FUTURE KING

By the time Goldman and family appeared, they had honed their lean urban formula. The first rule: Always buy a critical mass of buildings in the target neighborhood, and buy them cheaply. So they spent two years quietly assembling 400,000 square feet in thirty buildings, mostly along NW 2nd Avenue.

They then began to expand the artsy content of the neighborhood and build the brand of the Wynwood Arts District, leasing
space to art galleries for incredibly low rents of six and seven dollars
a square foot—even giving Miami's Museum of Contemporary Art
a massive annex for one dollar a year for four years. "Most landlords
would never think to do something like that," says Jessica Goldman
Srebnick. "But it was in our interest to say a big important museum
was staking their claim here." By 2006 more than forty new galleries
had opened in the area.

The Goldmans did not, however, anticipate the real estate collapse of 2007 and 2008, which put a damper on any new development in Miami. The city became a poster child for condominium
overbuilding and the real estate bubble that finally burst. This slowed
things down until about 2010, when the economy began to improve
and Tony Goldman came up with the idea of Wynwood Walls.

What makes Wynwood distinctly urban is its density, with
contiguous warehouses fronting the streets. In this close-packed
environment, Goldman created what amounted to a public park—a
grouping of large, open courtyards between and behind his warehouses, with an inviting gated entrance on NW 2nd Avenue (now
also known as Tony Goldman Way).

"We felt it was really important for people to have a place to
congregate and interact and be inspired," says Jessica. "It had been a
gravel parking lot and the backs of all our buildings. We lit them, and
prepared them, and invited the best artists in the world to come paint
them. It was an outdoor street museum unlike anyplace in the world."

To make sure the quality would be there, Goldman hired Jeffrey
Deitch to curate the walls. The results were spectacular, with world-
class artists such as Shepard Fairey, Ron English, Miss Van, Domingo
Zapata, Maya Hayuk, and Mexican street artists Saner & Sego,
attracted by the opportunity to paint the largest works of their lives.
It was the chance to be Diego Rivera, or even Michelangelo. And the
mural mania spread through the neighborhood like a viral video—

though not, perhaps, at the same quality level as the museum-like Wynwood Walls.

The phenomenon of the walls was Lean Urbanism in the literal sense, creating value (murals) from a low-cost input (paint) via individual creativity and hard work (the act of painting). It also followed the lean maxim of working within the local vernacular. While most of the warehouse walls in Wynwood were blank or splashed with odd Caribbean colors (foam green or mango yellow), there was a history of primitive-art product placement—painted images of footwear, fabrics, and appliances, a spillover from the hams, chickens, and cans of soda painted on the walls of grocery stores in nearby Little Haiti. There was also a tradition of gang-scripted graffiti on the more tattered edges of the neighborhood.

"Goldman incorporated something that already existed in the neighborhood—the signage and the graffiti—which he then elevated. He elevated the popular to high culture," says Behar, the installation artist who began renting his studio in Wynwood three years before Goldman "discovered" it. "He was very smart. He provided a public space that did not exist in the neighborhood. No one was willing to do that, not even the city, and he did so with a level of quality that provided a visual identity to the neighborhood."

CURATED INDIVIDUATION

The advent of the Walls was a uniquely lean and creative solution to some tough hurdles facing the reclamation of Wynwood from urban wilderness to live-work-play environment.

From the start, the settling and transformation of Wynwood was a disjointed process, determined to a large extent by the physical layout. While the buildings worked well as galleries, museums, and even performance spaces, their huge size and lack of windows were not conducive to the kind of places where entrepreneurial retail businesses could get a low-cost footing. They did not lend themselves easily to the variegated fabric of streets so dear to Jane Jacobs in her vision of *The Death and Life of Great American Cities,* where the diversity of the small and unique play such an essential role.

In addition to the impact of swiftly rising property values, Wynwood's evolution of street-side retail by New Pioneers was hampered by other constraints. The first was the district's lack of a residential population. Except for a small community of Puerto Ricans who lived in the substandard housing built for warehouse workers, and a handful of maverick artists, Wynwood had no residents. It was an industrial area with very little infrastructure for residential housing.

"Wynwood inherited this fabric, with gaps, of one-story windowless warehouses," says urbanist and former Miami zoning attorney Andrew Frey. "The adaptive uses that you can put a building to depends on the buildings themselves. There are only so many things you can do with a one-story, windowless warehouse. And one of those is not residences." The other "not" is small retail, including eateries. Both require an infrastructure of storefronts and small spaces.

By comparison, both Soho and South Beach had excellent bones for both residential and retail: multiple floors, street-front spaces for stores, and smaller units. "You could do a lot of stuff with those buildings," says Frey. "Wynwood had the limitation of its building stock."

The problem became a chicken-or-egg conundrum. Without residents, it was hard to create the foot traffic required for streetscapes of interesting retail. Without compelling (and requisite) retail, nobody wanted to live in the area, even if they could. And because of the Goldman-induced gold rush of galleries—and his reputation for transformation—real estate values escalated above what creative, risk-averse artists and entrepreneurs could afford. Those who had made the area compelling and engaging were already being priced out. Even with relatively low rents, capital-poor creatives could not afford to build out raw spaces for something like a restaurant or a coffee shop—let alone acquire the proper zoning.

Then several things happened. First, Goldman used his clout as a name developer in Miami to get a zoning overlay down the NW 2nd Avenue corridor where most of his properties were, making it easier to put in restaurants—which he did in 2008 with Joey's, an indoor/outdoor Italian place named after his son. It was the first place to eat in the neighborhood.

A year later, in 2009, Miami adopted a new citywide zoning code called Miami21, which had a provision that made a huge difference for Wynwood: so long as square footage was not increased, any adaptive reuse of a building would be exempt from additional parking requirements. In a flash, the cost for legally redeveloping an old warehouse dropped dramatically. When Goldman converted a 40,000-square-foot building on NW 3rd Avenue into his headquarters and a location for retail businesses, for example, he didn't have to add eighty more parking spaces required under the previous zoning. "A significant amount of Wynwood's success is based on that one leniency," says Joe Furst, president of Goldman Properties.

Miami21 also permitted live/work space in Wynwood, but limited density to thirty-six units per acre. The idea was to keep the area light industrial, but this stymied the ability to build small residential spaces, a necessity to bring a twenty-four-hour population to the area. You could live in a tiny apartment only if it was stashed in the back of an increasingly expensive warehouse; even the density of low-rise loft buildings like Lombardi's Wynwood Lofts were prohibited under the new zoning.

It was in the midst of this conundrum that Tony Goldman came up with the Wynwood Walls, opening a Pandora's paint box across the district. In one stroke it created a fascinating area to walk around and put a kind of happy face on an area that once resembled a war zone.

"What replaced the [creative retail] was the paintings on the walls," says photographer Walker. "That became the tourist attraction, that became the draw that made this neighborhood so bizarre, weird, wonderful, surprising, shocking—all those things that out-of-towners and locals couldn't believe when they walked into it. But that still didn't mean you could buy a cup of coffee."

You might not be able to get a cup of coffee, but you could finally get a drink. The year after Joey's opened, a speakeasy and outdoor bar called Cafeina opened on a side street off NW 2nd Avenue. The following year—2010, the year of the Walls—Goldman put in another restaurant, the Wynwood Kitchen & Bar, which bracketed the entrance of the walls and opened onto the first of its courtyards.

CURATED RETAIL

It was not until 2011 that you could actually get a good cup of java in Wynwood, at Panther Coffee. And the only reason you could do that was because Goldman Properties realized that it was in danger of killing the goose that laid the golden egg. Because prices were now marching from the $100-per-square-foot level to the $500- to $600-per-foot range by 2015—twenty to sixty times what the first lean artists and pioneers paid—Goldman realized that uncapitalized bohemian entrepreneurs were going to have a hard time starting up in Wynwood.

Wynwood was also attracting more attention from the city—especially after the zoning overlay that allowed it to become, in effect, an entertainment district. City inspectors were suddenly looking things over and the days of operating under the radar were ending, which meant more financial resources were needed to launch a "legit" enterprise.

So Goldman Properties began to curate small and creative enterprises, and to incubate them like a shared coworking space. That became their mission and their tactic: to artificially sustain a lean urban environment with low entry barriers. Starting with Panther, they created lower-than-market deals for the kinds of companies they thought captured the Wynwood zeitgeist.

Panther Coffee was just that, a subsidized artisanal bohemian coffee shop that ground its beans from family farms in Nicaragua, Ethiopia, Brazil, and Rwanda. Its dark, wood-lined interior and tree-shaded courtyard (a single Poinciana tree, rare in Wynwood) was immediately jammed with millennials and their mobile devices.

That same year, 2011, Goldman underwrote a small theater called The Light Box. It opened in the Goldman Warehouse for the Miami Light Project, a prestigious local performance nonprofit. Another start-up, a high-tech incubator called the LAB Miami, was itself incubated inside the Goldman Properties HQ building (a space later filled by the Miami Boutique Café) before it expanded to 10,000 square feet in 2013, adjacent to The Light Box. With high-tech newbie start-ups like Klangbox, Infinixsoft, and Loigica, the LAB Miami offered everything from a place at a desk in the main room for $265 a month to a glassed-in office for $1,600. It also offered cheap space for TED-like talks and presentations.

"I would say, maybe somewhat arrogantly, that the content of what people think about when they think about Wynwood are businesses that we've seeded, given sweetheart deals to, and helped get funded," says Goldman properties president Furst. "Panther, the two restaurants, all the artistic programs that we have done, the LAB, Miami Light Box—we absolutely put the content well ahead of rental rate."

Furst says his favorite project was Zak the Baker, "an unfunded guy with a great talent" that Furst and Goldman Properties approached in his baking facility in working-class Hialeah. "We put him in business here. We were the landlord and the lender. We gave him a very favorable rate with an upside for us."

Zak the Baker, which serves sandwiches as well as loaves of bread, became an overnight sensation in Wynwood, with lines out the door. Now Furst is expanding Zak from 2,100 square feet to 7,000 square feet, with plans to create a glass-walled street theater of baking. "I think it will be one of the great deals in Wynwood, a great community giveback deal, a production baking theater—pastry, bread, the whole thing—where you as a client will be a participant."

Zak Stern, the baker in question, readily admits he could not have relocated to Wynwood without the help of Goldman Properties, which not only financed the build out but also tied his rent to his performance.

"They know what they need to do to activate a neighborhood," he says. "They need to get independent artisans in here to give it some soul and then later can charge whatever they want. It was clever and it worked."

Furst and Goldman Properties are not alone in their attempt to create an artificially lean environment to lure new and interesting businesses.

Several blocks away on Miami Avenue, a cluster of restaurants has emerged following the installation of Jimmy'z Kitchen, a casual gourmet restaurant on the ground floor of Cynergi, the only residential building that went up in Wynwood during Miami's condo craze. Jimmy Carey, a longtime Miami chef who had made a name for himself in a tiny takeout place on Miami Beach, was able to create a location there only because of the landlord's willingness to artificially depress the rental rate and to pay for infrastructure that included a $200,000 ventilation system.

Even so, says Carey, "The first year [2010] was scary as hell. It was a crapshoot, and we didn't know what to expect . . . but I had a lot of trust in Tony Goldman and I saw what he was doing with the Walls." In the ensuing years, says Carey, the foot traffic increased dramatically—so much so that the landlord is now trying to triple Carey's rent from its original seventeen dollars a square foot.

Developer Lombardi did his part as well. In 2014 he cheaply leased an empty lot to a drive-in movie theater company from Austin, Texas, called the Blue Starlite (since relocated to a larger space in Coconut Grove), and in 2015 subsidized an open-air restaurant called The Annex, an almost self-conscious pop-up parody of lean, pioneering urbanism.

Located down the street from the Rubell collection, The Annex was a bar and restaurant assembled on a 3,000-square-foot cement slab. Overhead: A tent "roof" on a metal frame. On the two sides: dozens of wooden French window frames of all sizes, panes intact, screwed together lengthwise. The back and front of the restaurant are open; the back faces a warehouse wall with a giant Blatz Beer neon sign; the front opens onto a gravel courtyard. On one side of the courtyard is a food truck kitchen where the cooking is done.

The Annex was a partnership between Lombardi and an antique dealer named Steve Haribel, who used district warehouses to store an immense collection of nineteenth- and twentieth-century furnishings from the French countryside. These supplied The Annex's furniture, warmly lit by strings of old-fashioned lightbulbs under the tent: old French apothecary chests, leather chairs and sofas, and wooden tables of different sizes, all kept cool by huge fans that move Miami's balmy air through the open space.

INSTITUTIONALIZED LEAN COOL

By 2015, Wynwood was home to more than two dozen bars, cafés, restaurants, and breweries, along with more than a dozen retail boutiques selling clothing and housewares. Several new collections—most notably Gary Nader's Latin American Art Museum—joined the scene, along with the independent O Cinema. There was even a hair salon, a bank branch, and a florist.

The speed of the neighborhood's transformation, especially from 2013 onward, was breakneck; the smooth evolution from desolation to destination was artificially accelerated, manipulated in a way that dropped a few chapters from the lean casebook, like a gearbox missing a couple of teeth; it still worked, but with an irregular motion. The result was a hugger-mugger neighborhood with odd couplings: an old repair shop for truck motors catty-cornered from a bikini boutique; a new steak and ale restaurant across from a homeless shelter; a Caribbean shoe import/export warehouse facing an intersection with three art galleries. The district fractured as it hurtled toward the future, leaving fascinating splinters in its wake.

In an attempt to make sure that the cool, raw motif of Wynwood was preserved as it blossomed, in 2013 Goldman Properties and Lombardi (with ninety properties between them) formed their own Business Improvement District with other area investors. While not omnipotent, the Wynwood BID does control funding for public parking (fees paid by new buildings) and has its own design review board. Its aim is to make sure that landowners in Wynwood do not rent out to bland national brands.

"Now we are all tied to the same mast," says Goldman's Furst, who is also the president of the BID. "We as a BID are trying to keep the things that make Wynwood a little bit edgy and a little bit off and a little bit weird . . . we want to encourage [other property owners] to do similar deals. We want to work collaboratively, we don't necessarily want to be the loss leaders for everyone else's success."

So far, the collective shield has held—at least in the sense that most new businesses in the district are small and interesting, though their degree of funkiness varies.

On the one hand, there is a newly occupied alleyway off NW 2nd Avenue with pretentiously trendy stores that sell designer stationery (Wynwood Letterpress), chic sunglasses (Wynwood Shades), tony home furnishings (INIVA), and savory gourmet items to eat and drink (Jucy Lu life market). It feels like the fall retail collection from *GQ* or *Vanity Fair.*

On the other hand, a few blocks away sits the new Concrete Beach Brewery, a twenty-barrel brew house, with enormous brass tanks of beer behind the circular glass walls of an indoor/outdoor "social hall" that can accommodate musicians and small theater groups; the exterior walls that line its courtyard consist of rebar cages crammed with broken concrete. And over on Miami Avenue, twenty-somethings drink and take turns on a half-pike for skateboards while losing their hearing to deafening music at a new bar named Nugbrand, in deference to a bud of marijuana.

And while rents of forty and fifty dollars a square foot are nothing like the seven and eight dollars a foot once available, they are still much lower than the $175 a square foot in the nearby Design District or the $300 a square foot on Miami Beach's Lincoln Road pedestrian mall. And though the new rent thresholds do not permit truly funky start-ups, they do permit interesting places that, with good financing, can make inventive use of the huge, high-ceilinged places they occupy.

Even this middle ground of an artificial lean may not last long, however. In its final march to generate a local population, the BID is pushing through a new zoning package for Wynwood. The current zoning permits only thirty-six units per acre; the new zoning will allow for 150 units per acre, which means that developers can build units that are 500 to 660 square feet and rent for $1,300 to $1,500 per month. The new zoning also allows five-story buildings on side streets and eight-story buildings on the main avenues of Wynwood, with variances up to twelve stories.

When this zoning goes into play, Wynwood will reach its final destination as a walkable, bustling, live-work-play world. On the one hand, it will have finally legislated the construction of small residential units. But the goose that laid the golden egg will most likely consume its own entrails, tearing down the CBS warehouse walls that are now so fulgently covered with art, replacing them with the glass walls of condominiums and designer shops.

"When you look at this neighborhood in three years it will be unrecognizable," says developer Lombardi. "The murals will be on the walls, but the tenancies will be unrecognizable. There will be boutiques and cafés, but we won't have sixty galleries. We might have twenty. The little guys will have nowhere to go."

And yet this is the ironic goal of all New Pioneers, and the way in which Lean Urbanism achieves the creation of wealth for its original stakeholders. In the same way that the architects and carpenters of Seaside were paid with buildable lots that were later valued at close to one million dollars each, so will the original New Pioneers of Wynwood cash out. Gallery pioneer Brook Dorsch, who bought his warehouse in 2000 for $120,000, sold it in 2015 for $3.5 million. His new location: Miami's economically marginalized neighborhood of Little Haiti.

"It's only when it is illegal that it makes sense for artists to live in a commercial or industrial or inner city kind of place," says photographer Walker. "Because the minute it becomes legal, it's no longer affordable for artists. Yet they are the ones—the artists and the creatives—that create the foot traffic and the interest, the hip quality that suddenly makes the neighborhood a desirable place to be."

chapter four

NEW ORLEANS: A TALE OF TWO CITIES

How People Succeed Where Government Fails

The destruction of New Orleans in 2005 by Hurricane Katrina, and its subsequent rebuilding from scratch, provides startling contrasts for understanding the New Pioneer concept of the citizen builder, and for appreciating the idea that common sense and doing it yourself trumps the rules and regulations of the professionals. Ten years after the storm, certain neighborhoods in the city were entirely rebuilt while others still languished. The metrics of success or failure fall into several categories, but one conclusion is salient: When rebuilding came from the bottom up, based on individual effort and ingenuity, success came quicker and at a lower cost than when rebuilding was engineered from the top down. This proved true regardless of whether the top-down solution came from the private or public sector, and despite immensely greater resources from above. Where regulation receded, individuals succeeded.

A big problem with top-down orchestration is that it seeks to impose a set of idealized solutions created in vitro— in the lab, so to speak—which are then imposed through all-encompassing codes. In New Orleans, the Make It Right foundation (MIR) embodied "top-down" solutions by the private sector. MIR spent inordinate amounts of money installing LEED (Leadership in Energy and Environmental Design) Platinum–certified "green" homes that capriciously ignored the traditional vernacular of New Orleans housing. In the public sector, "top-down" was embodied on a much vaster scale by the Road Home, the $9 billion federal program that squandered most of its resources trying to regulate the rebuilding process.

Contrariwise, where citizen builders either ignored the help from above, or ignored the strings attached, rebuilding occurred faster and more efficiently. The largest example was the Vietnamese community in New Orleans East, which eschewed government help and rebuilt in record time. Other examples included the many small-scale, volunteer-driven solutions that resulted in far more housing, per dollar, than well-funded answers from above. All demonstrated the power of the New Pioneer.

Two Sides of New Orleans: Building from the ground up in the Vietnamese community (above) proved far more efficient than expensive top-down solutions like this $450,000 high tech "shack" of less than 1,000 square feet (below).

AFTER THE FLOOD

If you drive through the streets of the Versailles neighborhood in New Orleans East, you can't see any signs of 2005's Hurricane Katrina. The middle-class, single-story brick homes that line the main east-west corridor of Dwyer Boulevard are well kept and neatly landscaped. They are accessorized like any middle-class neighborhood: multiple cars in the driveways, bicycles strewn by front steps, basketball hoops sprouting next to garage doors. If you cruise up Michoud Boulevard, which crosses Dwyer and connects the neighborhood with old Highway 90 to the south and Interstate 10 to the north, you can see posh cul-de-sacs of multistory homes. These are protected by iron filigree gates but built with the same ubiquitous rose-maroon brick as their more modest neighbors. The only clue that this is not your typical American residential streetscape is the women who walk down the streets wearing their traditional conical Vietnamese nón lá hats—that, and the fact that numerous front yards sport elaborate statues of the Virgin Mary.

About six miles west, in the Upper Ninth Ward, the scene is completely different. Cruise down Louisa Drive from I-10 toward the Mississippi River and you will see a checkered moonscape of empty lots and damaged homes, interspersed with houses that have been repaired and elevated. The streets are still buckled with plates of broken concrete and tarmac. A rough estimate would be that perhaps a third of the housing has been restored or rebuilt, even though it has been more than a decade since the flooding caused by Katrina inundated 80 percent of the Crescent City. The remaining homes still standing are in various states of disrepair, bracketed by empty lots where former homes were demolished and replaced by weeds and wild shrubs—what the locals call "jungle land."

What makes this divergence all the more glaring is the fact that Versailles, home to New Orleans' Vietnamese community, was entirely rebuilt in the year following Katrina with no federal assistance. The rest of the city still needs work in virtually all of the wards that flooded, despite the influx of $11 billion in federal reconstruction aid. And nowhere is the need for rebuilding more pressing than in the Ninth Ward, especially the Lower Ninth Ward, where tens of millions have been spent with surprisingly little to show for it.

The disparity between these two neighborhoods is the contrast between the do-it-yourself spirit of Lean Urbanism and the New Pioneer, unhindered by regulations, and the cumbersome weight of restrictions and conditions that come with investments from above.

FROM LEAN TO LEANER

New Orleans has never had a reputation for doing things the "right" way. It is a city with a scurrilous history, of rough-hewn trappers and deported criminals, of pirates and blockade-runners, of corrupt politicians and notorious eccentrics. It is a city of mavericks, an outlier, a Caribbean footprint on US soil with its own culture and customs. It is a harbor for obdurate individuals who proudly do things their own way, certainly not by the book. As Keith Twitchell, the president of the Committee for a Better New Orleans (CBNO), puts it, "I think a lot of people here don't even know what permits are."

In its own unique way, New Orleans is a perennial showcase for many of the principles of Lean Urbanism and the New Pioneer. It has a reputation as a city that scorns regulations, a place where people build as they see fit, on a small and individualistic scale. The result is a metropolis of organic development, an urban tapestry that shuns outside chains and cookie-cutter developments. You will not find a McDonald's in the French Quarter. Its culture of street music is a tangible display of low entry barriers for artists and entrepreneurs.

Hurricane Katrina dramatically affected New Orleans as a laboratory for Lean Urbanism and the New Pioneer. Similar to Detroit, the city suffered physical destruction on a massive scale. Most of the city flooded—though not the "sliver along the river" of high ground where the city was first established along the Mississippi River—

causing vast injury to its residential areas and an unprecedented diaspora of citizenry, from which it has yet to recover.

The numbers tell a big part of the story. According to the US Census Bureau, New Orleans had already been in decline prior to Katrina, having slipped from a peak of 484,000 residents in 2000 to 455,000 in 2005. After Katrina, the 2006 population fell to below 209,000, meaning the city lost more than half of its inhabitants in the wake of the storm. By the 2013 census, the city had only grown back to 379,000—still 100,000 fewer souls than before Katrina, 20 percent down from its antediluvian population.

With the impeccable if perverse logic of fewer intact houses, the destruction of the city did not destroy the real estate market as it did in Detroit. Average prices for single-family houses in good condition actually rose 20 percent in the first quarter after the hurricane, and another 15 percent in the next quarter, as demand exceeded supply. Consequently, New Orleans also saw little of the national drop in real estate prices following the subprime lending debacle of the mid-2000s. Today, housing prices in certain neighborhoods are reaching historic highs as the city's recovery accelerates.

The flood did, however, lower the barriers of entry for start-ups and new business, attracting young people, artists, entrepreneurs, etc.—the New Pioneers who arrived to rebuild the urban wasteland. Similar to other cities that have experienced an urban apocalypse (yes, Detroit), the city was gutted by economic and physical destruction. Written off by large-scale, mainstream investors, the playing field was leveled for small businesses.

The result has been a bonanza of entrepreneurial activity. According to a Brookings Institution report released in August 2013, New Orleans exceeded the national average for new business start-ups for the three-year period ending in 2012 by 56 percent. Its annual Entrepreneurship Week conference, launched in 2008 by local incubator The Idea Village, is now the largest crowd-funding event in the world. The 2014 iteration of the conference attracted more than 5,000 entrepreneurs, business executives, investors, and MBA students.

The city's cultural life has also escalated. New Orleans now has more than double the national average of arts and culture nonprofits. Likewise, reports the Brookings Institution, quality of life has also increased: bicycle lanes and pathways, for example, have grown exponentially, from less than eleven miles before Katrina to more than fifty-six miles today, all made possible by the overnight gutting of the urban landscape.

Perhaps most significantly for the city's future, public education has been reinvented. As of September 2014, New Orleans became the country's first all-charter-school system, with smaller, locally focused schools replacing the mammoth, unwieldy pre-Katrina institutions that were considered among the worst in the country.

"One way to look at Katrina is that it created a clean slate for the radical reinvention of the schools," says Scott Cowen, the president of New Orleans' Tulane University. "Why try to rebuild a system that was clearly failing to begin with?" With little other choice, the city instead encouraged the growth of autonomous schools (i.e., charters), decentralizing control and trusting the ingenuity of local charter operators. Instead of issuing specific instructions, the city outlined ten principles for education reform, including empowering local schools, engaging the community and parents, and creating safe environments for learning. The result has been a dramatic improvement in academic standards.

On the higher education front, Tulane University itself received more applications in 2010—44,000—than any other private school in the country. Students everywhere wanted to attend a school in the heart of New Orleans and be part of its renaissance. Subsequent to Katrina, in fact, Tulane created a Center for Public Service, through which every student had to enlist in a volunteer program to help the city, ranging from tutoring kids to building houses and public gardens.

A HISTORY OF STARTING OVER

The idea of working from a clean slate is actually something of a New Orleans tradition. In September 1722, four years after its founding, a hurricane hit the ramshackle, unplanned cityscape and literally erased it. This allowed city engineers, who considered the storm a godsend, to plot out the grid of the French Quarter and establish an elegant metropolis.

What's worth noting is that right after that hurricane, and subsequent to other hurricanes and fires that have periodically devastated the city, the people immediately "set to work to repair the damage done" as one historian observed. The people themselves did the rebuilding, just as the parents and grandparents of today's Lower Ninth Ward residents built their own homes. And there was no hiatus during which residents waited for someone else to rescue them; they acted without hesitation or approval.

After the great fire of 1788, for example (which, similar to Katrina, wrecked 80 percent of the urban landscape), the city experienced a construction boom and expansion; by the time the next great fire hit in 1794, the city was entirely rebuilt, with the addition of the French Market and the city's first theater. After both conflagrations, temporary structures were immediately built to house the population, and direct loans were made straightaway to help people rebuild their homes. After Katrina, residents were not allowed to return to their homes for many months, let alone build temporary structures; trailers from the Federal Emergency Management Agency (FEMA) that were intended to provide interim shelter took nearly a year to arrive.

The response to Katrina was unique in New Orleans' history in terms of its lethargy.

Part of the fault lay with city government, which took seven months to come up with a master plan that everyone could agree upon. There was even a heated debate in Congress as to whether the federal government should help New Orleans rebuild at all, a position spearheaded by Speaker of the House Dennis Hastert. But much of the blame lay with the federal bureaucracy, which was so overburdened with its own regulations that it could barely function.

"It was soon clear that FEMA couldn't manage itself out of a paper bag," observes Cowen. "FEMA administrators, many of them lawyers, felt safer playing by the rules. But after Katrina, those rules were useless. We were operating in a new environment . . ." Jurisdictional regulations, for example, prevented Navy and Coast Guard vessels from entering the Mississippi River to help victims after Katrina. The deployment of some 2,000 firefighters from across the country who volunteered for rescue operations was delayed for several crucial days because FEMA regulations required them to be trained for, among other things, awareness of sexual harassment.

Compare this to the response to Hurricane Betsy in 1965, in an era with astonishingly fewer regulations. President Lyndon Johnson—LBJ—arrived in New Orleans the day after Betsy hit, convening a team that included the head of the federal Office of Emergency Planning, the Secretary of Agriculture, the chairman of the American Red Cross, the Surgeon General of the United States, and the head of the Small Business Administration, the president's vehicle to issue commercial and residential loans.

Ignoring the red tape, LBJ ordered food to be distributed by the Department of Agriculture and the Red Cross at once. He ordered the Army Corps of Engineers to begin debris removal that night. He announced the immediate allocation of funds to rebuild streets, highways, bridges, public buildings, docks, hospitals, and schools, and he ordered the immediate supply of federal equipment to begin. LBJ also suspended mortgage payments for VA loans. He ordered the SBA to begin processing the first long-term reconstruction loans *the next day.*

President George W. Bush, by comparison, did not return to the White House from a vacation in Texas until two days after Katrina hit. He did not tour the Gulf area until four days afterward, which is when he saw the extent of devastation and authorized federal aid. He did not visit the city of New Orleans itself until more than two weeks after Katrina hit. But, worst of all, he put FEMA—an agency designed for short-term emergencies—in charge of rebuilding.

THE HARDEST HIT

When Katrina slammed into New Orleans on August 29, 2005, the damage from wind and rain was heavy but not lethal. What swamped the metropolis, literally, was the breaking of levees along the industrial canals that cross the city to connect the Mississippi River with Lake Pontchartrain. It was not until a day after the hurricane made land-fall, in fact, that the storm surge breached the levee system and began to flood the lower-lying neighborhoods. Four major breaches of the city's canal walls took place, along with scores of smaller fractures.

Some of the 1.2 million people who evacuated the greater metropolitan area had already started to return when the flooding began. Father Vien Nguyen, the pastor of Mary Queen of Vietnam Church in New Orleans East, remembers calling members of his flock the day after the hurricane hit and telling them not to come back yet because the "waters are rising." Ultimately, the flooding caused $109 billion in damages (2005 dollars), making it the costliest natural disaster in the history of the United States.

One of the hardest-hit areas was the Ninth Ward, especially the Lower Ninth Ward, a predominantly African American community about two miles east of the French Quarter. The Lower Ninth is par-titioned from the rest of New Orleans by the city's largest industrial canal. It was this canal that was fatally breached the day after Katrina hit. The homes in the Lower Ninth were literally swept away by the rush of water, creating the ultimate icon of the disaster: the sight of "house-riders" who desperately clung to the roofs of their floating residences for days. Many of New Orleans' 1,577 fatalities from the storm occurred here.

Another hard-hit area was Father Vien's New Orleans East neighborhood. It is partitioned from the rest of the city by the same industrial canal that abuts the Lower Ninth Ward. Long considered a backwater of the city, New Orleans East contains an area known as Versailles—aka "Village de l'Est"—home to approximately 5,000 ethnic Vietnamese immigrants who settled the area in the mid-1970s after the fall of South Vietnam. Their homes, built principally from brick, did not float away during the hurricane (one thinks here of the three little pigs and the huffing and puffing wolf). There was, however, enormous damage from wind and the rising waters that engorged the neighborhood with several feet of mud.

The recovery of these two communities from Katrina speaks volumes about the pioneering spirit of the Vietnamese immigrants and the principles of Lean Urbanism. The hard-hit Ninth Ward looked to the federal government for help, a not uncommon reaction in a declared disaster area where local government resources are overwhelmed. The Versailles neighborhood, on the other hand, did not expect, want, or ask for any help from the feds. Its people had long ago experienced the fickle nature of aid from the US government.

GOOD MORNING, VIETNAM

In the heart of the Vietnamese community in New Orleans East stands Mary Queen of Vietnam Church, a whitewashed, modern-looking building complex that faces south onto a huge grassy expanse. This open ground across from the church was once designated for public housing but is now home to a soccer field and an urban farm. It is also used for parking, since Mary Queen is one of the busiest Catholic churches in the United States, with more than 5,000 members. On any given Sunday, four or five masses are given in Vietnamese, as well as in English and Spanish.

The people who live nearby and attend the church are descended from several towns in what was then North Vietnam, themselves descendants from Vietnamese Catholics who were converted by missionaries in the fifteenth and sixteenth centuries. When the war of independence from French colonial rule succeeded in establishing North Vietnam in 1954, the inhabitants of these towns—coastal fishermen by trade—fled south to avoid communist rule. They settled in villages on the China Sea, where they lived until the fall of South Vietnam in 1975 compelled them to flee again—this time to the United States.

The Vietnamese Catholics settled in various places in the United States, but a preponderance moved to Gulf of Mexico communities where shrimping was good, such as Galveston, Texas, and New Orleans. In New Orleans East there was a rambling low-cost apartment complex known as the Versailles Arms; it was a perfect place for the first families to settle, located not too far from where shrimping boats could be docked, and in a distant, low-lying area of the city that was of little interest to other New Orleans residents.

Over the years, the industrious Vietnamese community thrived, growing to some 1,600 households, but never really assimilating. They kept their own language, customs, food, etc., and became a self-reliant immigrant community.

When Katrina hit, the residents of Versailles (as the whole community came to be known) evacuated along with everyone else. They moved to temporary shelters in cities like Houston and Dallas, and relocated to other locales in California. And, like everyone else, they were initially prevented from returning home by the National Guard.

Tony Tran, now fifty, was a teenager when his family left Vietnam for the United States. When Katrina hit he evacuated with his two sons, while his wife stayed behind in the hospital where she worked as a nurse. Tran says that despite resistance from the authorities—and from National Guardsmen assigned to protect the city from itself—a large number of Vietnamese returned within two months.

"We came back to all sorts of things, like gun barrels and soldiers trying to kick us out of the city," says Tran. "They said it was because of safety issues and lack of services, but our people said, 'In Vietnam we didn't have electricity, we didn't have toilets. Why so many regulations to stop us from coming back?' So they came back anyway, two months after the storm." The water had already receded, pumped out after two weeks, leaving behind several feet of mud.

Almost immediately, the people of Versailles began to rebuild. "During that time, city hall didn't have a system to give out building permits, so they said, 'Just go ahead and gut your houses and build whatever you can,'" recalls Tran. "And so the Vietnamese people, with a mentality of survival, did so."

Unlike other areas of New Orleans, where the focus was on shelters for individual residents—including the long-delayed FEMA trailers—the initial efforts in Versailles were aimed at bringing back public buildings and common spaces so the community could organize itself. "Instead of focusing on their houses and themselves individually, the first thing the Vietnamese did was to organize at the churches and their community centers and get those up and running," says New Orleans urban planner Ann Daigle. "And then they got their fishing boats up and running."

The Mary Queen of Vietnam Church became the de facto community staging area. "The people came back but couldn't live in their homes, because of the mud and mold and devastation," says Tran, who now works for the church as a parish assistant. "So they came out here to the church parking lot. They just camped out. [The church] became the main gathering center for food supplies, and the Red Cross brought us a lot of food." In other areas of southern Louisiana where there wasn't flooding, church congregations cooked food and brought it over. Church services were conducted from an open stage, with a throng of 3,000 folding chairs for the outdoor masses.

For the next six months, groups of residents went from house to house, gutting them, cleaning them up, and putting them back together. Those who knew how to do things—like carpenters and masons—showed other homeowners how to do the work. There was no place to purchase home-rebuilding materials in the area, so teams would go out and buy lumber, cement, and Sheetrock from home supply centers hours away and haul them back to the neighborhood. "It was amazing, but they did it," says Tran.

One of the Vietnamese who returned was a (now) seventy-two-year-old named Tanh, who initially evacuated to Dallas. Like many of his neighbors who fled under the mayor's order for mandatory evacuation, Tanh returned as soon as he could to rebuild his home. He worked to repair his roof, replace wallboard, and mix mortar for brickwork, all the while living in a tiny attic crawl space provided by a neighbor. "We rebuilt everything ourselves," he says. "I rebuilt my own home, with a hammer, a saw, everything. After about six months I was living here again." During the rebuilding process, neither he nor any of his neighbors were accosted by inspectors, or felt any need to involve city officials.

Today Tanh and his wife work on the fruit and vegetable farm located across Dwyer Boulevard from the church, created as a post-Katrina community-development project. There are about three acres under cultivation. It is a rich and immaculate site, with thick rows of bright green plants springing from dark soil. A few dozen yards from the road are a toolshed and a canvas tent framed by wooden poles, where the farmers wash the vegetables and escape the sun's glare. The food is sold weekly at a farmers market in the parking lot of a strip mall at the entrance to the community on Alcee Fortier Boulevard; the rest goes to a cooperative that sells the produce outside the community.

Not far from the farm and the church is a huge grassy square, the Village de l'Est Park, a sort of community commons that locals refer to simply as "the Viet." It is lined with houses and encompasses, on its eastern edge, the local Einstein charter school. In the middle of the Viet are several buildings, including a large community center that was among the first structures to be restored.

Today the community center functions as a place where classes are offered and neighborhood events are staged. Elderly residents practice Tai Chi at the center, for example. One of the staff members at the center is Jennifer Tran (no relation to Tony), who was fifteen when Katrina hit. Her family, like others, jumped right into the rebuilding effort.

"My dad put up the Sheetrock and did everything himself," says Tran. "We didn't really get a lot of help. We had help from churches in other states, but most families bought the materials and did it themselves." Like many other residents, Jennifer's father had no formal training in building. "My dad is a mechanic, and wasn't in construction," she says. "He learned how to do it by doing it."

"The Vietnamese were able to organize and rebuild their community faster, smarter, and more economically than any other neighborhood in the city," says Pamela Bryan, who serves on the New Orleans City Planning Commission. "It was a model of rebuilding that everyone else aspires to." As for permits or inspections, says Bryan, "We had no code enforcement here. The city was broken, completely broken . . . Code enforcement? It was like the Wild West."

Among other things, the Vietnamese completely ignored the federal mandates for elevating homes. This height, a prerequisite for all homes built or rebuilt using federal funds, took a year to determine, and was another factor in the delay of rebuilding the city. The Vietnamese, free from government assistance or regulation, were able to ignore this three-foot height requirement, which would have added huge costs to rebuilding. "If they go back under water, they'll just have to rebuild again," says Bryan.

The only government interactions with the Versailles community following Katrina were by and large negative. First came the refusal by the government-regulated power company to turn the electricity back on in the area. That gave rise to organized protests from the Vietnamese, who were required to prove they were actually living in their homes again.

The second was the city's decision to create a massive dump for the millions of tons of hurricane debris—much of it toxic—on the doorstep of the community. It took sustained community demonstrations to finally halt the dump, which by then had accumulated 300 million tons of debris. Most of that has since been relocated.

About the only institutional assistance that the Vietnamese accepted came from Tulane University, which helped the Mary Queen of Vietnam Community Development Corporation repurpose an old post office as a health clinic. The only government presence remains in the form of the original Versailles Arms apartments where the Vietnamese immigrants first lived. After the owner received a large insurance payment and departed, the city took over the property but has done nothing with it. Today it remains an abandoned, gutted residential complex behind chain-link fences. It is the only structure in the neighborhood that remains damaged.

THE SAGA OF THE LOWER NINTH

To reach the Lower Ninth from Versailles, or from any other part of the city, you have to take a bridge across a heavy industrial canal that borders the ward. From atop the levee that lines this canal, you can look down on the area that suffered the city's greatest destruction. Unlike the rest of the metropolitan area, which endured a steady rise of floodwaters that slowly subsumed homes, the Lower Ninth was slammed by the deluge rushing from the breached levee. The surge literally swept houses from their foundations.

Robert Green was one of the victims. He lost both his mother and his daughter, unable to pull them onto the roof where he had taken refuge, and where he survived for several days before emergency crews were able to rescue him. "All of this was destroyed, everything. It was all just washed away," he says.

Today Green lives in one of the hypermodern "sustainable" homes built in the neighborhood by the Make It Right foundation, a charitable group founded by famed actor and New Orleans native Brad Pitt. Pitt arrived two years after the flood, stunned to see so little in the way of rebuilding in the predominantly African American Lower Ninth.

Pitt raised millions of dollars (the total eventually exceeded $45 million) from private sources to rebuild, from scratch, the area directly in the path of the breached levee. From twenty-one renowned architecture firms worldwide, Pitt solicited designs for homes that could earn Platinum LEED certification and yet somehow be cost-effective for low-income residents. By 2015, MIR had built 105 of the 150 houses Pitt pledged to construct for those who "lost everything."

The results have attracted national as well as global attention: a village of dramatically shaped and brightly colored homes that appear to have been helicoptered in from the future. It feels like an architectural laboratory, which is not far from the truth: the MIR goal was not merely to rebuild the demolished homes of the Lower Ninth, but to create a healthy community of "affordable, high-quality, environmentally sustainable homes."

Green's home, for example, can be sealed as tight as a submarine to preserve the cool air from its efficient air-conditioning system. It has an array of solar panels, as do all of the MIR homes, which reduces monthly energy bills to about the cost of a haircut. It uses a tank-less water heater; its plumbing is nontoxic; its toilets can flush either solid or liquid waste (the latter saves water); and its countertops are made from recycled post-industrial glass bound by an "environmentally friendly resin, which comes in part from corn oil."

All of this may be commendable, but what is immediately apparent is that most of the houses ignore the lessons of the simple, cost-effective architecture developed over hundreds of years by the pioneers who actually built and lived in New Orleans. It's not that the homes don't have traditional elements. It's that these components have been scrambled and reassembled, as though by an alien who tried to construct human habitats from all the correct parts but without understanding how to correctly assemble them. In culinary terms, the houses resemble the way a French chef would deconstruct a key lime pie, separating the elements and arranging them randomly on the plate.

Green's house, like traditional New Orleans homes, has a front porch—only its front porch is overhead, hanging above the front door, a narrow, second-story apparition that can only be reached by a child-sized spiral staircase located in the master bedroom. The same staircase also leads to a narrow, shelflike balcony in the bedroom itself that has no apparent function. Needless to say, the staircase is almost never used by Green or his family.

Across Tennessee Street from Green's house is a home designed by London-based firm David Adjaye Associates: a rectangular block of house painted Tuscan red, with a wide, dramatic stairway leading to its front door. On closer examination, the grand staircase is actually bifurcated, placing a standard-gauge staircase adjacent to an expanse of giant-sized steps. These were apparently designed for planters or as a stylized, oversized stoop, where people were supposed to sit. Unfortunately, there is no porch roof to provide shade; that element covers the home's flat roof above, which is designed as a large second-story porch. Despite its dramatic appearance, however, the second-story porch fails to perform its most basic function: to provide an accessible roost where residents can sit and interact with neighbors who pass by. It requires you to yell down to the street—if you could see the street, that is. Instead of typical balusters, the exterior wall that wraps around the roof porch is waist-high and solid; you can't see the street while sitting.

The side of the house also reveals one of its "green" attributes—the ability to retain cool air—accomplished by reducing the only two windows to tiny apertures. They are part of what makes the house environmentally "efficient" by allowing the residents to seal it up tight. What they actually accomplish is to reduce the amount of light entering the home and eliminate any cross breeze.

Next door is the home of Melvin Andrews, a retired serviceman who lives with his mother. At first glance the GRAFT-designed (a Berlin firm) house is more traditional, with an actual front porch. But then you notice details—that the porch roof overhang has been drawn back in a rakish "designer" angle that attenuates to a tiny lip. It provides no shade; even the balustrade is tilted inward at a similarly rakish angle, thereby reducing the amount of sitting space. "I live here because Oprah gave us the house," says Andrews, "and I'm very thankful. But I miss the old one, and my mom does, too." The old home had been constructed by Andrews' grandfather and not by professional designers or builders.

The neighborhood is filled with similarly recombinant residences, with conceptual elements that seem to have forgotten their purpose. Some of the homes look like Rubik's Cubes, others like miniature corporate headquarters. Most of the trees were swept away by the flood, which makes it feel like the early days of Long Island's Levittown, a suburb built on open fields where potatoes once grew. The big difference is that this neighborhood is overshadowed by an ominous concrete levee, oddly reminiscent of the wall built by survivors in Pitt's 2013 movie *World War Z*.

Resident Green, meanwhile, is not dismayed by the bizarre configuration of his home. He is inordinately happy to have been given his abode by MIR. Otherwise he would not have been able to afford it. With little sensitivity to the income levels of the residents, the MIR fantasy homes were built with financial abandon. The first homes to go up, with their unique elements (such as curvilinear exterior walls), cost well over $400,000 each to construct. Seven years later, with designs deliberately simplified, MIR says the costs were brought down to $220,000, though this does not include the solar panels or other LEED extras, like expensive environmentally sensitive appliances. The math, however, does not lie: $45 million, along with additional millions of donated materials, was consumed to build just over 100 homes.

Not all of the architectural firms approached for prototypes of "affordable, sustainable" homes missed the point. One of them was Concordia, a local New Orleans company. Its principal, Steven Bingler, recalled his experience in an op-ed article that appeared in the *New York Times*: "Early in the process, Make It Right's founder, Brad Pitt, invited a few returning residents to critique the designs, most of which tried to take a basic form, the single-family home, and squeeze it into the latest style, with little consideration of local needs or the local vernacular architecture. The residents weren't impressed, and asked perfectly logical questions: What's with the flat roofs—you know it rains a lot here, right?"

Perhaps because Bingler was a local who understood the native genre, his Lagniappe House—still LEED Platinum—was among the most traditional in appearance and function, with big windows, a wraparound shaded porch, and peaked roofs. Not surprisingly, it was the most popular design chosen by residents.

"We started with cross ventilation and high ceilings and deep front porches, because that's another room. One comment I heard was, 'Why are these people designing four-foot balconies? My rocking chair alone is three feet,'" says Bingler. "These passive and culturally proven, natural solutions are the ones that need to be at the head of the pack. This fasciation with materials and mechanization makes it impossible to keep it simple."

Proponents of MIR—including Bingler—applaud Pitt's efforts to bring the neighborhood back into existence; in fact, the first master plan that city officials proposed after Katrina earmarked the area for a return to its natural state of swamp. Residents who wanted to return saw Pitt as their savior.

Nonetheless, MIR's clutch of 105 new homes is at the heart of a debate between community leaders, urban planners, preservationists, and just about anyone else invested in the restoration of New Orleans. Even in the zero-sum game of rebuilding, the gratuitous contributions of MIR are seen as a waste of precious resources and a bizarre application of abstract design principles. As a January 2014 article in the UK's *Guardian* put it, "The project's ambition and achievements are admirable, but its self-conscious architecture and idealism seem jarringly aspirational in a place that would simply settle for being functional."

SMALLER, CHEAPER, SIMPLER

The rift over MIR is as simple as north and south. Pitt's fantasy village is on the north side of St. Claude Avenue, the main commercial boulevard that runs through the ward. To the south of St. Claude is the Ninth's Holy Cross neighborhood, a collection of historic housing nestled on higher riverfront land that mostly survived, though was heavily damaged by the flood waters.

"Our argument was that instead of coming in up there [across St. Claude], where there was nothing, where literally everything was gone, that he [Pitt] should have come in here, spent a fourth of the money, and renovated the old, damaged houses," says urbanist Daigle. "This is what the Preservation Resource Center wanted. This is what the city wanted."

The Preservation Resource Center (PRC), originally the Preservation Alliance of New Orleans, was founded in 1974 to promote the preservation of New Orleans's historic architecture. After Katrina, it set up offices in the Lower Ninth Ward and funneled private funding to restore homes in Holy Cross. While the area still sports houses that are damaged and unrestored, along with some empty lots where homes were razed, the historic area is now spangled with architectural gems fully restored for the black families who lived there.

City planning commissioner Pamela Bryan was the director of Operation Comeback at the PRC from 2007 to 2011. Her mission was to raise private and public funds to restore houses in the historic Holy Cross neighborhood. "Part of our proposal was to rebuild them as sustainably as possible, utilizing a lot of salvaged materials, and putting in weather stripping and insulation," she says. "If we could incorporate solar panels we would, but only at a very low cost . . . It was an extraordinary challenge to do this because it is a low-income area and people can't afford to buy houses if their cost per square foot is too high."

Bryan has mixed feelings about the MIR project. "After Katrina . . . no one was paying any attention to the Lower Ninth Ward, especially the place where MIR came in," she says. "The water came in and took those houses right off of their foundations. So it was just vacant, with houses toppled on each other and cars toppled on each other. A lot of people just drowned right there. So in one sense it's an incredibly generous act of Brad Pitt to start this nonprofit Make It Right because no one else was going to do anything."

On the other hand, could the money have been used more efficiently?

One of the principles of Lean Urbanism that is second nature for New Pioneers is the idea of recycling and of staying within the spectrum of "native"—native materials, native ecologies, native design, etc. Not only are these indigenous solutions more authentic, they are more cost-effective. Lean architecture and the spirit of the New Pioneer implies more for less. It implies an economy of effort, a lean way of doing things. What bothers Bryan, from this perspective, is the expense of LEED certification for MIR's "affordable" housing. "How long can these houses exist?" asks Bryan. "Can these homeowners maintain them? What is their price point?"

Absorbing the cost overruns, MIR offered its houses for $150,000 to residents. Even at that price, it so exceeded the ability of the low-income residents of the Lower Ninth (who received $60,000 on average from FEMA to rebuild their homes) that the city had to intervene with "soft" mortgages for half the cost. These mortgages are entirely paid by the city—so long as the residents live in their new homes for a minimum of five years. In other words, through its dedication to LEED requirements and the whimsy of its designers, what MIR has created is not *affordable* housing but *subsidized* housing.

Bryan's own encounter with LEED-certification requirements remains abandoned at the intersection of Lizardi and Dauphine streets in Holy Cross: a community center the PRC was unable to complete. "It was going to be kind of an educational tool on sustainability and wonderful technology," says Bryan—it had been designed via charrettes with local residents and top architects and engineers. Its LEED Platinum requirements, however, ultimately proved too expensive. "I was working in a low-income area and the costs are prohibitive for anything that had any kind of LEED certification . . . we were never able to complete it because [of] the costs." Meanwhile, across town at the Viet Square, the community center was rebuilt inexpensively—and immediately—in the old way.

This was clearly not the case with the Pitt project, which approached its mission top-down with little interest in sourcing the language of lean, local solutions. There was also an attitude of "whatever it costs, pay it, and we'll figure it out later." Take the paint used, for example: Benjamin Moore Aura, both interior and exterior, which at sixty-eight dollars a gallon is the most expensive paint on the market. Yes, it has extremely low levels of toxic VOCs (volatile organic compounds), but, according to *Consumer Reports*, there are paints with similar levels that cost half as much.

"We certainly would not try to argue that, if your goal is to build as many or to restore as many homes as possible, this is the right approach," said Tom Darden, executive director of MIR. "It's more than just providing shelter, which of course is fundamental, because people need shelter. But once you are providing that shelter, why not strive for the best quality shelter, even for very poor people? That was an aspiration for us."

Darden says that many of the expensive environmental technologies that MIR developed and used have come down significantly in cost (solar panels being one example), and that the MIR project was also a testing ground for new ways of building green.

"It was not as simple as building as many as we could. Maybe we could have built twenty-five more homes, or maybe fifty, I don't know," says Darden. "But that's still just a drop in the bucket. The Lower Ninth needs thousands of homes, so our mission was to be aspirational, and to make a statement about the importance of high-quality homes for low-income families. I would like to think that we achieved that in terms of elevating the bar for other affordable housing developers."

In the end, however, the issue of cost rankled critics. "You can't talk about that like it's affordable housing," says Laura Paul, whose lowernine.org rebuilt seventy-five houses for about $1 million, compared to 105 houses that MIR has built for $45 million. "It's insulting to those of us who are actually building affordable housing."

"It just amazes me," says urbanist Daigle. "If they had spent all that money here [Holy Cross] instead, getting these gorgeous houses back up, letting people renovate them, they could have made triple, quadruple the impact. Plus that would have been truly green and sustainable because, number one, this is higher ground, and number two, it would have been recycling. These materials are probably two or three hundred years old. So they are solid, hard pine and cypress— wood that even the termites won't eat."

In an embarrassing contrast to such native lumber, MIR instead used high-tech "environmental" TimberSIL wood, which is infused with glass to prevent rot without relying on chemical treatments. By avoiding these "toxins," the wood could be mulched at the end of its useful life, and hence recycled. In a story that broke at the end of 2013, however, residents reported that the wood was "rotting from the inside out," with some homeowners saying the wood had turned gray, then black, and had mushrooms growing out of it.

Make It Right spokeswoman Taylor Royle admitted to the press, "It was unable to withstand moisture, which obviously is a big problem in New Orleans," and MIR replaced all of the rotted wood with traditional yellow pine, which it has used ever since. Nonetheless, as the local alternative paper *The Advocate* observed, "The situation is a cautionary tale for nonprofit home builders and others interested in using cutting-edge, sustainable construction techniques . . ."

MIR was not alone as a champion of high-tech green solutions. Another organization, Global Green, took the same approach in Holy Cross, building five high-tech "green" single-family homes for low-income families. The first house built (LEED Platinum, of course) cost a reported $1 million, but then subsequent houses dropped in price. "Everything they could shove in the house they did," says Michelle Pyne, the Global Green project manager for New Orleans. This included state-of-the-art geothermal heating and cooling systems, using ground pipes to draw on the year-round constant ground temperature of seventy degrees. "Part of what we were doing was materials testing," says Pyne. "By the time they built the last homes, they were using local Louisiana wood."

Like the Preservation Board, Global Green tried to build a LEED Platinum community center, which also became too expensive. While across town elderly Vietnamese practice Tai Chi in their spacious, non-LEED-certified Viet community center, the Global Green complex languishes on Douglas Street, still unfinished years later.

Compare this to Project Home Again, a nonprofit housing initiative funded with a $20 million gift from Barnes & Noble chairman Len Riggio and his wife, Louise. They stuck with Craftsman style, the traditional housing in the Gentilly neighborhood where they built: deep eaves, front porches, and columns. When executive director Carey Shea was hired in 2008, she immediately fired nearly all of the consultants on the team in order to preserve resources for the homes themselves. She also shed what she called "green bling"—things like solar panels—in favor of more cost-effective passive heating and cooling, such as low-cost insulation, screened-in porches, and large, double-hung windows that allow cross ventilation.

They built 101 houses by the end of 2011, many of them larger than the MIR houses (some 1,500 square feet with four bedrooms), for half the expense. They were also given to the new homeowners with a soft mortgage that was forgiven after five years of payments.

THE ATTITUDE FROM HIGH ALTITUDE

The artisanal, low-tech approach of native New Orleans architecture embodies a hallmark of Lean Urbanism and the New Pioneer spirit—that affordable, organic housing grows from the ground up, with an implicit notion that people can themselves build by using local materials and local solutions. When things are dictated from above in exhaustive detail, the implication is that people cannot be trusted to build, let alone use common sense. The result is that on-scene flexibility and creativity are killed.

In his book *The Rule of Nobody*, Philip K. Howard illustrates this with the example of nursing homes. In the US, where nursing homes are regulated with astonishing detail, residents are frequently treated with insensitivity and cruelty in the name of sticking to the rules. In Australia, where nursing homes are regulated by a few guiding principles for compassionate care, residents receive far better treatment from the on-scene staff, empowered to find adaptive, individual solutions.

Howard also notes that when people are entrusted to solve a problem or complete a task, they become empowered and rise to the occasion, usually with unique, parochial solutions. The problem with overcodification is that it stifles the ability of those entrusted with the task to use his or her judgment, rather than the prescribed rule. While Howard is talking about government, his principle rings true—that it is always better to stipulate *what* needs to be done, rather than dictate *how* it needs to be done.

The sense that MIR imposed a vision from above in a precise and almost condescending fashion creeps into the very fabric of their communications. Make It Right maintains a lovely, well-built website, for example, that speaks volumes about its project. The section "What We've Learned" has a library that is "a free resource where we share what we've learned about green building." An "In Depth" section on Floor Coverings starts as follows:

> "Carpet - Vacuum often. Use short, slow movements, about 2-3 strokes over each spot, for maximum soil removal. High-traffic areas may require frequent cleaning in order to maintain the upright position of the nap. Spills should be wiped up immediately and stain spots treated promptly. Always dab the stain, never rub it . . ."

It goes on like this for nearly every subject. Ceramic tile? "To clean, use an appropriate cleaner applied with a damp sponge or mop." Thank heaven that Make It Right did this important research.

Rather than being led by the nose, the pioneer mindset is one of do-it-yourself. It is also a "just do it" philosophy, of taking action rather than studying the subject to death in order to create perfect solutions with no sloppy edges. The consequence is that, at least on the scale of private residential structures, the lean, pioneering approach is not only less expensive but faster. The top-down approach both costs more and takes longer.

A TALE OF TWO CITIZENS

A few blocks from the candy-box houses built by MIR is the home of Terry Adams. Like Robert Green, after the Industrial Canal levee broke, Adams rode the top of his house for three days before being rescued. For the first year after the flood, he was unable to return home. Finally FEMA supplied trailers for people to live in, and he inhabited one on his property for about a year—until FEMA discovered high levels of formaldehyde in the trailers and pulled them out.

In the second year after Katrina, Adams received financial assistance from the Road Home, the program designed to distribute FEMA funds to individual homeowners to rebuild. Rather than wait for an MIR home, Adams decided to rebuild by himself. He had experience working in construction, and his father had been a carpenter, so he was not without basic building skills—though he had to contract out the electrical and plumbing work.

Adams built a straightforward New Orleans shotgun house, long and narrow with a porch on the front and a peaked roof. He says the house cost him $80,000 to build; at 1,600 square feet, it is 30 percent larger than the typical MIR house.

"I built the house on the same spot it was, a stick house," says Adams. "We call a traditional house a stick house, because you buy all

the wood yourself; it doesn't come prefab. You build it all from sticks."
The MIR houses, he says, arrived in pieces by truck. "It was very
unaffordable [an MIR house]. A lot of people had to get mortgages
to pay for them . . . If they just built the old stick houses, everybody
would have come back. Now it's less than a third that came back."

One reason why Adams was successful in his personal effort to
rebuild was that he acted quickly; those who hesitated, or waited
for further assistance, were caught up in a regulatory nightmare that
got worse as time passed. The regulations that Adams faced in the
beginning were fairly straightforward and made sense, he said. "The
city came with new codes, that you had to have foundations and you
had to screw the house down to the foundations. You might spend
$10,000 or $15,000 just on concrete alone [but] the city wasn't going
to approve you not doing that part right."

As the federal funds for Katrina relief began to disseminate,
however, the regulations became stricter.

One homeowner who got caught in the regulatory grind lived
just a half-dozen blocks from Adams. His saga is so emblematic of
overkill codification that he became the poster boy for New Orleans'
frustration, with stories about him in the *New York Times*, on PBS,
and even in the British press.

The cautionary tale is that of Errol Joseph, sixty-three, whose
father had built their nine-room home on Forstall Street in the Lower
Ninth. Joseph had a mortgage in good standing and was insured for
the damage. But after the flood washed away his home, the mortgage
lender demanded repayment of the loan, which consumed his flood
insurance settlement. Joseph returned home when residents were
allowed to come back into the Lower Ninth (a year after Katrina)
and gutted his home. He then applied for a reconstruction permit,
which took until 2009 to obtain, since he had to convince the city
bureaucrats that his home was salvageable.

Joseph was at that time armed with $26,000 from a second
insurance policy, a $55,000 grant from the Road Home program to
rebuild, and a $30,000 grant to elevate the home (after the federal

experts decided on a three-foot elevation requirement, they realized that the added cost required an additional pool of funding). A flooring contractor, Joseph felt he had the skills needed to rebuild his home himself. He used the grant money to buy supplies and elevated the frame of his house on wooden cribbing. Before he continued, however, he contacted the state for an inspection. He was told that he needed to wait for "a letter of continuance" or he would lose his federal grant. The following year (2010), he was told that the rules had changed and he wouldn't be allowed to do the work himself.

When he finally got approval from FEMA to build in 2011, six years after the flood, he was then told that he'd been overpaid by Road Home and owed the organization $40,000. That was changed the following year, when he was told he did not owe the money. But by then most of the materials he originally purchased had deteriorated, and the weathered framing for his house was being threatened with demolition by the city.

Joseph finally began rebuilding again in 2014, nine years after the flood. But damage to the exposed elevation platform cost an additional $20,000, for starters. So he turned finally to Laura Paul's volunteer lowernine.org group, which helped him rebuild. "If I had not dealt with the Road Home program, I would have been back in my house years ago," he says.

What snagged Joseph was the glacial process and ever-changing regulations for distributing the post-Katrina federal funds, a boondoggle of monumental proportions.

THE HEAVY HAND OF HELP

Besides being the biggest natural disaster in US history, Hurricane Katrina was a profound embarrassment to then president George W. Bush. Ten days after Bush told FEMA director Michael Brown, "Brownie, you're doing a heckuva job," Brown resigned in disgrace, the nation aghast at broadcast images of chaos and human suffering in New Orleans.

Determined to make good his administration's shortcomings, Bush finally authorized some $85 billion in federal aid to the coastal states impacted by Katrina, including Mississippi, Alabama, and Florida. Despite the federal largess, however, the process of implementing relief and rebuilding New Orleans and the Gulf area was anything but rapid or smooth. Like a bear trying to fix a wristwatch, there was a lot of muscle but little finesse.

The Army Corps of Engineers alone spent $14.5 billion to rebuild the levees and flood walls of the city, and took eight years to complete the work. FEMA meanwhile dumped $19.6 billion into Louisiana's post-Katrina communities to "rebuild and protect their property against future hazards." Of that amount, $11 billion went to public assistance funds, with $9 billion disbursed directly to more than 100,000 residents, money that came through FEMA from HUD (the federal Housing and Urban Development authority) for the Road Home program. The rest was spent on rebuilding roads and bridges.

The Road Home program was born in then governor Kathleen Blanco's office. It was a "direct to homeowner" reimbursement plan to pay individuals the pre-Katrina value of their homes (minus insurance and other payments). The valuation part turned out to be flawed, however, leading to a discrimination lawsuit because property values for white homeowners in pricier neighborhoods were higher than for black homeowners in poor neighborhoods; it was later changed to reflect replacement costs.

Beyond that, Road Home was not a bad plan. It was a reimbursement plan, with the governor determined to learn from the mistakes of Louisiana's sister state of Mississippi.

Mississippi had gotten federal relief for homeowners right away, some $5 billion (for a quarter of Louisiana's damage) thanks to the added pull its Republican governor, Haley Barbour, had in Washington. That money went straight to the people who had lost homes, no strings attached, and most of them took the money and ran. Many of the recipients were elderly, and not interested in rebuilding the historic homes and communities wiped clean by the storm surge. Instead, the Gulf casinos had record takes for three years.

Louisiana's Governor Blanco wanted to make sure the money went into the ground. So the Road Home plan, first drafted in December of 2005, was chewed over for months. When finally approved by the Louisiana Recovery Authority in March 2006—seven months after Katrina—Road Home was primed to reimburse homeowners for the cost of rebuilding their houses. The money was to be distributed by banks working with homeowners. In May, HUD approved the plan, and in June, the state of Louisiana chose the private firm ICF International to administer the program.

At first, all went well. ICF had opened ten assistance centers across the state by August 2006 and, with 1,500 new employees, began accepting applications. It was a year after Katrina, and less than half of the city's population had returned home, so it was time to get things moving.

At that point, the federal government abruptly changed the rules. Almost as soon as the program started, it was halted for a once-over that fundamentally changed the way the problem of rebuilding was to be solved. "The government threw out the plan, after massive expenses," says Scott Ball, who worked as an administrator for the Louisiana Recovery Authority and then ICF. "We built the program and it was approved and then it was thrown out. It was undoubtedly a decision made by a bureaucrat in a windowless room."

What FEMA did was to change Road Home from a reimbursement, loss-compensation program to a building-grant program, with the rebuilding process controlled in minutia. Their motivation? Louisiana's reputation for political corruption was so potent that federal regulators wanted to make sure the money was not pilfered. That reputation may or may not be deserved—Mayor Ray Nagin of New Orleans was, after all, convicted of corruption in the post-Katrina cleanup—but the result was a suffocating blanket of regulations.

As Ball puts it, "There was a great deal of concern about fraud in Louisiana, but can you imagine [the federal government] tracking receipts from 250,000 building projects?"

But that is just what they did, along with making the application process hugely complex and opaque. "They were so afraid that Louisiana was going to steal all the money that there were something like seventeen layers of checks and balances in the cutting of a check," said New Orleans developer Kenneth Bickford. "They sucked up an enormous amount of that money just to make sure that none of it got stolen." As for the regulations themselves, Bickford—who had close friends in the governor's office—described them as "one set of handcuffs after the next."

The difference between the plans was more profound than just the quantity of regulations in place, however. They reflected disparate philosophies of how to rebuild.

In a lean urban scenario, what is important is the result, the quality of the building to be achieved. There is an inherent belief that pioneer citizen-builders are capable of creating safe, attractive structures. Contrariwise, today's world of heavy coding emphasizes process rather than result. There is an inherent belief that citizen-builders are not capable of creating safe, attractive structures without being closely supervised and managed.

In the governor's plan, homeowners were not told how to build. Their only requirement was that they actually build, in order to get the money. "There was an owner's covenant, recorded against the title, that the money had to be spent on rebuilding the house," says Ball. The money was to be released in stages by banks, as they built. In the federal plan, the money was granted up front—usually after a year's worth of tedious paperwork—but with regulations controlling every step of the rebuilding.

In other words, in the governor's plan what mattered was *if* you built, not *how* you built. In the federal plan it didn't matter *if* you built, it only mattered *how* you built. The governor's plan called for compensating residents for their costs; it was a reimbursement plan.

The federal plan released the money up front—creating the illusion of progress—but then controlled in fanatical detail how it was spent, with delays built in.

Of course, no set of rules, no matter how detailed, can cover every eventuality. In a perverse law of nature, overly articulated rules can be manipulated to produce results quite contrary to the intentions of their authors. As CBNO president Twitchell puts it, "There is no law that has ever been written where somebody can't twist it to produce the opposite effect." And in New Orleans, such twisting is a local sport.

Height elevation is a good example. After much deliberation, the federal administrators determined that all new or rebuilt homes that Road Home funded had to be elevated three feet—something that made little sense for extensive areas that had been subsumed under eight to ten feet of water, and even less sense for areas that experienced only a foot or so of water. This was precisely the kind of regulation the Vietnamese community sidestepped in order to quickly rebuild.

Because of the added cost, FEMA set up a separate fund for elevation expenses, ultimately disbursing almost one billion dollars for just that. The result, says developer Bickford, was a "shark feeding frenzy" by builders. "FEMA would pay a certain amount to tear down the old house and put in the foundation for the new house, somewhere around $30,000," he says. "Some of the worst people in this town are now millionaires, trashy people who have gotten rich on this. The houses were torn down and elevated foundations were put in, but they're still waiting to be rebuilt."

Another federal rule put in place was the requirement that homeowners use licensed contractors rather than rebuild by themselves. (Amazingly enough, most of the homes destroyed in the Lower Ninth had been built by the pioneer parents and grandparents of the pre-Katrina residents—without general contractors or architects or inspectors.) Since there were far too few legitimate contractors in New Orleans at the time, this requirement spawned a class of rogue contractors who took advances from Road Home grantees and then disappeared. Attempts by the residents to seek restitution were stymied by the federal regulations, which made it almost impossible to prove fraud as long as the "contractor" had at least set foot on the premises.

Even on the application side of things, the rules were not clear. "For the Road Home awards, we were working with two families, almost adjacent to each other, with both homes washed away," says MIR director Darden. "The one family got $150,000 awarded, the maximum you can get for the option to come back. The other family got a $5,000 award because of a paperwork glitch—simply because of the way the papers had been filled out."

With such prodigious and confusing controls in place, the pace of disbursement was painfully slow. "The actual dispersal process followed a very complicated set of policies, with a not very attentive or friendly federal government," says administrator Ball. In December of 2006, four months after ICF opened its doors, just eighty-five grants had been closed from 88,414 applications received. Three months later, in March of 2007, just 2,780 grants out of a total of 111,887 applications received had been closed. (Despite this trickle of actual help to displaced homeowners, ICF itself was thriving. After getting the Road Home contract it went public in September of 2006, and saw its shares soar as fourth-quarter revenue doubled.)

Because Terry Adams reacted quickly, when the Road Home program had just started, he was able to get his funds with fewer strings attached—although he still had to meet all of qualifications for approval. "At first it wasn't complicated and it was a fairly simple process," he says. "As time progressed, and they saw that people weren't doing the right things and trying to do shortcuts, they started making restrictions." The one that required use of a licensed contractor is what stopped Errol Joseph from rebuilding.

At the end of the day, however, even the multitude of regulations could not ensure that Road Home recipients would use their grants to rebuild their original homes. Many bought or built in other areas, while still others decided to not return, spending the money to set up new lives elsewhere. In the end, the topsy-turvy, regulation-heavy federal program merely added layers of expense, a far cry from the Lean Urbanism principle of economy. And nowhere was this more apparent than in the effort to produce what came to be known as Katrina Cottages.

FROM COZY TO COSTLY

Jeff Hebert, now the executive director of the New Orleans Redevelopment Authority, was director of planning for the Louisiana Recovery Authority after Katrina. Like many, he was aghast at the waste inherent in the way FEMA distributed the funds for rebuilding New Orleans. "There were a tremendous number of strings attached to those funds that made redevelopment extremely difficult—environmental laws, compliance with paperwork, regulations, etc. Basically, it's more expensive to use federal funds to rebuild than anything else."

Among other things, Hebert was in charge of the Katrina Cottage program for the state. "The governor wanted us to be creative. We did an RFP [request for proposal] to get the best design, and DPZ [Duany, Plater-Zyberk] was selected as the architecture firm." DPZ designed inexpensive prefab houses along the lines of the traditional shotgun house. They could be built for eighty dollars or less per square foot and were, says Hebert, "a great example of affordable housing." That was before FEMA regulations intervened.

Despite the fact that the Katrina Cottages were designed to fit on trailer trucks, FEMA was not equipped to think of anything beyond literal trailers. While some Katrina Cottages were manufactured—and "the communities built with these ended up looking spectacular," says Hebert—FEMA instead built thousands of "mobile" trailer homes. The idea was that these trailers could be pulled out and recycled once the emergency was over, whereas the Katrina Cottages would become permanent. As potentially permanent structures, the cotttages did not fit the FEMA regulation format for temporary emergency housing, despite the fact that they were attractive, affordable, and superior places to live, and could actually reconstitute the devastated communities where they were placed.

Besides looking like the worst sort of mobile homes in a trailer park, in the end, the FEMA trailers were all sold for scrap metal after tests proved that they emitted hazardous levels of the toxic chemical formaldehyde—a level equal to what a professional embalmer would be exposed to while on the job, resulting in headaches, nosebleeds, and breathing difficulties. By 2008, barely a year after tens of thousands of the FEMA trailers were installed, they were all removed.

Ironically enough, some of the few Katrina Cottages that did get built were installed with great success, creating urban spaces that are thriving today. One such area is along Landry Avenue, between Hendee Street and Shepard Street, in the heart of the Algiers neighborhood across the Mississippi from downtown. "Because of that development, it spurred people to fix up their homes in surrounding areas," says Hebert.

Of course, by the time the Katrina Cottages were installed, the "soft cost" of government regulations, red tape, paperwork, staff redundancy, administrative expenses, etc., had driven up the price tag astronomically—to as high as $350 a square foot, by the estimate of New Orleans architect John Williams, who is now in charge of master planning for the Lower Ninth Ward. "They ended up spending ungodly amounts on Katrina Cottages. It was all a mess," he says.

Nonetheless, says Hebert, "At the end of the day it was a much better product than what happened [with the trailers]."

FIX IT YOURSELF

It is nearly impossible to determine how many homes were actually rebuilt after Katrina. The common estimate of 200,000 homes destroyed or badly damaged is probably an exaggeration, since there were only about 220,000 residential structures at the time (statistics are sparse). The city's Community Data Center estimates the damage at 134,000 "occupied units," which includes those in multifamily housing. A good estimate of buildings made uninhabitable is probably closer to 110,000, a number that reflects the actual reduction of population and loss of active mailing addresses.

Of these homes, as many as 30,000 were repaired or rebuilt in the first two years after the storm (though none faster than the 1,600 homes in Versailles). Most of these were in affluent, higher-elevation neighborhoods, where houses took less damage and repairs were covered by homeowners' insurance. Six years after the storm, a survey of the 109,335 recipients of Road Home grants—disbursed mostly in 2008 and 2009—reported that about 40,000 of those homes were rebuilt. Even if another 5,000 Road Homes were completed after that, that leaves 35,000 homes still damaged or destroyed.

Now, since Road Home spent $9 billion for the 45,000 homes rebuilt under the program, that meant it spent $200,000 on every house. Yet the average grant given to the owner of a damaged or demolished post-Katrina home was about $60,000. Since roughly half of the grantees did not rebuild—stymied by time and deadly regulations—you can say that each house actually represented a disbursement of $120,000. The remaining $80,000 per house went to the overwrought machinery that administered the grant. That means $3.6 billion was spent to make sure that $2.7 billion was actually spent rebuilding homes in New Orleans, with another $2.7 billion thrown away on unfinished homes.

In contrast to the bloat of top-down, overly regulated efforts to revive New Orleans, the leanest recovery was executed by volunteer organizations. In many ways, these poorly funded volunteer efforts—with names like United Saints Recovery Project, Operation Noah Rebuild, and HandsOn New Orleans—accomplished the most. As Tulane president Cowen notes, "True recovery started only when nonprofits and local groups began to create a grassroots movement that cut across all segments of the community; this groundswell, from the bottom up, produced an organic and unified vision of the city that embraced, and indeed grew out of, the context of unique neighborhoods."

Like the Vietnamese recovery, a lot of the volunteer work was organized around churches. The Southern Baptist Convention, through its North American Mission Board, assembled thousands of volunteers from across the United States. The First Baptist Church of New Orleans worked with Habitat for Humanity in rebuilding homes in the Upper Ninth Ward. Their Baptist Crossroads Project, with 200 volunteers from twelve states, built thirty houses by the first anniversary of Katrina; another ten were up by the following spring, and another forty after that.

One highly visible volunteer project was Musicians' Village, with Habitat for Humanity teaming up with Harry Connick Jr. and Branford Marsalis to build seventy-two single-family homes and five "elderly friendly" duplexes on the 8.2-acre site of a former high school. Again, thousands of volunteers—many from the Baptist ministry—helped build the homes for displaced musicians.

In terms of sheer numbers, few could top Trinity Christian Community in Mid-City. Immediately after the storm, they set up a circus tent near their church where volunteers gathered and formed teams to renovate homes, ultimately bringing back 1,600 structures. Like the efforts by Habitat for Humanity and the Baptist ministry to build seventy-two houses in what is now called Musicians' Village, these efforts resembled nothing less than barn raisings by America's early pioneers, where entire communities—often united by the local church—built new villages with their own collective hands.

One exemplary volunteer organization was (and remains) the aforementioned lowernine.org, founded in 2007 by a Maine boat-builder named Rick Prose. With extremely modest funding—their 2013 budget was $149,000, for example—lowernine.org has rebuilt seventy-five homes in the Lower Ninth Ward.

"We've been averaging about ten houses a year," says executive director Laura Paul, who uses unskilled volunteer labor from across the US (including groups of college students) whom they train in basic carpentry skills. Paul says she has long given up going the "proper" route to get things done.

"I have had experiences with the city zoning and permitting office that are hugely frustrating," she says, like having a thirty-page application for a handicapped variance thrown out and returned to sender, along with cancelled payment, to begin a reapplication process because of one missing document. "So we don't pull permits. If there is a piece of paper in the window [of a house they are rebuilding] we don't pay a lot of attention to it."

In one case, lowernine.org asked for a permit to take down part of a blighted house that was threatening to collapse onto an adjacent, newly rebuilt house. "We reached out to the regulators for permission and got laughed at. So we decided not to ask and just did it. No one in the city was going to investigate this. Technically—legally—we were not on solid ground, [but] we just went out and did it, and took out the part of the property that posed the threat."

With this "just do it" mentality, lowernine.org found out about Errol Joseph's unfinished house and, with a donation of siding, completed the exterior in mid-2014. Now Paul has gotten a letter from Road Home demanding the return of $10,000 of Joseph's grant because there is no occupancy permit. "This is what makes me insane," she says. "There is no occupancy permit because the house isn't rebuilt yet. Yet I got this threatening letter—to us, a nonprofit, doing free labor on this house."

CONCLUSIONS OF A CAUTIONARY TALE

The story of New Orleans' reconstruction presents a high-contrast juxtaposition of lean versus fat urbanism, set in a city with a tradition of citizen-builders in the mold of America's early pioneers. It is a city of residents who basically don't like being told what to do. As developer Bickford puts it, "New Orleans is a great city for figuring out creative ways to get around the rules. It's a point of pride for the citizens." That's if they even worry about it. Bickford recalls one project where he asked if a permit was needed to clear and burn brush. "'You get a can of gas, that's your permit,' I was told . . . Everything down here is done with a wink and a nod."

A big reason why the denizens of New Orleans like to fly "below the radar as much as possible," says Twitchell of the CBNO, is because of local zoning codes that are "currently unintelligible and unenforceable." A lot of permits are enforced purely to produce income, he says, thanks to state restrictions on what the city can do to raise revenue. "It's gotten out of control. There are reasons why a lot of these codes exist, but we seem to be mistaking the map for the road."

One New Orleans resident who has a good take on Lean Urbanism and the city's pioneering spirit is Richard Sexton, a world-renowned photographer who specializes in imagery of the Caribbean. (His book *Creole World* couples photographs of New Orleans with photographs of cities in Latin America. The similarities are remarkable.)

"The idea of a house today is smaller, more efficient. We're not as affluent as we used to be," says Sexton, who lives in the Marigny district of New Orleans in a 1,000-square-foot restored house that was once the home of freed slaves.

Like most of the old homes in the area, Sexton's incorporates local solutions to the problems of climate. It is built from nail-hard cypress, and despite being one story, has a high, peaked ceiling, which makes it feel spacious and acts as a draw for hot air. The house is also built in shotgun style, open in the rear to create a miniature wind-tunnel effect for breezes. "Modernism," he says, "has to reinvent itself because it has overly embraced all of that technology."

Twenty years ago, the Marigny district where Sexton lives was a slum, filled with unkempt Greek Revival housing from the early and mid-1800s. Because it was constructed of impervious cypress and pine, it endured. Artists, gays, and bohemians moved into the area as New Pioneers and recycled the housing. Down the street is The John, a bar that was formerly a battery repair shop. Nearby is the Indywood Cinema, a former Laundromat that now shows art flicks for patrons who sit in upholstered chairs. Three blocks away is the Wasabi restaurant, once a welding shop.

This is Lean Urbanism in practice, and the fruit of the New Pioneers: redevelopment along the frayed edges of a city, where residents rebuild without the heavy hand of regulation. These are marginalized areas, forgotten patches of the urban landscape. Like the Vietnamese Versailles neighborhood, they have fallen off the grid and no longer come under scrutiny. Cities with limited resources either look the other way or just can't be bothered. And what you end up with are charming, livable neighborhoods filled with character and value.

chapter five

COTTAGE SQUARE AND THE GULF: LANGUAGE AND RECYCLING

Playing the Name Game to Beat the Rules

The mission of the New Pioneer is not to rewrite the restrictive codes of a given municipality. That is too large and complex. Rather, the pioneer's mission is to work around those codes, to find the seams and loopholes that permit building and rebuilding to take place in a way that makes common sense.

On the Gulf Coast of Mississippi and Alabama, two projects—Cottage Square, a 4.5-acre "square" of small cottages, and The Gulf, a 6.5-acre whimsy of stacked and connected storage containers—exemplify this creative approach to code busting. Cottage Square exists as a residential enclave today because it called itself a commercial development. The Gulf exists as a hugely successful beachfront restaurant-bar complex because it called itself a "temporary" structure.

Both projects also exemplified the Lean Urbanism and New Pioneer precept of working with existing, local materials, recycling and repurposing them rather than liquidating them in favor of a solution "from above." External solutions typically cost more and raise thresholds by requiring large, up-front cash investments. Organic, artisanal solutions to local building problems, developed by pioneers new and old, are typically simpler, more intuitive, more cost-effective, and more attractively unique.

Both developments were also successional. Cottage Square started out as two cottages, then four, then twelve, etc., adding buildings gradually over a five-year period. The Gulf began similarly, with first four shipping containers, then eight, and then twelve altogether, along with trees, walkways, and grass paths added as it grew.

Finally, both are also excellent examples of a single, persistent pioneer with a vision of how to create usable, people-friendly spaces from raw property, using as little capital as possible—always a hallmark of the lean approach.

Cottage Square: Housing that is affordable because it is built small, using the vernacular of the old coastal South.

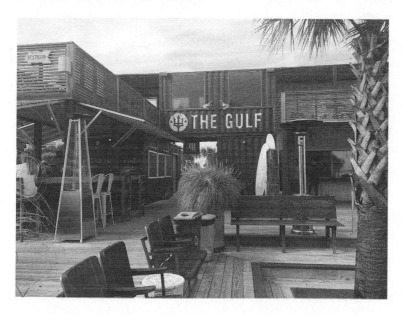

The Gulf: How to beat the system by changing the language to get past zoning issues and build with cargo containers and theater seats.

THE COTTAGE KEEPER
OF OCEAN SPRINGS

Bruce Tolar was no stranger to the straitjacket of local coding when he began what was to become Cottage Square in Ocean Springs, Mississippi. It was 2006, and Tolar had been practicing what he called "traditional architecture" in the city for twenty years.

This had not been Tolar's career plan. As a young architect and graduate of Louisiana State University, he had been inculcated in the school of modernism. As a student he swore he would never design traditional architecture. But as a fresh graduate, he needed work. So, when a community-minded philanthropist wanted Tolar to design in the vernacular style of the city's vintage downtown, he took the job.

"Woody Blossman was a well-off entrepreneur here in town who owned some property up by the highway," says Tolar. "He wanted me to build some houses similar to what was in Ocean Springs' old downtown." At the time, much of the city's historic core had survived from its heyday in the 1890s, when it had been a bustling Gulf Coast resort. "Back then people came here from New Orleans by train for vacation. So our historic district had that kind of Queen Anne–cottage feel of a second-home place. My client—and he was my main client for a long time—wanted that sort of thing out on our highway, where no one saw what Ocean Springs looked like as they drove by at sixty miles per hour."

The highway in question—old Highway 90 and not the interstate three miles north—was lined with generic cinder-block buildings that housed an Applebee's, a Wells Fargo Bank, a Krispy Kreme, a McDonald's, and so forth.

"That's when I started my 'delve' into trying to do traditional architecture under current coding," says Tolar. "Ocean Springs had a thing—it still does—where every commercial building has to be built to a central-business-district, fire-district level of codes. So that means your exterior walls have to be noncombustible load-bearing walls." Which means you had to use metal or cement blocks, not the traditional element of wood that the area's pioneers had used. Among other things, the requirement for "noncombustible load-bearing walls" increased costs for materials and work crew.

Tolar began what became a thirty-year sparring match with city officials, trying to figure out ways around the code. "If you did it out of concrete block or metal building materials, you satisfied the code," he says. "But the building code official was undereducated as to what other options were . . . I was doing everything I could to make traditional architecture fit the established code. It was just ridiculous. I was so tired of going to city hall."

Like other regulation-challenged small builders, Tolar had to become an expert in the city's codes in order to get around them. "They would bring out the little blue book and say you can't do this, and you can't do that . . . I could at least come in and fight them and say, I *can* do it because here in this section it shows what also works for fire resistance, or whatever. And they couldn't argue with me."

One year Tolar stayed in a vacation cottage that his patron owned near Destin, Florida. Blossman wanted him to stop in a place called Seaside and see the town they were building. "I went and saw it and said, 'This is hokey. This isn't a real town. They are trying to re-create a real town, whereas I live in a real town.' But Woody wanted to build small little cottages and put businesses in them as incubators. And for South Mississippi, that was very advanced thinking."

It would be years before that vision could be realized, but in the meantime, Tolar got plenty of practice as an architect in Rosemary Beach, where he opened an office. Rosemary was another New Urbanism town on the Gulf Coast of Florida's Panhandle, laid out with a form-based code by the same architects behind the planning of Seaside.

Then Hurricane Katrina struck. In its wake, all sorts of possibilities emerged. While it brought destruction to the coasts of Alabama,

Mississippi, and Louisiana, it also created gaps that could be reconstituted in a more intelligent, New Urbanism way.

Like other towns on the coast, Ocean Springs was hit by a surging wall of water that scooped out low-lying areas. Fortunately, the historic downtown was on higher ground. But even the high ground got wet. "We all had damage," says Tolar. "I was at an eighteen-foot elevation in my home, but we still had three feet of water, so it was a twenty-two-foot surge."

Tolar joined dozens of New Urbanists, led by Seaside planner Andrés Duany, who had gathered in the blacked-out city of Biloxi; Tolar recalls having to get past National Guard troops with a pass to join the meetings. "I came there to listen and learn, and I was sitting at a table next to Marianne Cusato, Steve Mouzon, all these guys who were drawing these little cottages," recalls Tolar.

Cusato, who in 2006 would win the Smithsonian Institute's Cooper-Hewitt Design Museum's People's Design Award for her work, recalls that their goal was to design a 200- to 400-square-foot alternative to the FEMA trailer. "Those little tiny trailers with three windows were not humane," she says, deliberately designed *not* to be so comfortable as to become permanent. "Part of the reason they did trailers was because it was illegal for FEMA to build a permanent structure. When you are talking tens of thousands of homes lost to Katrina, the numbers don't work. The volume meant these wouldn't be temporary, that people were going to live in them a long while."

In the end, the FEMA trailers would be withdrawn after a year, due to toxic levels of formaldehyde. Fortunately, however, Mississippi had built 2,800 prefab housing units based on the designs of Cusato, Mouzon, and their colleagues that came to be known as Mississippi Katrina Cottages, or more simply Mississippi Cottages, paid for with a $280 million federal grant.

Tolar was familiar with the Lean Urbanism trope of building small, and had been working on ideas for modular buildings and self-built homes that could be used as infill for storm-damaged southern Mississippi. "At the time I was trying to implement ideas that weren't cottage neighborhoods so much as they were about building density in a neighborhood," especially those with gaps created by storm damage. "I came back from Biloxi saying, 'This is something I can do.'"

CODE-BUSTING TIME

As a result of the Biloxi design sessions, a prototype of Cusato's "Katrina Cottage" was built in Mississippi state capital Jackson and showcased at the International Builders' Show in Orlando, Florida. It ended up being the seed for Cottage Square.

"Our mayor at the time was into New Urbanism and had gotten the ear of Andrés [Duany] and convinced him to bring the cottage to Ocean Springs so we could show it off," says Tolar. Duany welcomed the mayor's suggestion but turned it up a notch. He wanted to showcase not only Cusato's Katrina Cottage, but also all of the lean designs the Bixoli architects had come up with to replace FEMA's ugly and toxic trailers.

"The concept was that each of these architects was coming up with a design, so let's build them and make a neighborhood out of them and have people come in, like to a showroom, to see them," says Duany.

Tolar agreed to spearhead the effort, and found the perfect site: two acres of dense overgrowth behind an auto parts store on the main boulevard—Government Street—east of the historic downtown. Future residents would be able to walk to a grocery store, a YMCA, churches, parks, and medical clinics. It had sewage and water lines on the property edge. It was also across the street from an elementary school. And it was owned by a friend who would sell it for a fair price.

"This is where I started to get into Lean Urbanism," says Tolar. "The property became available and it was all about how to develop it. I began to see ways around and through the maze of codes."

To begin with, Tolar was not a developer—though he had designed one small subdivision that led to his "hatred for the typical subdivision laws that we have here." And like most New Pioneers, he had the handicap of little up-front capital. "I couldn't afford to put in all the streets, and all the sewer and water, like you would in a traditional subdivision—where you have to do all that first, before you can turn your first spade of dirt for any buildings."

Then it hit him—since the property was zoned commercial, he would seek to have his Cottage Square permitted as a shopping center.

"In a shopping center you can do parcels, and there are no commercial subdivision regulations. You plat your property and build it as you go," says Tolar. This would allow him to build a small-scale successional development, a microcosm of the kind of organic build-out-over-time developing that the Cotton District and Seaside had practiced. It meant that he didn't have to tarmac a grid of streets in place, with a network of water pipes and electric poles, but he could add houses one at a time along a gravel surface.

"I told the town planner I was going to treat it like a shopping center. And he said okay, fine, because he was all for getting it [the Katrina Cottage] on site, and the mayor was all for getting it on site, too. And if I didn't have to go for any variances in the ordinances, I didn't have to talk to any aldermen, I didn't have to talk to any of the other planning commissioners . . . I could keep it out of their vision and I could get it done quickly."

GOING NATIVE

Another purview of the New Pioneer (and tenet of Lean Urbanism) is adapting to the locale, and recycling its intrinsic elements rather than ignoring them and superimposing an outside concept.

This came down first to the flora. As the two-acre parcel was being cleared, Tolar made sure the mature trees were left standing—frequently running out to instruct workers accustomed to blindly hacking down everything—and altered his plans accordingly. "We found out where the trees were located and immediately went back and did another version of the site plan," he says.

For Tolar, the retention of an umbrella of indigenous trees was already in his DNA as an architect. "I built my first house in a neighborhood with trees," he says. "Instead of cutting them down I fit my house in between. That was in 1980 and I was considered weird for that, though today it makes a whole lot of sense for people . . . That was the way I was with this site." The result is a shady setting with a canopy of live oaks and magnolias, which makes Cottage Square feel authentic and organic rather than immaculate and antiseptic.

Preserving the natural setting was just the first challenge. Even with the shopping center work-around, Cottage Square was faced with ongoing opposition from municipal bureaucrats. The first pushback was from regulators who would not permit residential units in a commercial district.

"This was another thing I was always fighting with the planners about," says Tolar. "Fortunately, they allowed for live/work in the downtown. And this was the chink in the armor. After decades they finally said that if you had a second floor in a downtown building, they'd allow that for living. And that had been changed in the code. But first-floor units were still not allowed."

Consequently, when the Cusato Katrina Cottage was relocated to the site, and joined by a Lowe's prototype cottage on the same first "street," both were one story and had to be used as commercial structures. So the Lowe's cottage became an insurance agency and the Katrina Cottage a hair salon—at least, the front room did.

With that regulation met, the next problem was the fire code. Because the project was zoned commercial, its structures required metal or concrete siding, something clearly absurd for the two first wooden cottages.

Fortunately, even by this early stage, Cottage Square had caught the eye of certain powerful patrons. One was lumber and building-supply company Lowe's, which had agreed to become a sponsor and donated a kit for the second cottage. The other was Mississippi Governor Haley Barbour, who, a year after Hurricane Katrina, presided over a ribbon-cutting ceremony for the first two cottages. He liked what he saw, and said as much to then town mayor Dorothy Geeben.

Tolar, by then a veteran code bender, used the momentum of the governor's visit; he immediately went to the planning board, which reluctantly permitted the wooden buildings to stay—so long as they were retrofitted with sprinkler systems. "So, that fixed the original cottage, and it fixed the one next to it, and the others after that," says Tolar.

BABY STEPS

The following year, Tolar built two more cottages next to the first two. One was entirely his design, slightly larger with dormer windows and an upstairs (which became his office), and the other a two-bedroom MEMA (Mississippi Emergency Management Agency) cottage that was funded as a prototype for the state's designs.

"At that time we had one side of the street complete, landscaped, and available for touring," he says. But little else.

Then opportunity struck. By this time—2008—the state had built thousands of one-bedroom Mississippi Cottages to replace the FEMA trailers. While they were far more attractive and livable than their toxic predecessors, they were still under FEMA jurisdiction. And FEMA regulations did not allow them to become permanent. As permanent housing solutions were being found, the cottages were taken back and warehoused, waiting for the next emergency (ultimately most were auctioned off or demolished).

Tolar requested ten (he eventually got eight) of these Missis-sippi Cottages for permanent installation. "I wanted to put them in Cottage Square, to show that they could be put on permanent foundations, so you could bring people in here and take pictures and show them what could be done," Tolar explains. "The state was willing, even FEMA was willing, but the NIMBY factor [Not In My Back Yard] had come up. Their thinking was, 'Oh, it's a trailer. It doesn't belong on a permanent foundation.'"

In Ocean Springs and elsewhere, there was serious pushback from local officials who were against permanently installing such small housing units, for fear they would lower property values. Just the association with the word "trailer" was enough to sour the public perception of these 400- and 500-square-foot homes.

The other problem was that as a private developer, Tolar couldn't benefit from any public funding. In order to acquire the cottages, he had to partner with Enterprise Community Partners, a nonprofit that supported affordable housing and community development. The cottages had to be in the nonprofit's name.

To use these one-story cottages as affordable housing, however, Tolar was still faced with the code requirement for a first-floor business in a commercially zoned project. "So I went before the planning commission to ask for a special use [variance] for the cottages. And you'd have thought I was asking for their use as whorehouses," he says. "But I made it through the process. As long as it's just those eight, they said. But the rest had to be commercial."

With the addition of these eight cottages on its northern flank, and another two gems ("Tiny" and "Kernal," designed by architect Steve Mouzon) installed in its center, Cottage Square gave the impression of a small community. "We became one of the first little neighborhoods [to use Katrina Cottages]," says Tolar. "And this was the vision that Andrés [Duany] had for this location, that people could come from other places and say, our downtown could look like this, or my neighborhood could be like this."

What Cottage Square provided was a low-threshold entry point for young people to rent their first homes. Later, when two-story, two- and three-bedroom cottages were built in a mirror project that doubled the size (and tripled the unit count) of Cottage Square, families as well as single people could move in to what amounted to Ocean Breeze's most affordable quality housing.

"We aggressively went after rentals when rentals were out of vogue. That's what pushed me to go after the state for those [eight] cottages. They were going to sell them off," says Tolar. "The people living in them couldn't really pay for them at the time, but I thought they would be needed in rental neighborhoods."

Working with his nonprofit partner, Tolar has kept the buildings of Cottage Square affordable, with rents for one-bedroom cottages at $600 a month, $1,000 for a two bedroom, and $1,200 for a three bedroom. These are prices well below average for the space they provide—not to mention their quality in the peaceful, elegant community created by the "square."

INFECTIOUS SUCCESS

Like many of the homesteads of the New Pioneers that emerge in blighted or neglected areas of the urban landscape, Cottage Square not only created affordable space for residences and small businesses, it also engendered improvements in the surrounding streets. In particular, it jump-started a mirror development called the Cottages at Oak Park that enhanced and completed Tolar's tiny village.

Thirty-six years before Katrina hit the Gulf Coast, Hurricane Camille lashed the same area. An ugly barnacle from the recovery effort was a trailer park adjacent to Cottage Square. "It was the worst eyesore in town," says Tolar, but its owners had refused to sell. After Katrina they softened up and sold the property, by serendipity, to a friend of Tolar's who bought it precisely because it was adjacent to Cottage Square. And he gave Tolar the job of designing it.

Tolar did not want to repeat the one-story, one-bedroom shotgun houses already in Cottage Square. "We had also learned that too much of one scale done in one place starts to get overdone," he says. So Tolar turned to another concept born in the post-Katrina flurry to rebuild coastal Mississippi—a so-called "eco-cottage" developed by Professor Michael Berk at Mississippi State University. With a FEMA grant of $5.8 million, Berk had designed two-story "Green-Mobile" homes. With small footprints, they were energy efficient and inexpensive to build. But no one had bothered to put one up.

"As much trouble as we were having to get these [Katrina Cottages] placed in towns, they couldn't get any of the Mississippi eco-cottages he had designed built. They were too different, too radical," says Tolar. But not for the architect of Cottage Square, who used the adjacent Oak Park to showcase the eco-cottages as concepts for affordable housing. "We were awarded money to develop two sites . . . The only stipulation was that they had to meet LEED Silver [criteria]."

Taking a page from his code-hacking experiences, Tolar attacked the LEED regulations in the same way. He found ways to earn LEED points without resorting to expensive high-tech gizmo-green solutions. Because the project was located on a public transportation axis, it earned points; because it was a repurposed brown field, it earned points; because it had subsurface drainage that didn't add to runoff (thanks to Tolar's lean and less-expensive use of gravel and crushed limestone instead of asphalt surfacing), it gained points.

"We were building the same way we did the other units, smart building practices that had nothing to do with being LEED at the time," says Tolar. "We were trying to find systems that made things more efficient—better air-conditioning systems, better roofing systems—but the next thing you know I was talking at green seminars because our cottages were meeting those standards."

When finished, Oak Park added 2.5 acres to the existing two acres, and also tripled the number of units—adding twenty-eight cottages to the existing fifteen (one final "Louisiana" Katrina Cottage had joined the Cottage Square collection to save it from demolition). Oak Park also effectively completed the "square," lining all four sides of the now 4.5-acre compound, including a row of five cottages facing the elementary school across Government Street on the south side; this row was immediately the most handsome piece of Ocean Spring's main-street urban fabric. The only gap to the 4.5-acre square was an automobile repair shop next to the five cottages on Government Street. Fortunately Tolar left a copse of trees standing behind the shed, filling that part of the "square" with dense greenery.

In the center of the great 4.5-acre Cottage/Oak Square, Tolar added a row of seven cottages, all two stories, next to the two small Mouzon cottages. Together they now form an L-shaped cluster with the trees in the center of the square, and frame a small gravel space for Cottage Square parking; Tolar doesn't allow cars to park in front of the houses, to protect their charm and walkability. Adjacent Oak Park does an even better job of this, placing cars behind the homes or in a rear corner of the compound.

LESSONS OF THE SQUARE

Cottage Square is a case study in what a single New Pioneer can accomplish by bending the rules and regulations that make simple, elegant affordable housing impossible in most of America. The municipal codes that Tolar faced make it illegal to do what any pioneer could once do on his or her property: build a small, energy-efficient cottage.

Tolar did benefit from the post-Katrina environment, to be sure. The initial cottages were available for next to nothing, collateral from the recovery programs. Cottage Square also received various donations. Lowe's donated a truckload of picket fencing, which the development team sliced and diced to create different looks. Paint manufacturers also donated paint, while wood and window companies lowered their rates.

But the critical element for Cottage Square was its lean, pioneering approach.

First, like the Cotton District and Seaside, it was successional. This means that you start with a single building, and then grow a community over time. It means that you don't need a vast amount of capital to begin with; that you can create worth over time, with value that builds on itself. "What's important is the incremental value, rather than the initial value of the buildings themselves," says Duany. "If you achieve one good one, the rest increase in value—there is a multiplier effect." Places where the regulations are light will lower the threshold for small-scale successional development; if they aren't light, the codes have to be hacked.

Next, Cottage Square demonstrated not only the power of small-scale development for the entrepreneur, but the idea of small itself—the physically small. Among the dominant trends of the twenty-first century is the drift toward smaller housing, one solution to sustainability in a world of diminishing resources.

In this vein, small is a theme of the pioneer, to build affordably using local resources. Like Thoreau at Walden Pond, the idea is to "simplify, simplify" and live in a modestly sized residence that you could build yourself instead of consuming your life to pay for.

What Cottage Square shows is that you can create affordability without sacrificing quality. This depends on good design, of course. But the architectural detailing of small cottages—from peaked roofs to porches with columns and balusters—combined with attention to ceiling height, open floor plans, and landscaping, makes them eye-pleasing, attractive places to live.

"I don't think it's about people having to live in small spaces. If you frame it that way it sounds punitive," says Katrina Cottage designer Marianne Cusato. "It's that people choose to live in smaller spaces. When you're taking stock of how you want to live, maybe a thousand square feet is fine. There is less to clean and less to heat and cool."

The important thing, says Cusato, is not square footage but what comes up from the ground. "It's about tall ceilings, with lots of light and connection to the outdoors. Imagine a 2,000-square-foot house with one window and eight-foot ceilings. You'd feel like you were in a prison."

In the end, however, what made Cottage Square exemplary of Lean Urbanism and the New Pioneer was Tolar's creative approach to the language of local coding. In some cases, he knew the codes well enough to figure out work-arounds. In other cases, he changed the words he was using to evade the code.

"Over and over again, the established codes—I call them the dumb codes—create typical subdivisions and urban sprawl," says Tolar. "In Ocean Springs they didn't fit because they killed the character of the old town."

As for Cottage Square, Tolar says he was just trying to create what the city actually needed: quality, affordable, urban housing for young families. "What you see here is along the same lines as Lean Urbanism, we just didn't call it that. We thought of it as affordable urbanism," says Tolar. "As a developer I wanted to see what we could do without really having a budget at the time. We were reacting on a daily basis to what we needed with what was available."

ORANGE BEACH: LANGUAGE AND THE RECYCLER

Eighty miles due east of Ocean Springs lies the coastal community of Orange Beach, Alabama. It is a town of high-rise retirement/vacation condominiums—beige columns dropped onto the Gulf of Mexico shore and surrounded by pools of parked cars. The towers may as well be mausoleums, condo coffins stacked to the sky. There is no life to them. Their residents may be alive, but they are all segregated, separated, and boxed off from each other.

Toward the end of the town, about a mile from the Florida border, there is an exception to the monotony: a dozen ocean cargo containers painted bright blue and stacked at right angles to each other, enclosing a half-dozen acres of sandy beach contained by a seawall.

Welcome to The Gulf, a loose arrangement of stacked shipping containers repurposed as a restaurant, bar, and groovy gift shop. Within this oasis of life are clusters of people talking, drinking, eating, laughing, and playing. Old Motown songs—"My Girl," "Tracks of My Tears," "I Heard It Through the Grapevine"—waft from speakers strategically placed amid palm trees (themselves repurposed) and an eclectic mix of chairs, tables, benches, picnic tables, even some old theater seats. People of all stripes—young families, conservative seniors, trendy millennials—mingle seamlessly, eating grouper sand-wiches, sipping beer, fishing, chasing kids in the sand.

In a town that is otherwise dead, The Gulf is the liveliest of venues.

"People will drive from an hour away just to spend an afternoon here with their kids," says Courtney Brett, the architect of The Gulf. "People are really enjoying the space. We didn't expect this kind of popularity in our projections."

Brett has clients in eight different states but maintains her offices outside of Mobile, where she is involved with infill projects to bring life to that city's downtown. The Gulf, which was initially completed in late 2012 (it has expanded since then), was a project that came her way via Shaul Zislin, a cofounder of the annual Hangout Music Festival in the adjacent town of Gulf Shores.

Zislin owns the 6.5 acres where The Gulf is situated, a spit of land that abuts a large county parking lot at the base of a large coastal bridge. The bridge spans an inlet from the Gulf of Mexico to Bayou Saint John. Zislin had intended to develop the land as a five-story, mixed-use project with retail, restaurants, and residences. Unfortu-nately that could not be permitted, due to the weakness of the seawall retaining the sandy property. So Zislin turned to Brett, a wunderkind with a growing reputation for innovative solutions (now twenty-five, she was the youngest person ever to become a licensed architect in the United States).

"The idea had been to make this a gateway to Orange Beach," says Brett. "Then the department of transportation came in and said you can't have any major construction on the property until we replace the seawall." The only problem: funding for the seawall was not in the department's newest five-year budget.

"Even without a mixed-use project going in, we thought there must be some way to get people out here fishing, and eating, and having fun," says Zislin. "We did it with the music festival, so why not here?"

Brett's was the Lean Urbanist solution of a work-around: Since no buildings could be permitted, she instead advanced the concept of calling it a temporary structure, bypassing most of the code. "We wanted to energize this property, so we started with a basic idea of getting a little food truck community out here," says Brett. "Just pull up some Airstreams for people to camp on the beach. Build something that is purely on wheels that we can wheel out later."

The City of Orange Beach would have none of it, however, fearing the land (originally a nine-acre public-private partnership) would turn into an ugly trailer park. "The city said no to food trucks, nothing on wheels," says Brett. "So we jokingly said, fine, we'll take the wheels off."

That idea, which seemed absurd at first, became more credible in light of the ready availability of empty shipping containers stacked high at the nearby Port of Mobile. They could be purchased for $1,500 apiece, and were built solidly enough to meet local hurricane wind codes. The city council, impressed by the presentation and by the Zislin's growing reputation as a magnet for tourist dollars, said yes to Brett's application to build a temporary structure.

"Our goal, if this were to be truly temporary, was to have zero construction waste," says Brett. "We wanted to be able to pick the whole thing up, put it on the back of trucks, and assemble it all again in an underused space. That was our original idea, to pick it up without wasting anything."

BUILDING WITH FOUND MATERIALS

Because The Gulf was a temporary structure, Zislin wanted to invest as little as possible. So, in lean, pioneering style, Brett employed the materials at hand. This is what the first pioneers did, building from the trees, the stone, the turf—whatever was locally available. In the world of Orange Beach, this meant using as much recycled material as possible.

Beyond the containers themselves, recycled from storage depots on Mobile Bay, Brett used discarded window glass—broken or excess from construction projects or hurricane damage—from beachfront condominiums. The containers were retrofitted with holes cut to match the shape and size of the pieces, and because the glass was hurricane resistant, it met code. Had it not been recycled glass, but cut at the factory to fit various design specs, Brett estimates the cost for all the containers would have run as high as $60,000.

"We sorted through hundreds of pieces of glass to find ones we could use. The same with the wood," says Brett. "We were kind of collectors for a while, figuring out what we could make of it."

The weathered wooden fences that had surrounded the site were repurposed as walkways and platforms. Tables and chairs were made from recycled boat wood. Some of the chairs were recycled from an old theater, wooden chairs with fold-up seats that turned out to be extremely weather resistant. Even the palm trees planted around the tables are repurposed from Zislin's HangOut Music Festival, where they are trucked in to create intimate, VIP seating enclaves, and then discarded or offered to locals for planting.

Adding to the natural feel of the compound, much of the ground surface immediately surrounding the containers was covered with hydroponically grown grass. This surprisingly durable surface was donated by a farm in nearby Foley that grows it for Turner Field, former home to the Atlanta Braves. At the end of the season they sometimes have leftovers, which they offered to The Gulf.

"The original plan was to put the grass on the upper levels of the containers," says Brett. "In this climate, containers can become like little ovens, so we put the hydroponic grass on the roofs to keep them cooler on the inside. But it grew out of control. We ended up with a forest. And we didn't expect this many people, so we ended up with a forest on top but ruts in the sand where people were walking." Now those paths are covered with a carpet of the surprisingly resilient hydroponic grass, which is almost as tough as Astroturf.

The result is a family-friendly environment that is also popular with older patrons and young adults. There is a comfortable lankiness to The Gulf, with its open breezeways and overhangs. There is also the energy of being in a creative space, with clever configurations for the rectangular containers. One container is dedicated to restrooms; another is a bar that protrudes toward the sea, cut open on three sides; still another is the open, shaded "porch" of the restaurant/kitchen, its roof the floor of an upstairs seating area.

"Part of the open design of the structure is so that the wind and water will blow through it," says Brett. "The only fully enclosed structure is the kitchen, so that it can be protected. The rest can be hosed off and the wood replaced."

Similar to recycling efforts in other cities where New Pioneers are homesteading is the idea that sweat is equal to or better than cash equity. In cities like Detroit and Phoenix, urban pioneers are finding that low-tech solutions can solve problems with labor supplanting the high expense of gizmo materials.

"If you wanted to just come in and spec it and build it without the effort of looking for the pieces you need, it would cost more per square foot," says Brett. "This is technically cheaper, but it wouldn't have been without all the grunt work to find the components."

The Gulf symbolizes Brett's pioneering mission to bring architectural design, differentiation, and local authenticity to the mundane buildings of everyday street life, which are being mass-produced and layered across the surface of America.

"I see so much money pouring into [the building] industry from a segment that architects have ignored or don't want any part of," says Brett. "These are not big beautiful things but are nonetheless developed on a national scale. We think we can add value to projects that add to our sense of community. And that's what is important about these buildings at The Gulf. We don't want to see another rash of Pizza Huts that become other things but still look like Pizza Huts."

In order to make that happen, it's going to take some pioneering efforts. Such as lifting arbitrary restrictions by the creative use of language, calling a now five-year-old building a "temporary" structure. Or by thinking way out of the box, by seeing where the new wilderness—the urban jungle—can be hacked back. Among other projects, Brett is working on repurposing old big-box retailers, literally cutting them to pieces and adding street frontages and landscaping to the new open grids.

Like any good pioneer, new or old, Brett is also operating in a part of the country where the threshold for innovation is lower than in more established metropolitan areas. Having worked in New York City for Skidmore, Owings & Merrill, one of the largest and most influential architecture firms in the world, she headed instead for the Old South. There, the rules and regulations are not as omnipresent, and the weight from above not as oppressive.

"At Skidmore Owings I had just enough introduction to the expediters, to the building departments, to the unions—to the whole complexity of the organism up there that was needed to get something in the ground," she says. "I knew that if I really wanted to test my ideas I needed to be in an area that was a little more flexible ..."

chapter six

TWO SCHOOLS OF THOUGHT: GOING SMALL, RURAL, AND URBAN

The Lost Art of the Citizen Builder

Self-reliance was a hallmark of the pioneer throughout American history. When it came to building his home or business, the American pioneer became a citizen builder. Long before there were licensed architects or engineers available to advise them, somehow the immigrant pioneers built the early towns and cities of America. And they were well built. Those artisan abilities are now lost in the endless flight to expertise, and our sense of self-reliance has atrophied into helpless dependence on the regulators.

There are two maverick architecture programs in the United States that teach their students how to become citizen builders again. Both use their immediate environments as testing grounds, and both are surrounded by structures designed and built by their students. Both are also centers for iconoclastic thinking founded by visionary pioneers.

The first is the Rural Studio in Newbern, Alabama, 130 miles west of its mother ship, Auburn University. Located in one of the poorest counties in the United States, the studio's aim is to teach young architects how to actually build—and how to lower the barriers to affordable housing by using recycled materials and the local vernacular of home construction.

The second is the MRED school at Woodbury University in urban San Diego, a branch of the main campus in Los Angeles. Its goal is to teach architects how to become developers in a metropolitan landscape where the term "affordable housing" is an oxymoron, removing critical layers between the architect and his or her creation.

Both schools teach revolutionary, lean approaches to architecture. By facilitating students to dirty their hands in fieldwork and financing, both programs remove entry-level barriers for young builders to actually build, rather than merely sketch concepts at large firms. And both focus on creating dwellings that are less expensive to build, one through parsimonious use of materials and the other through cracks in the code.

Experimental Homes: Rural Studio architecture students with no regulations or codes build houses for poor families from recycled materials.

Finding the Seam: Avoiding cost in San Diego by making a large building from smaller ones separated by 3-inch gaps (plugged by rubber strips).

IN THE LAND OF THE FREE: THE RURAL STUDIO

Anyone who believes that America has become culturally homo-
genized needs only to drive down State Road 69 in rural Alabama,
from Tuscaloosa to Greensboro. Along the roadside are churches that
sport giant crosses out front—outlined with strings of luminescent
bulbs, and clusters of ponds where locals grow catfish for dinner and
sale. The walls of convenience stores are lined with animal heads, and
eateries have names like the Bates House of Turkey and Poppa's BBQ.
On the radio you can listen to the *Rick and Bubba Show* play the latest
local hit with its refrain, "God Is Great, Beer Is Good, and People Are
Crazy." On the local news you can see a weekend feature story about
the latest slingshot squirrel hunt, where kids are taught the historic
importance of slaying, eating, and pelting the forest rodents.

It was here in western Alabama, in destitute Hale County,
that architect Samuel Mockbee first established the Rural Studio
in the early 1990s. The setting for James Agee's 1941 book about
Depression-era sharecroppers, *Let Us Now Praise Famous Men*, Hale
County hasn't changed much since; 40 percent of the population
still lives below the poverty line. Many live in shacks on par with the
worst *favelas* of Latin America, with dirt flooring and no plumbing.

Mockbee came to Hale County on a mission: to return architecture to its role of serving the public. He wanted to teach young
architects how to create buildings that answered the needs of the
average citizen, affordably, instead of merely entertaining wealthy
clients with brilliant designs. As Mockbee said at the time—when he
walked away from a thriving private practice to start the Studio—he
felt compelled to act on the dichotomy delineated by Renaissance
architect Alberti, who instructed students to "choose between for-
tune and virtue."

Fortunately for Mockbee, his friend D.K. Ruth shared that vision.
At the time, Ruth was the chairman of Auburn's school of architecture and hired Mockbee as a professor. Together they successfully

secured a grant from the Alabama Power Foundation, which focuses on community projects within the area served by the eponymous utility company. Their matching grant of $215,000 launched the Rural Studio in 1992. Mockbee picked Hale County because it was so desperately poor, and because it was distant enough from Auburn to separate students from the distractions of campus life. It was also completely free of building codes and building inspectors, making it a perfect laboratory for pioneering innovation.

After several temporary facilities, the Rural Studio was permanently established in Hale's tiny hamlet of Newbern (population 189, give or take), nine miles south of Greensboro. The Studio was headquartered there in a circa-1890 Victorian farmhouse called the Morrisette House, donated by William Morrisette, a retired businessman and Newbern native who thought the Rural Studio would benefit his hometown.

The Morrisette House was where the first students lived. It's now the administrative center; students reside in a string of experimental cottages on the property built with recycled materials, and in apartments in nearby Greensboro. Classes were also first conducted in the farmhouse. They are now held half a mile down the road in a voluminous former grain warehouse on the edge of "downtown" Newbern, which has also been transformed by commercial structures built or repurposed by the students. These new civic buildings represent a further step in the evolution of the school's mission, which began with the goal of constructing low-cost homes using recycled materials. This was the singular focus of the Rural Studio when it first started: to use donated, salvaged, and recycled local materials to build houses for the rural poor.

DOWN BY THE RIVER

One of the defining principles of Lean Urbanism and the New Pioneer is to use regional vernacular—to employ low-tech solutions that have matured over centuries, rather than adopt expensive, high-tech solutions designed by experts. As Mockbee put it, "The best way to make real architecture is by letting a building evolve out of the culture and place. These small projects designed by students at the Studio remind us what it means to have an American architecture without pretense. They offer us a simple glimpse into what is essential to the future of American architecture: its honesty."

About twenty-five miles from Newbern, down a dirt road that ends in a curve of the Black Warrior River, a community of four extended families called Mason's Bend can be found. The land is red clay and the houses are clustered together amid copses of hickory, oak, and cottonwood trees.

It was here that Mockbee's students took on their first new-house construction. The house was built for the Bryant family, an elderly couple who were raising three grandchildren in a ramshackle shed without plumbing or heating. Now called the Hay Bale House, the building exhibits all the hallmarks of an early Mockbee domicile—the ingenious use of scavenged building materials (that would never meet municipal code) assembled in a design incorporating parochial principles.

The Hay Bale House was just that: a house whose walls consisted of eighty-pound bales of hay, wrapped in wire and polyurethane, and stacked like bricks. Its front porch, an echo of antebellum mansions, is shaded by sheets of translucent corrugated acrylic that are ribbed with wooden slats and held up by wooden beams on concrete block posts. Recycled cross sections of an old round silo provided three half-barrel rooms for the grandchildren at one end of the 850-square-foot house, which centers on its original woodstove.

The cost for all materials in the house: $15,000, paid for by grants and donations. A smokehouse out back, built by a fifth-year architecture student, was constructed mainly from rubble—curbs torn up by the Alabama Department of Transportation, plus old bottles cemented into the cracks to let in light. The cost: $140 in materials.

Another half-dozen structures in Mason's Bend, all built by students, exhibit the same inventive use of materials. One is constructed of carpet tiles that are compactly held together by steel rods. Another, the 600-square-foot Butterfly House, uses sharply angled sheets of recycled tin, which collect rainwater for the house cistern. One astonishing edifice is a community center that uses automobile windshields, layered on each other like fish scales, to create a peaked structure oddly reminiscent of Le Corbusier's Notre Dame du Haut chapel.

The intention of these home-building projects, says current Rural Studio director Andrew Freear, is to put students back in touch with the relationship between materials and design—and provide the experience of building something with their own hands. Freear, an Englishman who replaced Mockbee in 2002 after the latter's death from cancer, says the Studio's location is the perfect place to impart the lost art of the citizen builder.

"That is one of the attractions of a place like this, surrounded by farmers. There is very much of a can-do attitude around here. You've got a barn that needs fixing, you go fix it. You've got a truck that needs fixing, you go fix it," says Freear, who looks as though he could be a working farmer himself; like his students, he dresses for the rural elements in boots, blue jeans, parkas, and sweater vests.

"The profession (of architecture) has been encouraged to get further and further away from taking any responsibility for doing any building at all," he says. "The great thing about being a student here is the delight that it is *you* who's going to be building it. It's not about designing it and letting someone else worry about putting it together. We figure out how to put it together, and that influences how it looks."

With today's practice of training architects to become professional studio designers, says Freear, contractors have usurped the function of doing the actual building. "The understanding of how to put things together—we are giving that away to contractors who don't even get an education in building . . . We go through this extremely intensive and long education, and then we give it away."

Courtney Brett, a graduate of Auburn and the Rural Studio, was one of the student builders who constructed houses in Mason's Bend.

"When we worked on Miss Lily Bell's house, they dropped us off and said we wouldn't have any power tools," she recalls. "They said that we needed to learn how to do everything by hand before we earned the privilege of doing anything with more sophisticated tools."

Among other things, Brett and her fellow students spent time with the families before building their homes. "These houses belong to the world they are part of, so we had to learn how people lived before designing houses for them ... We learned who would be living in the house and what would be salvaged. Miss Lily Bell wanted to keep the old woodstove that belonged to her father. That's how they heated the house and that's how they heat it today. We had to figure out how to incorporate it."

THE ERECTOR SET OUT BACK

In addition to building homes for poor families in the area, students also constructed their own housing on what amounts to the Studio's campus quad: a muddy field behind the main Morrisette farmhouse. The field is bracketed on its north side by a long open structure with a tin roof, affectionately known as the Super Shed. Student houses—300-square-foot cottages—line the outer edge of the Super Shed, which provides a kind of collective front porch (as well as protection for materials, machines, tools, etc.).

On the east side of the field, a long raised platform with a tin roof is attached to the back of the farmhouse itself. This is the studio's outdoor dining area. In the open field formed by this right angle of Super Shed and dining platform, a great wooden skeleton is used to test one of the studio's new ideas. With ribbed wooden braces and a long-necked tower patched with different materials, it looks like the framework for a Trojan horse.

"This is the mockup graveyard," explains Natalie Butts-Ball, Rural Studio's director of communication and official tour guide. "This is where we build and test everything." The skeletal wooden horse is an experiment in lamella, a construction technique that allows a few individual workers to build a sizeable structure by bolting together smaller components—typically short sections of crossbeams—so that a crane is not needed to put larger elements into place.

On the south side of the field, opposite the Super Shed, a one-story wooden house is under construction by a team of third-year students; the building will act as a curing and storage house for food that is grown on the seven-acre property. Those students, on campus for only one semester, are the residents of the row of curious cottages that line the Super Shed. These diminutive domiciles—which Ball refers to as "pods"—are each a model of how to use salvaged materials.

"These pods were built in the late nineties, one of them from wax-impregnated cardboard," says Ball. "They were interested in testing temporary-relief disaster housing so that if a hurricane came in, or a flood, they could easily put up a house. And they were interested in seeing how durable they could be."

So far, so good. Fifteen years later the cottage made from bales of wax cardboard was still in surprisingly good shape, with a bed, desk, and couch cozy and dry inside. Other cottages were made from recycled barn lumber, broken halves of cement blocks, and odd bits of tin and plastic. One of the sheds, a two-story pod where Mockbee lived, was sheathed in recycled license plates, their silvery undersides facing outward. A communal shower, built by three female students in 1997, looks like a Roman oven, open to the sky.

"These provide us great examples of what to do or not to do. Here you can see how things are aging," says Ball. "Every year Andrew [Freear] takes the students on a tour of these projects to critique the work. It's like having a living library or encyclopedia. You can go through and dissect the details, why one thing worked and another didn't . . . The main thing with our clients, both public and residential, is that we have to minimize the maintenance, because no one can afford it. If you can see the work from fifteen years ago you can say, okay, we shouldn't do that next time."

Closer to the main administrative farmhouse is a huge greenhouse. It's another of the Studio's efforts to grow more of its own food—and another case study of reclaimed materials. While the framing is a skeleton of standard-issue aluminum struts, the front and back walls consist of rows of metal drums. These are barrels formerly used by a mint oil company based in the area. For whatever reason, the FDA wouldn't allow the barrels to be reused once they'd been emptied. So the company contacted the Studio to see if they wanted them—since it was easier to ship the barrels to Newbern than dispose of them.

Now long rows of the oil drums face south, each filled with water. The low winter sun heats them, and the thermal mass is released at night, stabilizing the temperature of the greenhouse in chilly months. Meanwhile, a culvert along the greenhouse is designed to catch rainwater from the greenhouse's plastic-tarp roof; the water is then funneled by solar pump to a large tank for later use, to irrigate the plants.

HOW TO BUILD A TOWN

After the passing of Samuel Mockbee, the focus of the Rural Studio began to shift away from residential homes using recycled materials to larger-scale civic structures that combined salvaged materials with standard components. The methodology also changed; rather than assigning fifth-year students—who stayed on campus for a year—with multiple tasks, students were put into teams and given a specific project to design and build.

Several of these projects now comprise "downtown" Newbern, creating a village square framed by a new fire station, a barbeque pavilion, and the town hall. Across and down the street, past the Rural Studio's grain warehouse–cum–classroom, a new library is, itself, a repurposed community bank that had been shuttered for decades. What boggles the imagination is that each building was constructed by a team of just three or four students using mostly their own muscle power.

The most impressive of the buildings, for both its size and its impact on Hale County, is the Newbern Fire Station. It was the town's first new building in 110 years, and it was designed to fit into the existing town morphology of narrow-fronted buildings facing the street. It was constructed from recycled barn wood and $100,000 in donated materials. The firehouse aptly resembles a husky, oversized barn with a huge "front porch," where fire trucks can emerge and pause before lumbering onto Highway 61, Newbern's main drag.

Like a barn, the building is not insulated and uses no internal cooling or heating systems. Instead, it relies on natural cooling and heating, including a south-facing wall composed of opaque plastic (polycarbonate) that lets in winter light to heat the concrete floor, which stores and radiates that heat to prevent the pumper truck's water from freezing. The structure is supported by twin "beams" along each flank, constructed by students from three two-by-twelve-inch timbers bolted together and trussed by steel rods. The students constructed these on campus, and then assembled the skeleton of the building in a single barn-raising kind of day using a borrowed crane.

The impact on the community was immediate.

"Before the existence of the Newbern volunteer fire department [housed in the new building], homeowner's insurance was very difficult to get and very expensive, because it would take thirty to forty-five minutes to get a fire truck to your house," explains Ball. "Your house would burn down before they could get there. So they got a grant for a fire truck and equipment, and even have an ambulance jammed in there."

In principle, the use of a crane was a violation of the build-it-by-hand philosophy of the Studio, but was necessitated by the frequency of tornadoes in the area—the students were worried that a freak windstorm could wreck the building if it took too long to complete using a more traditional but time-consuming scaffolding approach.

Nothing but hands were used, however, to build the Newbern Town Hall opposite the fire station. It was constructed from untreated eight-by-eight-inch cypress beams that were locally milled. The students assembled them like puzzle pieces, sliding them onto steel rods embedded in a concrete platform, creating stout eleven-foot walls. Because the untreated cypress (read: less expensive) will shrink as it dries out over the years, the windows and doors are mounted outside or inside the walls on slotted bolt holes that allow the building to contract without shattering the glass. Similar to the fire station, glass walls on the south side allow the winter sun to heat the cement flooring.

These buildings are just two examples of more than a dozen civic structures that Rural Studio students have built in Hale County. Among them are a county animal shelter, a boys and girls club, a rural heritage center, a learning center, a hospital courtyard, and a series of public structures in two public parks.

All of the architecture demonstrates innovative, low-cost alternatives that hearken back to a pioneer way of thinking, of building simply and using the materials at hand. Today this includes recycling the buildings themselves. Newbern's one-story 1920s bank building on Main Street—now the community library—recycled its ceiling wood (replaced with sound-absorbing tiles) for the floors and walls of small reading rooms on the north side of the building. Half a dozen layers of brick that lined the old vault were likewise used for an adjacent courtyard.

Reflecting the artisanal, hands-on approach to their projects, Rural Studio students are also taught to pay enormous attention to detail. Former student Brett recalls how, in the construction of an outdoor pavilion at a public park, she and other students painstakingly aligned all the screw heads. "They were square-headed stainless steel screws, the kind with a square on top," she says. "The idea that everything down to the tiniest detail mattered was imparted to us so completely that those screws line up, every square, every edge, along the length of the building. You can find things like that, almost as secret jokes, on all the Rural Studio projects."

In the work at the community bank–cum-library, the two students who were tasked to build its bookshelves spent scores of hours carefully applying polyurethane and lacquer to the edge of each shelf. "A lot of the plywood [for the bookcases] was precut, and did not have a finished edge, so we are making sure it has a finished edge that is very durable," said Ashley, a graduate of the school who stayed on after graduation to finish the project. "Craftsmanship is very important at the studio. We are meticulous."

At the same time, thanks to the absence of code, the students have been able to build with latitude. At Perry Lakes Park, where students created the aforementioned pavilion along with a covered bridge, an observation tower, and three "nature-view" public toilets, they also constructed an elevated walkway. What makes the walkway unique is that it has no railings. It looks like it's floating over the ground. At three feet high, it poses little fatal risk to its users, and the absence of railings makes it delightfully open and natural, not to mention less expensive to build. In typically code-heavy, litigious-wary communities, this would not be permitted.

Nonetheless, says Studio director Freear, the civic structures being built by students are constructed with the International Building Code in mind. "The studio in its inception twenty years ago was doing single-family houses very much under the radar, with lots of improvisation," says Freear. "But since the program has gone toward making buildings in the public realm, that has changed the game in terms of the kind of materials that we use—and relative to our position on 'code' in the regulations books."

Working in a county with no funding to police a building-permit process, the Rural Studio has become, in effect, its own policing agency. While Freear acknowledges the excesses of today's municipal codes, he believes in the fundamentals that address safety. "The basics of the code book were about the health, welfare, and well-being of the individuals living in those buildings," says Freear. "Now, whether they have lost sight of that is another question."

For the last half-dozen years, students at the Rural Studio have been asked to embrace the International Building Code, bringing in special instructors—including structural engineers—for workshops to explain the IBC. "Getting the students to not be frightened of it is a challenge, because they immediately believe it to be restrictive and boring . . . But we don't see it as being restrictive. Of course, it's different for us because we don't actually have to go and sit down and explain our choices to anyone relative to any ambiguities that are in [the IBC]. We sort of sit down, write down our understanding of the situation, and then go forward."

Because there is no one to present their plans to, the Rural Studio does not have to pull any permits. Nonetheless, it keeps documentation, basically for the intellectual honesty this engenders. In fact, local municipal and county administrators come to the Rural Studio for zoning guidance since they don't know how to deal with new commercial development that is encroaching on historic homes.

More than the intellectual rigor that comprehending the IBC provides its students, however, the Rural Studio is compelled to understand and crack the code for its next phase, going mainstream with low-cost housing.

THE DAWN OF AFFORDABLE HOUSING

There is an old rubric that basically goes like this: It's impossible to make anything fast, cheap, and good. If you build it cheaply and rapidly, it won't be a quality product. If you build it well and rapidly, it won't be inexpensive. And if you build it cheaply and well, it won't be done fast. You can only have two out of the three.

The Rural Studio's mission for the future is to shatter that paradigm with something it calls the 20K House. While times have changed sufficiently in the decade since the project was conceived—it's now closer to a 25K House—the target is essentially the same, just with that slight uptick in cost: to design a 600-square-foot house that can be built with about $16,000 worth of off-the-shelf materials, about $4,000 in labor, and about $5,000 in profit for the developer/contractor.

On a plot of donated land about a mile from the main Morrisette House campus, two small, trim houses sit in a clearing of Alabama longleaf pine trees. The gray one is called McArthur's House, named after the original owner for whom the building was designed. It is rectangular in shape, with a wide set of steps descending from an indented center porch on one side. The white one is called JoAnne's House, also named after the owner for whom it was designed. The house is square shaped, with one corner carved out for a balustrade-wrapped porch.

"The goal for these is that anyone could go to their local hardware stores and buy what they need to build the house for themselves," says Ball. "So it's not about using recycled materials at all."

While they use off-the-shelf modern materials, however, the designs are historic and time-tested—in other words, they follow the local vernacular. The ceilings are all ten feet high, so that warm air will stay above the height of occupants. Large windows on all sides provide cross ventilation, and the combination of tall double-hung windows and transoms above the doors allows residents to evacuate hot air as it rises. A narrow space between the ceiling and roof provides insulation and also channels rising warm air. Roof edges overhang to protect the walls from heat and the open windows from rain. The houses are also raised off the ground so that air can pass underneath.

"All of these great things, which have nothing to do with code or any of that stuff, come from just observing how people survived in those days," says Freear. "We've taken some of that—and none of it is rocket science, by the way—and asked, 'How can we make a contemporary version of this so that people can live within their means, keep the heating and energy bills as low as possible, in a comfortable, beautiful home?' That's been the mantra for these houses."

"We basically use traditional methods that the South has been using for generations, so it's not really new technology," says Ball. "We use what works well. It's why the traditional buildings are still here two and three hundred years later."

The 20K Houses, says Freear, represent "sustainability with a small *s*," which means building climate-sensitive, energy-thrifty, and easily maintained houses using low-tech methods and hardware that can be easily repaired by local people with basic skills.

The Rural Studio maintains that the houses can be built for around $25,000—so long as there is a relatively easy site to build upon. That does not, for example, include land improvements or remote sewage and water hookups.

"Twenty thousand was a kind of idealized number that we sort of drew out, where we tried to ask, what could the poorest of the poor afford?" says Freear. "We looked at folks living on welfare and said it looks like they can afford about one hundred dollars a month. They may already be paying that in rent. When you equate that to some form of mortgage, it basically translated to twenty thousand dollars that they could afford—about one hundred dollars a month over thirty years."

The problem that Freear and the Rural Studio now face is finding someone who is willing to construct the homes. While you may be able to build a house for $20,000 or $25,000, once completed it gets appraised at double that price. "The builder is clearly not going to keep selling it at the price it was built for. If it gets appraised at $50,000, then they're going to sell it for $50,000. So all the time, there is pressure on us to kind of raise the number . . . It's really a struggle."

This catch-22 immediately manifested itself when the Studio "faux" bid the houses to several Birmingham contractors. Despite the fact that the materials costs were in line with their projections, "where they blew us out of the water was the suggestion of what it was going to cost to build it. These are little houses that need only very basic supervision. We thought, 'Are they just thinking of a number here?'"

Freear says he had the same experience when trying to promote the idea of building small wooden houses, back in his native England, for materials that cost $20,000 to $25,000. "Their reaction was more about the expectations of what you're supposed to pay for a house. It's not exactly thinking of a number; it's more like, well, this is what it costs. Whether it's built of mashed potatoes, concrete block, or wood, it's just, 'This is what it costs to build a house, right?' So it's a struggle to find people who actually want to build it for an affordable price. That's the truth."

THE CODE WHISPERERS:
SAN DIEGO'S MRED MAVERICKS

The city of San Diego was named after a Catholic priest whose main claim to fame was the miraculous healing of an heir to the Spanish throne in 1562—one century after the priest had died. The cure took place when Franciscan monks carried the corpse of father Diego de San Nicolás del Puerto to the bed of Don Carlos, son and successor to King Philip II. Don Carlos was near death from a traumatic head injury. He miraculously woke from his coma the next morning and Father Diego—or what was left of him—was immediately canonized as San (Saint) Diego.

The image of San Diego's namesake as a fossilized priest, a saint frozen in time, is strangely appropriate for this most southern of Southern California cities. Known for the exquisite bay that attracted Spaniards in the first place (still a favorite harbor for the US Navy), San Diego is one of the most hypercoded cities in the country. It is so layered with neighborhood, city, county, state, and federal regulations that it is almost impossible to build anything small, innovative, or inexpensive. It is a city ossified by the status quo.

San Diego has numerous charms—a year-round temperate climate, quaint historic precincts, well-manicured neighborhoods, and handsome hotel and convention facilities—that add to its allure for Rust Belt tourists and retirees. San Diego is not, however, known for its affordable living.

In the decade prior to the Great Recession, which began in 2007, single-family home prices in San Diego more than tripled. As a result, the city has one of the country's worst ratings in the Housing Affordability Index (this National Association of Realtors ranking measures the percentage of US households that can afford to buy a median-priced home in a given area). In the first few years of the twenty-first century, it fell to below 20 percent for San Diego.

Like most overpriced cities that rode the great real estate bubble of the prerecession years, San Diego saw its housing prices drop precipitously when the economy collapsed. In the end, prices fell by more than a third before they started climbing back. Today they are on the rise again; according to the Zillow Home Value Index, San Diego home prices in 2015 had reached 94 percent of their prerecession level.

The result then and now is an extremely high entry barrier for young households with moderate incomes. "Affordable or attainable housing is our biggest problem—a crisis really," says Howard Blackson, an architect and one-time city planner who now runs the San Diego office of engineering firm Michael Baker International. "I think there is a resort-plantation mentality that keeps us very, very tight, with little change."

Leading the charge to change that state of affairs is Armistead "Ted" Smith, the founder of the Masters in Real Estate Development (MRED) program for California-based Woodbury University's School of Architecture. Smith—a professor and maverick developer of small, affordable homes in San Diego—created MRED just over a decade ago to teach architects how to design, finance, and build their own projects. By doing so, he has trained a cadre of innovative graduates, New Pioneers who are building a new San Diego of small, infill residential structures that defy the phlegmatic norm.

CRACKING THE CODE

Founded in Los Angeles in 1884, Woodbury College—now University—opened a satellite campus in San Diego in 1998 to offer bachelor's and master's programs in architecture. Six years later it birthed a further San Diego offshoot, Smith's tiny but revolutionary MRED program.

By the time Smith convinced Woodbury to open its MRED program in 2004, he had already developed a nonconformist reputation in San Diego for his GoHomes program—a Lean Urbanism approach to affordable housing that cracked the city's zoning codes. Back in the 1980s, the "city" of Del Mar (a coastal residential enclave that is actually part of San Diego's vast municipal footprint) was looking for a way to buffer its commercial strip from its high-end homes. What local city officials had in mind was multifamily housing.

Smith came up with a unique solution that took advantage of two regulations regarding single-family homes. One was a zoning statute that defined single-family homes as those with a single kitchen. It could have a dozen bedrooms, but as long as it had only one kitchen, it was designated as single family. The other regulation came from a ruling made by the California Supreme Court in the 1980s, which stated that a family doesn't have to be blood related or given a numerical cap.

These were both critical to creating GoHomes, which were legally zoned as single-family homes while actually containing six different households. These "households" consisted of six one-bedroom suites, each with its own bathroom and exterior entrance. They shared a single kitchen, and were legally defined as an extended "family."

This zoning legerdemain cut costs dramatically. Characterized as single-family homes, the GoHomes avoided steep parking requirements as well as the real estate expense of commercial, multifamily housing lots. "And so you could have affordable housing in Del Mar, where you could buy a 'little' house for $50,000—a sixth of $300,000, which is what homes cost in 1980," says Smith.

Smith and his colleagues also worked for years with city planners on what the threshold definition of a "kitchen" was, so as to allow hot plates and small refrigerators in the separate suites. "We used these incredibly complicated ordinances to make it clear that it was legal to do what we were doing," he says. "It was a great way to make affordable housing."

Smith and his partner Kathleen McCormick then took these Lean Urbanism principles—of gaming the definitions in zoning and building codes—to denser areas of the city. In particular they were involved in the resurrection of San Diego's Little Italy, which was something of a slum in the 1980s.

In the mid-1990s, the city launched its Little Italy Neighborhood Development (LIND) program, designed to buy up entire city blocks and deliver them to single developers. Smith and McCormick, along with five other architects (including current MRED staff), proposed taking one of those blocks and subdividing it into six separate properties for compatible but diverse buildings. The city agreed, and Smith and McCormick used their GoHomes concepts to construct an apartment building called "the Merrimack."

Originally from Virginia, Smith was something of a Civil War history buff. An iconic moment of that war was the emergence of the ironclad ship, the first of which was the Confederate vessel *Merrimack*. It was a game changer in naval history, and marked the beginning of the end of the wooden-ship era.

"We named the building the Merrimack, because [that ship] was the first ironclad to actually go to war, so it was a status-quo changer," says Smith. "When we did the Merrimack [building] we thought enough of ourselves that we were doing a status-quo changer, and that the building would be a model for other developers who didn't want to build an underground garage and all the trappings that come with it."

One of the tools of Lean Urbanism that levels the playing field for New Pioneers is called "thresholds." By understanding precisely what triggers the next level of regulation, it is possible to avoid heavier costs by pushing the envelope to the edge of that threshold.

In textbook lean style, Smith avoided the code-driven requirement for a parking garage by calling the Merrimack a "double duplex." Even though the building contained twelve living units (which Smith called "suites") he used the codes for kitchens and bedrooms and shared spaces so that it was legally defined as containing just four units. This took the building below the five-unit threshold that automatically triggered the expense of building a parking garage.

The double-duplex designation not only reduced parking requirements but also helped with financing. "We realized there was a financing magic for four units. Five units became a commercial loan, whereas four units was a residential loan," says Smith. This was a huge advantage because commercial loans call for periodic renewals that make it impossible to lock in long-term interest rates; residential loans are predictable and easier to pay off.

Three years after the building was completed, Smith—then an instructor at San Diego's New School of Architecture—jumped ship to Woodbury and started the MRED program, using the Merrimack's roof as its campus. If you drive past the Merrimack today you will see a steel-and-glass addition sitting on top the original masonry (stone and cinderblock) building. This classroom complex, with exposed structural elements, no insulation, and a single stairway access on the side of the building, flagrantly ignores local building codes. It was approved, however, because it was called "a covered patio," according to former city planner Blackson.

MASTERS OF THEIR UNIVERSE

Inside a high-ceilinged classroom of the MRED school rests a model of the building itself. The model bristles with a row of cannons, a tongue-in-cheek reference to its ironclad namesake. In this and other rooms of the Merrimack, including a spacious design studio, six to eight architecture students undergo the MRED curriculum each year. The idea behind the program is multifold. The first is to create an architect-contractor-developer who can leapfrog the tedious years of "working in the back room of a big firm doing details, with little responsibility or client contact," says Smith. In the course of twelve months, each student attempts to develop a small project as his or her thesis—learning by apprenticing to faculty who are developing their own projects. "We want them to have the experience of actually build-ing," says Smith. "You need the real-life construction experience."

By assuming the roles of contractors and developers, students can also avoid conflicts that inhibit innovation. "The idea of being the con-tractor means first of all that the whole fight is gone, of contractor and architect blaming each other for problems," says Smith. "We've discov-ered that instead of holding the hand of the contractor and trying to keep him happy, we could just *be* the contractor. It's cheaper and faster."

As for being the developer, there is the obvious financial upside. But just as important is the creativity released. "The difference is that now we become the only cook in the kitchen," says Smith. "We are the contractor, the owner, the operator, and the architect. All of a sudden your liability is way reduced so you can innovate." In one of his buildings, for example, Smith tried what he calls "a fancy detail in the skylight" that used glass bricks with minimal caulking. "Well, it leaked, and we thought, 'What good luck that we still own the building because otherwise we'd be sued.' The whole idea is that you can try an unusual detail. An architect's not going to do it, not when they get this tiny fee along with a huge liability."

As would-be developers, students are taught a slew of related skills. Among them is estimating the cost of construction, includ-ing a "widgets and shells" studio where costs are estimated for odd-shaped shells or spaces, or for materials like a glass wall vs. a masonry wall. (The widgets are the elements like bathrooms, kitchens, and front doors, which are needed regardless of project size and shape.)

In addition to regular faculty, real-world experts lecture the students. Lawyers talk to them about partnerships and agreements and how to limit liability. Contractors lecture on how to manage subcontractors and construction sites. Accountants and bankers talk about how to keep the books and manage their shares in a partnership, or how to hide taxes in depreciation.

"One of the really important things is that you get an educa-tion in financial literacy," says David Saborio, an MRED graduate and now a member of the faculty. "People in architecture don't know about investment vehicles, like how loans or interest works, or what a ten-year bond is. It's something that used to never be taught, but it's a really important part of it . . . If you don't know how the money works, you're screwed."

Perhaps the most important thing students are taught at MRED—and what makes it a lean institution—is that by understanding zoning and building regulations, they can work around the system. "We get into the nitty-gritty on all the zoning ordinances and also the International Building Code stuff," says Smith. "Because those things—the physicality of the building and the zoning issues of the project—are the two big determinants, and we are looking for every advantage in those ordinances . . . If you know the ordinances better than the guy at the planning department, then you are going to be able to accomplish things you want to do."

For their final assignment, students are required to locate a site, design a building, and attempt to get it financed. In the lean spirit of lowering the barriers for young and impecunious pioneers, MRED teaches students that intelligence and ingenuity are their own capital.

"We try to teach that there are all sorts of ways to get involved with projects without having any money, like trying to do partnerships with landowners," says Smith. "We teach the students that the architecture fee, the contractor fee, and the developer fee are 30 percent of the project cost, so if a bank will lend you 70 percent of the cost, you can basically build these projects for free." While bank lending has substantially slowed since the recession, and only a few students succeed in launching a project at year's end, the process is nonetheless a learning experience.

In the meantime, the concept of code cracking is imbued as a fundamental tenet of real estate development and architectural design. "The advanced departments are about the advantages in the zoning ordinances, and how to beat [those] and the International Building Code at the same time," says Smith. "We have gotten more and more into specific zoning and International Building Code research, because that's the key to the whole thing."

AN URBAN LABORATORY

The neighborhood that surrounds MRED's Merrimack building, the formerly squalid barrio of Little Italy, is laced with buildings that illustrate the school's concepts of how to get around code—especially the block that Smith and his colleagues developed.

"This whole block has an interesting story," says Saborio. "Nobody wanted land up here in Little Italy. It was all TV and radio repair shops, parking lots, lots of seedy stuff. So the city had a competition for this block, and Ted [Smith] and some partners won the competition. It was supposed to be a prototype for what could be done on a typical city block."

Instead of creating a single megadevelopment, Smith's team did just the opposite by breaking the block up for smaller projects. "The first thing these guys did was to chop it back up, into simple row houses, mixed-use buildings, and affordable housing," says Saborio. "The redevelopment agency wasn't thrilled about it because they spent all this time consolidating the block."

Part of what Smith's team did with the block, besides the Merrimack, sits around the corner from the MRED building: a row of live/work townhouses, the first of their kind in the city. Designed and developed by MRED faculty member Jonathan Segal, at first glance the row appears to be a single building. But each townhouse is actually separated from the next by a three-inch space, hidden behind rubber stripping.

"See this seam right here? This is a building code hack, or trick, or whatever you want to call it," says Saborio. "Technically this is a completely detached structure. It's got its own foundation under it, and it's no different in theory than a suburban house. It stands alone. You could knock this down and it wouldn't effect the two [adjacent buildings]."

Had the row been constructed as a single building, it would have been designated a condominium, with all sorts of ensuing requirements—including an underground garage, a homeowners association, handicap access, etc. The additional expenses would have made the sale price prohibitive for small businesses.

A block away is another multiunit complex developed by Segal. These residences, constructed after the townhouses, were more densely stacked because of rising property values (thanks to the new buildings in the area!). But they were still affordable, thanks to code "advantages."

"These are all condos. But they still take advantage of the building code—you can see a seam between the buildings where they are literally separated," says Saborio. "So you get a bunch of duplexes, which is beneficial, because multiple duplexes are still under California residential code standards [for single housing]. If all of these were connected, you'd be talking about an elevator, you'd be talking accessible bathrooms, and you'd be talking about an underground garage. You'd be done; you wouldn't even bother."

A few blocks north and west, on a hillcrest near where Interstate 5 cuts San Diego in half, MRED's urban laboratory continues—this time with a multifamily apartment building designed by Smith on State Street. The top of the building includes a row of "mechanical rooms," each for a unit below, which allows the structure to exceed the local height limitations.

"Those 'towers' are playing the zoning ordinance game," says Saborio. "You *can* have an architectural feature built to house mechanical components for the building. If you end up not installing mechanical equipment later on, and are left with an architectural feature that may or may not be habitable, well, yay! They also serve as privacy dividers for rooftop balconies."

Even more innovative code jumping is how the building handles its requirements for parking and for access to units.

As a multiunit family apartment building, the building had to provide parking. But instead of digging a parking garage, Smith used the roof of a one-story retail and commercial space behind the building as its parking lot. Cars drive through a hole in the front of the building, up a ramp, and onto the roof. The parking roof also became a new "plinth" or street level for the building, a reset that helped the four-story building slash costs for access to upper units. First- and second-floor units needed no stairs or hallways. First-floor units are accessible from the street in front. Second-floor units are accessible from the parking level in back. For third-story units, there is a metal walkway that runs across the back of the building, with stairs down to the brick-surfaced parking plinth. For code purposes, the walkway runs along the level of a "second" floor, since it's only one story up from the parking surface. Fewer threshold codes are triggered for a second floor "balcony."

The final code work-around was figuring out access to the fourth floor. This was done by building stairways from the metal walkway up to each of the fourth-floor units. "Now you get into some building code fun," says Saborio. "Some of the doors open directly onto a unit, while some of them open directly onto a staircase that goes up ... All of those [fourth-floor] units up there are technically accessed from the second level."

These clever work-arounds dramatically cut costs for the building. First, there was no need to build an elevator, normally required in a four-story residential building. The work-arounds also meant no internal hallways that ate up space and needed maintenance, sprinklers, etc.

"The point is that this building has some forty units but no elevator, and the circulation system is why that's reasonable and according to code," says Saborio. "Here they used stairs as a kind of defining element of the building. Also, when you enclose a stairway, you can rent that square footage; it becomes part of your unit—compared to the wasted space of a public corridor that has to be maintained."

A CODE TO LIVE—AND DIE—BY

For ex-student Saborio, who became the school's de facto "code whisperer" after working for several years in the city's planning department, the layers of code that builders have to sift through is a mixed blessing.

On the one hand, they pose impediments that sometimes border on the surreal. On the other hand, they provide rules that act as solid guideposts. They can be gotten around, so long as they are understood.

"When you are talking about code, it's really important to distinguish between building code and zoning code," says Saborio. "Building code is primarily concerned with health, safety, and welfare, and I would say that most of the things in the building code are pretty reasonable, especially the International Building Code. You get into some silly stuff where things are more expensive because you've got companies lobbying to make the requirements for their products more rigorous, but for the most part the building code is not the enemy."

That role is taken by zoning ordinances, which have more to do with tastes, cultural values, appearance, and property values. And they are layered into San Diego's codes on a district-by-district basis as well as citywide.

"Every one of these ordinances has been written for a reason," says Smith. "But the reason may not exist any more, or it can be overdone, or it can be an overreaction. And this piling up of ordinances goes on every year. It's the 'old-society' syndrome, like the Roman Empire, where the bureaucracy becomes so thick you can't accomplish anything."

In San Diego, some ordinances affect only particular districts. Other ordinances are citywide. Then there are county regulations. The city is also under coastal regulations for the state of California, and California's state environmental quality act (CEQA).

"Our zoning code is ridiculous," says Saborio. "Each different community plan has its own planned district ordinances, and most of those planned district ordinances are about one hundred pages, plus or minus. So I feel pretty confident in saying that our land development code is literally close to one thousand pages."

Rather than lobby to change or discard the development code, however, MRED wants its students to simply know it better than anyone else. The alternative, says Saborio, is worse. "For zoning in California, there are two polar extremes," he says. "One is where everything is discretionary, and there has to be a decision maker about everything. The other is where everything is ministerial, or administrative. As long as it fits, it ships. And we love that."

What Saborio and Smith both abhor is a development process in which committees decide what is permissible. This is especially relevant for San Diego, home to powerful community groups that write ordinances affecting their districts, primarily for the sake of protecting property values and parking rights.

"What you really want is to have a hard set of ordinances that clearly say what you can and can't do," says Smith. "We don't want community groups to decide what our designs are . . ."

Once you know the rules then you can act accordingly. Among numerous examples by the alumni of MRED is a mixed-use project on 25th Street in the Golden Hill area of San Diego, designed by graduate Mike Burnett. Housing business offices, a yoga studio, and a hair salon, the building was constructed as an envelope around a former Texaco station—which sits like a time capsule in the building's courtyard.

"He took a gas station, and instead of tearing it down built a liner building around it," says Blackson. "By keeping the tanks in the ground he didn't have to do any soil remediation. And that saved money, and got around the rules, and was clever."

Burnett did the same thing—a wraparound—with another building that he constructed around a historic post office; by leaving it intact he avoided any conflict with San Diego's excessive historic preservation ordinances (all buildings built before forty years ago are protected as historic, for example).

As for urban pioneers building small and from scratch, says code-whisperer Saborio, it's all a matter of finding the regulatory tipping point.

"For the building code, you always want to watch out for the threshold that requires you to do the next dumb thing," he says. "Our goal is to read that damn code and know every threshold, so you can stay right under it. Knowing where that threshold is—that's how you avoid costing yourself a lot more money."

Nathan White, another MRED grad who now works for the city as a code reviewer, says he learned the threshold game the hard way. Under San Diego's ordinances, a duplex still qualifies as single residential housing; a triplex triggers the California Building Code and the next level of regulations.

"You want to [develop your project] under the California Residential Code rather than the California Building Code, because the residential code is substantially more lenient about everything," says White. "I did my own permit for a triplex, which is one above a duplex, and I had to go through every discipline—a mechanical review, an electrical review, a structural review, etc.—and had to pay additional fees for all of that. Plus provide handicap accessibility. None of that was required for a duplex. It was a good learning lesson."

Knowing thresholds also keeps you away from MRED's bête noire, community involvement that leads to modification of design. Which is why the school is so in favor of hard, lean, citywide rules that don't require discretionary input.

"Anyone interested in doing lean stuff or staying under the threshold is definitely interested in definitions. So, any time they [the city planning department] come up with a new definition for something, we applaud them, because it's one more threshold we then know," says Saborio. "And that keeps everybody out of a lot of community involvement."

The problem with community involvement is that it can add major expenses to a small project. Whereas a huge, city-block development can afford numerous community reviews—which are common because such projects frequently need a zoning variance—for small builders, such processes eat too much of the budget. It's much easier to avoid triggering red flags.

"PLACE MAKERS" AND THE IMPORTANCE OF SMALL

San Diego is a city that likes to do things on a large scale. It has a massive convention center. It has a vast marina on San Diego Bay. It has a large international airport smack in the middle of the city. It has a sprawling, world-class zoo. Its central Balboa Park, even after giving away 109 acres to freeways and 93 acres to a naval hospital, remains 175 acres larger than New York's Central Park.

What San Diego does not have is a sense of the small, especially when it comes to public space. While its central park is a behemoth, it has almost no public space in the urban core. The seeding of small parks in Manhattan and Brooklyn make these boroughs look like Swiss cheese compared to urban San Diego. The city is so alienated from its public pathways it does not even assume responsibility for maintaining street landscaping and sidewalks; those duties fall to the owners of private property fronting the streets, with predictably mixed results.

San Diego's civic leaders are becoming more aware of this absence of the small, and what it says about the city's mindset toward developing creative, entrepreneurial talent—and to lowering the entry barriers for new pioneers.

Ann Berchtold, the founder of Art San Diego, the city's annual contemporary art show, serves on the boards for both the Downtown San Diego Partnership and the Project for Public Spaces. Her concern is that young artists leave San Diego for Los Angeles because there are no "public canvases" for them, let alone affordable housing, studios, or galleries. Among her exploits was the Open Walls Project in 2014, where she wrangled a dozen highway billboards for twelve young artists to paint murals.

"Young people who are hungry to have what they are working on shown—you just give them a dirt lot and they can create wonders," says Berchtold. She and her colleagues did just that with an abandoned corner lot on El Cajon Boulevard, which artists transformed into a weekend marketplace. "You just create the opportunity for them and get out of the way," she says.

Berchtold is not alone among a handful of San Diego "place makers" who are trying to create small public oases in the city. Another ballyhooed project called Take Back the Alley started with a stretch behind El Cajon and has spread to several other trashed-out alleyways, adding color, art, and lighting to create community spaces.

Likewise, graduates from the New School of Architecture assembled a temporary village called the Quartyard Project. Opened in 2015 on land slated for future development, it used shipping containers to enclose a beer garden and dog run, and to house a coffee shop, bar, and sausage-centric eatery. The shipping containers will be relocated when the lot is developed.

These efforts are too few and far in between, says former city planner Blackson, who, along with Saborio, was part of the city's Civic Innovation Lab until it was shut down by a new mayor. A San Diego native, Blackson remembers a downtown denuded of residents, when everyone packed up and left for the suburbs. As an adult he witnessed the return to downtown living, only it came in the form of condominium high-rises and entire city blocks leveled and re-created as walled and gated "villages." San Diego's predilection for the large, he says, has followed the trend of every "great" US city in the twentieth century, from constructing civic buildings and freeways to creating downtown business districts and baseball parks.

Even the success of the Little Italy block that Smith and his colleagues designed and built—including the conversion of an old marine supply store on the corner into a local hangout called the Harbor Breakfast restaurant—did not change the mentality of the city, which decided that its model for full-block development was too complex to adopt.

An appreciation for small and individuated urban tableaux was not lost on MRED, however, nor on its cadre of thirty to forty graduates who remain in San Diego, determined to usher in a new culture. As former student Saborio puts it: "The more stakeholders per block, the more variation per block, the better the neighborhood."

In an effort to tilt San Deigo's zeitgeist toward the small, and in a departure from MRED's lean edict to navigate rather than change the rules, Smith and a consortium of cohorts and allies from San Diego's communities of architects, academics, artists, and urban activists finally pushed through—after fifteen years—a small lot ordinance for the city. The new ordinance allows property owners to build several separate homes on a single small piece of property, creating greater density with smaller, more affordable homes.

While in some ways the ordinance merely allows for the return of what's known in San Diego as "bungalow courts"—1920s-era clusters of separate homes on a single small property—it opens the door to cheaper housing and greater density without resorting to apartment buildings. Among other provisions, the new ordinance only requires each house to provide one parking space, which doesn't have to be covered, rather than a two-car garage in the bottom of the house that would add $200,000 to $300,000 to the cost.

This ability to create small, creative spaces that are affordable, says Smith, is the key to lowering the thresholds to entry for the young, entrepreneurial class of pioneers.

"What we are talking about are the wonderful people who make society fun but who don't get paid—the artists, musicians, and writers: the important players who are never rewarded properly," says Smith. "There are people who don't care what the rent is, stockbrokers and bankers and lawyers. I design for musicians and artists and architects, where you say the rent is going to be $1,200 and they say, 'Do you have one for $1,150?'"

chapter seven

PHOENIX: HOUSE OF THE RISING SUN

Making Small-Scale Pioneering Possible

Phoenix, Arizona, seems an unlikely laboratory for the fine-grained, walkable world of New Urbanism. It is a self-consciously "modern" city, at least by late-twentieth-century standards, with overly wide streets and high-rise towers set back from the boulevards to make room for more parking. It is not a city that merely deferred to the automobile; it is a city that flopped prostrate before the car, and was appropriately defiled.

Like Detroit, Phoenix had to suffer an economic meltdown before it could embrace the New Pioneers of lean. Further seduced by the siren of the great real estate bubble of the early 2000s—the froth on the cake after decades of sprawl—Phoenix followed the twin mirages of limitless suburban expansion and speculative condomania down the rabbit hole to economic collapse. When the real estate bubble burst, the city became a national poster child for overbuilding.

Phoenix's developers and investors stopped chasing their tails in 2008, by which time its leaders had realized the need for a new modus operandi. The "mega" approach to redevelopment was failing. Rezoning the entire downtown for high-rise development, like the city's botched bid to move Arizona's NFL team downtown, led only to more bulldozing and empty lots. A new mayor looked inward and found a cadre of urban pioneers who had been hacking the rules to save and rebuild the city's remaining old neighborhoods with new retail and edgy entertainment.

Phoenix mayor Phil Gordon, who took office during the final go-go years of the real estate boom, was among those who understood how the system was gamed for large-scale projects that nobody wanted to finance. The city had to disrupt its own rules to unleash growth from the ground up and level the playing field for a burgeoning community of New Pioneers. And that's just what a tiny cadre of young city officials, with the mayor's blessing, did. Their only problem: entrenched bureaucrats.

A City Repurposed: Keeping small-scale business alive, this converted motorcycle repair shop created an oasis along the new light rail corridor.

A CITY WITHOUT SHADE

The first thing any visitor to Phoenix notices is the incredible width of its major streets and the glaring absence of shade trees. The roadways are incomprehensibly wide, mercilessly scorched by a sun that elevates summertime temperatures to as high as 120 degrees Fahrenheit. It is an environment that is not merely pedestrian unfriendly. It is a city that's outright hostile to the citizen on foot.

This is not by accident. This is by deliberate design, the desiccated fruit of a multidecade policy to create a "city of the future" based on the automobile and the misbegotten notion of cheap, fossil-based energy without end.

The irony of this baked, shade-free city is that it was once called "The Garden City of the Southwest." In the 1920s and 1930s, it was verdant with shade trees and palms, street after street invested with foliage. A photograph of the main north-south thoroughfare of Central Avenue as late as 1950 shows a downtown rich with green streets and canopies of vegetation.

"When you look back on the pictures, it's heartbreaking," says Lyssa Hall, a young neighborhood specialist who works in the Phoenix Planning & Development Department. "We used to have massive trees that cut arcs of shade, so you could basically go from one end of the city to the other completely in shade. In the nineteen fifties we decided to invest in development and we basically widened all of our streets and removed all of our trees." The result was a city scorched by the sun.

Ironically enough, a similar situation had occurred seven hundred years earlier. The Hohokam civilization of Native Americans had flourished for two thousand years where Phoenix now stands. They had developed a network of canals and large interconnecting shade trees that together created a microclimate, a cool place for their people to survive the heat. At some point during the thirteenth century, however, the Hohokam civilization collapsed in a downward spiral of overpopulation and dwindling resources. Similar to what happened in twentieth-century Haiti, the city was deforested by its citizens. They also downgraded their complex agriculture to a monoculture of maize, the cheapest commodity to produce. The result was malnutrition, disease, and economic failure.

Beyond the parallel of a canopy demolished by the people it protected, dependence on an economic monoculture—a key contributor to the ruination of the Hohokam—resonates in the Phoenix of today. The city still suffers from its overdependence on real estate as the primary if not sole engine of economic growth. Whereas Phoenix was once propelled by the "Five Cs"—copper, cotton, citrus, cattle, and climate—it has been largely reduced to the final C of climate, mostly in the form of suburban expansion intended to lure Rust Belt retirees tired of the cold and the damp.

The perpetual-motion real estate machine that built the Phoenix sprawl worked for decades, becoming a self-fulfilling prophecy.

It created jobs and entire industries—as well as the all-powerful Homebuilders Association of Central Arizona. In a paradigm repeated nationwide, the urban core was abandoned as residents decamped for drivable suburban enclaves. City planners encouraged the new car-oriented culture, carving up older urban neighborhoods with interstate highways. Phoenix not only widened its main boulevards but also stripped them of on-street parking—everything was redesigned to get cars in and out of the downtown centers of employment and entertainment as quickly as possible.

All of this came to a screeching halt with the Great Recession of 2007. The emperor was suddenly revealed to be naked. No amount of pro-development rhetoric could restore the illusion that Phoenix could live forever on cheap farmland converted to housing developments. By 2010, with construction jobs evaporating, unemployment in Phoenix reached almost 11 percent. The veil had been lifted, and the city had to face facts and reinvent itself.

Part of that reinvention meant returning to some of the best practices of the past, lost in the headstrong plunge toward modernism. An even bigger part was for Phoenix to understand the value of doing things on a small, granular scale. Often these two forces intersected, converging the new and old, with an occasional creative assist from the city's youngest employees.

Take street width, for example. After decades of leveling trees and widening thoroughfares, the city realized the error of its ways. Beginning in 2012, Phoenix began a program of narrowing and replanting its downtown streets, adding on-street angle parking, landscaped "islands," and lighting. The cost: one million dollars per street, an expensive price tag for redemption.

Twenty-something neighborhood specialist Hall and others had alternative ideas. They pushed to narrow the streets using just paint, with no demolition or poured concrete for new curbs and island planters, etc. Using paint only, streets could be narrowed, bike lanes added, and on-street parking, once eradicated, restored. The cost: $70,000 per street.

"Investing one million dollars per block may not be worth it when you may have to come back in ten years and change it," Hall says. "Why not just do this [painting] so you can change the parking—which is what you need—then do the final street configuration when the area is more mature?"

With that lean approach in mind, Hall led an effort to "green" Grand Avenue, a former arterial roadway that cuts at a forty-five-degree angle across the heart of downtown. Long a drug- and prostitution-infested area, the street is now an edgy and hip arts district. In order to beautify Grand Avenue, Hall applied for a Greening America's Capitals technical assistance grant from the EPA, which paid for a consultant to come in and organize community meetings and planning. The result was a lean, inexpensive approach that the city approved and completed at the benchmark cost of $70,000 per block. Grand Avenue shrank from four to two lanes, adding bicycle lanes, LED lighting, and large, barrel-shaped planters decorated and maintained by local artists.

Because Grand Avenue had been part of the old US state highway system—as US 60 it had been the main state route through Phoenix—there was apprehension by federal Department of Transportation officials that the reduction in lanes would create a traffic snarl. "They were concerned that traffic Armageddon would strike," says Hall. "As it turned out, people just took alternative routes. But we had to have political support to convince the DOT to take a chance."

That political support is what makes Phoenix unique in the cosmos of the new pioneers. The idea of going leaner—of taking the megaplex mentality down a notch to embrace a smaller scale—is a result of pioneering activism emanating not only from the community, but from inside the government as well.

A perfect example is another of Hall's pet projects: Water Harvesting Tree Pockets. The idea came from a nonprofit group in Tucson called the Watershed Management Group. The idea was simple, elegant, and lean. Instead of allowing rainwater to drain into the sewage system at the end of each block, it drains the rain midblock through a hole drilled into the curb. The hole sends the water into a depression along the block, creating a mini-oasis.

"The storm water runs off and supports the landscaping," says Hall. "After a year and a half, if designed correctly, trees planted there can survive without any additional irrigation." The excavation work and curb "coring" is done by contractors paid for by the city; the landscaping work with soil, rocks, and planting is done by volunteers. Several blocks are now complete in the Garfield neighborhood northeast of downtown, an area once home to the notorious 9th Street Gang and currently witnessing an influx of urban millennial pioneers.

Hall herself is a perfect example of the new thinking that has been encouraged at city hall, first under Mayor Phil Gordon and then under his like-minded successor, Mayor Greg Stanton. They are by no means in the majority, but their efforts have begun to percolate. Hall started out as a maverick architect but decided to go into local government when she realized that "the city controls the shots via zoning," and that she could have more impact there. "It's such a young city and so transitory that you can come here and make a big difference. They let me do a lot of stuff. You're going to let me bore holes in the concrete and do a green street? I'm in."

GOING SMALL TO FILL THE HOLES

On a Wednesday morning in March 2015, about a hundred people assembled in an empty lot at the intersection of Roosevelt and 1st Avenue in downtown Phoenix. On hand were Mayor Stanton, several city council members, staffers from the planning department, and representatives from neighborhood coalitions—along with bankers, developers, and reporters from local newspapers, television, and radio. Even a food truck showed up.

In any other city, the groundbreaking for a four-story apartment building would not draw such a crowd. But this was big news in Phoenix, where empty lots are the bane of the city. As of mid-2015,

an astonishing 42 percent of Phoenix was composed of empty lots—a
virtual sea of them, on almost every street. They are not like the gaps
in Detroit or other cities faced with urban blight. All of the lots are
tidy, clean, and fenced. They were not bulldozed to erase crack houses
or make the neighborhood safe. They were emptied thanks to an ill-
considered combination of zoning ordinances.

"If you want to know why Phoenix destroyed its downtown, it
comes down to two things," says Emily Talen, a professor of urban
sustainability at Arizona State University in nearby Tempe. "The first
was that it was all zoned for high-rises. So nobody wanted to build
anything small. The land was too valuable. The second thing is the tax
code. Vacant lots are taxed at the lowest possible rate, 15 percent less
than if anything is on the property." That twin punch of up-zoning
the land valuation and downgrading the tax incentives to maintain
buildings created a body slam of destruction.

The result is a city missing nearly half its teeth. Everywhere you
look there are empty lots and gaps between buildings; like the wide,
shadeless streets, it is another symbol of a city unsympathetic to
pedestrians.

The particular parcel at Roosevelt and 1st Avenue, where the
mayor turned the first shovel of dirt in the spring of 2015, was newsworthy for a number of reasons. First, it had been vacant for more
than half a century. It was once a cluster of narrow, tree-lined streets
leveled in 1961 for "a parking lot to accommodate this auto-centric
area," noted Matt Seaman, the developer of the new project. It was
also newsworthy because of the property's inherent complexity. It
took three years of work and a loan from the Sustainable Communities Fund to untangle the project from a maze of impediments—
rights of way for access streets, underground utility issues, etc.

Mayor Stanton, an advocate for a walkable downtown, was ebul-
lient during the ceremony. "This is a great day to celebrate what is
going to happen to this crazy triangle. People thought it would be
vacant forever," he told the assembled crowd. Commenting on the

Herculean effort it took to bring a mid-rise project that actually addressed the street with retail storefronts, the mayor put it perfectly. "Yes, it is ironic that we make it easier to get permits and financing for a project on the outskirts of town than in the heart of the downtown like this."

The fact that Mayor Stanton became a proponent of small-scale mixed-use downtown development, along with historic preservation and adaptive reuse, betokens nothing less than a ground shift in Phoenix. It means that pioneers on the outskirts of policy making have infiltrated the highest ranks of government. In a topsy-turvy reversal, Stanton (like his predecessor) was using top-down pressure to reverse policies that had all but ensured a dead metropolitan core with oversized structures and empty streets. It was not an easy struggle and represented a generational shift on par with turning around the *Titanic* on high seas.

Prior to the Gordon/Stanton era, Phoenix City Hall believed in doing things big. Perfect examples are the creation of the city's two downtown sports stadiums, the US Airways Center and Chase Field. Both were built in the roaring 1990s, and both required the destruction of acres of buildings in what had been the warehouse district of Phoenix.

For both sports complexes there were viable alternatives. In the case of the US Airways Center (now called the Talking Stick Resort Arena and home to the National Basketball Association's Phoenix Suns), an older stadium suitable for renovation already existed on the grounds of the Arizona State Fair some two miles away. In the case of Chase Field, far less densely developed land was also available a few blocks to the east.

The controversy surrounding the development of Chase Field was not just sparked by the requisite urban bulldozing. The land acquisition and construction costs required funding from a countywide sales tax increase of a quarter cent—a tax enacted by the Maricopa County Board of Supervisors without voter approval. The issue was so volatile that County Supervisor Mary Rose Wilcox was actually shot and wounded by a man who argued in court that her support for the tax justified his actions (the shooter was found guilty of attempted first-degree murder).

The stock of warehouses demolished for these stadiums was, at the time, home to an incipient art community aghast at the decision, seen largely as an insider move by developers who profited enormously from the rise in preconstruction property values. To put this in context, the equivalent would have been for New York City to demolish the Soho warehouse district in Manhattan for Yankee Stadium instead of locating it on the fringe of the city. Spared destruction, Soho became a loft district for artists and students, then for art galleries, and finally for fashion boutiques. A quintessential example of wealth created by lean urban pioneers, Soho is now among the most chic neighborhoods in New York.

The city fathers of Phoenix, still enthralled by the ceaseless expansion of new suburbs, simply could not conceive of a downtown inhabited by residents other than monuments. But there were residents, and among them a die-hard cadre of artists and small business people, who set out to educate the city's leadership about the power of small things.

SOMETHING IN THE WAY SHE MOVES

Few people have had a bigger impact on the reinvention of Phoenix than pioneer Kimber Lanning. Ask any Phoenician how the city's most innovative programs came about, and most, from city officials to art gallery owners, will point you in the direction of Lanning. Her story is a microcosm of the city's awakening from its long, benighted sleep of bad urban planning.

Outside of her birth on Okinawa (her father was a US fighter pilot), Lanning is a native of Phoenix, having moved to the metropolitan region as a child when her dad was reassigned to Arizona's Luke Air Force Base. After graduating from suburban Glendale High

School, she resisted her parents' efforts to send her to an eastern college and went to Arizona State University in Phoenix instead. She studied architecture but was too restless to finish. Instead she left to start her own business—Stinkweeds records, a hip music shop on Camelback Road on the north central side of the city. That was in 1987, prior to the city's most ambitious campaigns to level its downtown.

"I was like a social worker disguised as a record salesperson," says Lanning. "All my customers were former classmates who would come by to complain. Almost all of them ended up leaving, and doing amazing things in other cities. This is what led me to the notion of place making, and why I have stayed here."

Over the course of her first decade in business, Lanning—who was deeply disturbed by the exodus of her classmates—did her best to create an oasis of local culture at Stinkweeds. She hung local art on the walls, and hosted live, local music in the store. "I was trying to provide an outlet for all these kids," she says. "It got to be five and six nights a week."

After a decade, Lanning purchased a building on Roosevelt Street, in the heart of a tattered downtown area with drug and prostitution problems. The only businesses open on the block were a liquor store and a hubcap shop. She called her establishment Modified Arts, and turned it into an art gallery and performance space for music, theater, and dance. For the next dozen years, Modified Arts functioned as one of the few small-venue theaters in all of Phoenix.

"Opening this was like a geyser; there was such a need. Here we were in this huge metropolis with fabulous programs at ASU in the arts, but the [region's] cities had all chosen to build massive, very traditional art institutions—the Tempe Center for the Arts, the Chandler Center for the Arts, the Mesa Center for the Arts, etcetera. There are like fifteen of them, all with a capacity of five thousand or greater, but absolutely nowhere for someone to start their career in a 350-seat professional theater. This did not exist."

By way of lowering barriers for young artists, Lanning rented her performance space for $175 a night, a price she stuck with for a dozen years. The artists could rent the room for that price and sell tickets for ten dollars each. Sell 125 tickets and you did well. "The audience was a mishmash of people from all over," recalls Lanning. "I used to get calls from parents asking, 'Is it safe for my kid to come down there?'"

A year and a half after Lanning moved in, a young couple—Greg Esser and Cindy Dach—bought another building on Roosevelt, about a block away, and opened the Eye Lounge art gallery. The two art galleries became the nexus for a gaggle of small businesses that opened on adjacent side streets in bungalows built in the 1920s.

While Modified Arts and Eye Lounge were commercially zoned, these small businesses on residential side streets—a coffee shop, a vintage clothing store, a used bookshop—were not. In the New Pioneer mode they operated under the radar, without commercial permits or licenses. But they created a core of "groovy" spaces that became the foundation for what is now the biggest monthly art walk in the United States.

"We'd promote this thing called First Friday, and be happy if three hundred people came down here. Now thirty thousand people come here on a monthly basis," says Lanning. Beatrice Moore, a gallery owner in the old warehouse district, had actually launched First Friday a few years before, but Roosevelt became its new home after the city leveled the warehouses for its twin stadiums. What the new artsy community on Roosevelt didn't know was that it was the city's next target.

The area south of Roosevelt Street occupied by these new pioneers was just east of the city's principal north-south Central Avenue corridor. It was a historic district known as the Evans-Churchill neighborhood. Once home to middle-class families that had long since fled, in the early 2000s it was occupied mostly by lower-income Hispanics. Sensing they would have little resistance from these Spanish-language residents with no political clout, the city under then mayor Skip Rimsza began to assemble the land for a professional football stadium. It was going to be the new home of the

Arizona Cardinals, the NFL team that had been using ASU's Sun Devil Stadium in nearby Tempe.

The methodology for razing the area was what turned Lanning into a full-fledged community activist. With little fanfare, a real estate agent who was a childhood friend and college roommate of the mayor went door to door, explaining to the Hispanic residents that a stadium was coming and that they had to sell. Once purchased, the homes were resold to the city for an immediate profit. "He lowballed everybody and sucked up seventeen homes, all of them demolished overnight," says Lanning.

Lanning and other area residents protested at city hall, but to no avail. "That was one of my early introductions to shadow government," says Lanning. "It caused me to get involved with how policy works. And it took me about three weeks to figure out that no decisions are ever made at city council meetings. The decisions are already made by the time the city council meeting comes around."

Lanning realized that only organized lobbying could influence policy decisions at city hall. So she began a coalition of local businesses called Arizona First, which between 2002 and 2009 grew to an organization of eight hundred members. By 2015 it had thirteen full-time employees, 2,500 members, and offices in Phoenix, Tucson, and Cottonwood. But in just a few years from its inception it had enough clout to begin altering policy—and to get Lanning an appointment on the city's Development Advisory Board.

THE TURNING POINT

Many of the policy changes that have begun to steer Phoenix toward a leaner approach to urbanism did not take place until after the advent of the Great Recession, that painful wake-up call for a city dependent on the economic monoculture of sprawl. But its refocus on innovative, top-down programs designed to lower thresholds for small businesses and small building developers was already seeded in the watershed year of 2005.

By that time, the effort to build the Cardinal stadium downtown had collapsed; for a variety of reasons the NFL team had decided to forgo downtown Phoenix and instead relocate to suburban Glendale. The city, having assembled its parcel on the bones of the Evans-Churchill neighborhood, decided to move forward with a biomedical campus that would integrate with ASU's science department. The two square blocks of Evans-Churchill that had remained intact along Roosevelt—the core of the artist colony started by Lanning, Esser, Dach, and other urban pioneers—were still in harm's way, having been designated as parking for the new campus. It all came to a head one night during a First Friday art walk. It was a night that gallery owner (and now museum curator for ASU) Greg Esser describes as "one of the most embarrassing moments" in the city's history.

"They had drawn a dotted line around everything they were going to tear down to create this biomedical campus and these two blocks were part of it," says Esser. "So in July of 2005 they send a multijurisdictional task force to the First Friday event." Comprising the task force were health code inspectors, building code inspectors, fire department personnel, police officers on horseback, squad cars with lights flashing—even a mobile SWAT command unit.

"It was like a tactical response, and their publicly stated purpose was to enforce underage drinking [violations], open-container violations, and illegal parking," says Esser. "They did none of those things. Instead they targeted each of the businesses that were operating in these two blocks on that evening. The same [First Friday event] was happening five blocks to the east and five blocks to the west, but there was no police enforcement evident in those areas whatsoever. So in hindsight it became obvious that they were trying to shake down this two-block area, because they wanted it for the planned development."

As it turned out, the enforcement efforts that night were ordered by planning staff within city hall and without the knowledge of the city council, a bizarre by-product of the Phoenix form of strong-manager government. And, as it turned out, the effort backfired.

Public reaction, as well as blowback from the increasingly organized community of small business owners, caused the newly elected mayor at the time, Phil Gordon, to reconsider the city's priorities.

Gordon had himself been a developer of small properties, including the restoration of historic buildings, and was aware of the difficulties independent developers faced with burdensome city codes. The tipping point came several months later, when arts activist Lanning used a $5,000 grant she obtained to organize a one-day educational symposium for the city planning staff and its elected officials. It was called the Adaptive Reuse Forum, attended by about forty of the city's most influential politicians, planners, bankers, and developers. And what they heard had a profound effect.

Among the speakers were Richard Florida, director of the Martin Prosperity Institute and proselytizer for walkable cities; sustainability expert Marsha Ward; Habitat for Humanity architect Debra Coleman; and Melvin Green, the architect-guru leading the charge to adapt building codes for existing and historic buildings. All came armed with facts and figures to talk about the economic benefits of small-scale development, and the need to lighten code requirements in inner cities.

"Phoenix evolved as suburban sprawl, with single-family detached homes. The code was built for that," says Esser. "Twenty years ago 'adaptive reuse' wasn't even a phrase uttered inside of city hall." Efforts to repurpose old buildings rather than tear them down were met with a blizzard of codes that all but ensured their destruction. The death knell was the pernicious phrase "change of use." As soon as a developer tried to upgrade, for example, an old beauty salon into a coffee shop, it came under "change of use." And that meant that the entire structure had to be brought up to code, regardless of any consideration for grandfathered use, relative cost, or actual user safety. And the codes were gamed for large, big-box developers.

A disheartening example was the code for restrooms equipped for the disabled. If you tried to repurpose a small 1950s strip mall, for instance, city code required every single tenant—right down to a tiny, 500-square-foot store—to install ADA-accessible men's and women's bathrooms. Meanwhile, large malls could have single "regional" ADA bathrooms, so that tenants like Forever 21 or the Gap were not required to put in their own facilities.

"I was told that we would never be able to change these codes because we had a really strong ADA community here that will fight you," says pioneer Lanning. Her response was to bring to the forum an attorney who represented the ADA. "He came in a wheelchair," she says. "He couldn't believe that the code was forcing these buildings to be destroyed." The attorney told the audience that a single ADA bathroom in one anchor store in a strip mall would be just fine. "'We don't want to cause any more buildings to be torn down,' he told them. 'We just want to know where the bathrooms are.'"

The same went for code that applied to the turning radius for fire trucks. Small city streets were being widened and their small buildings demolished to make room for large fire trucks. Lanning had a fire marshal address the forum. "I brought in this guy from the fire department. He said, 'We would much rather have infill. I'm tired of them straining our resources—we don't have the money to keep up with the sprawl. Plus if these buildings are occupied, they are way safer than if they are abandoned.'"

The result of the forum, in conjunction with the community's outrage at the attempted leveling of its art district (the popular First Friday walk was then in its sixth year), was a task force established by Mayor Gordon to examine just how Phoenix could restore vitality to its downtown. And what they came up with was a program that took the idea of Lean Urbanism and turned it on its head. Instead of young urban pioneers simply operating in a gray zone beneath the regulatory radar, the city would push a top-down effort to make it easier for small businesses to resuscitate older buildings and start new enterprises in dilapidated areas. The trick: bend back zoning codes that were strangling the core of Phoenix.

THE LEANING TOWER OF PHOENIX

It took several years before the conclusions of the task force were put into place, but the political will, on the highest levels, was now manifest. Even City Manager Frank Fairbanks, who had been in power for fifteen years and had overseen some of the worst periods of Phoenix's self-immolation, got behind the program. While Mayor Gordon gets much of the credit for championing the concept of adaptive reuse, it was actually Fairbanks who called the task force into being. He personally attended its initial meetings and charged every city department to work collaboratively with stakeholders in the community to come up with solutions. (That year, coincidently, he was awarded the National Public Service Award, the highest award given for distinction in public service by the American Society for Public Administration and the National Academy of Public Administration.)

One of the first things to come out of the task force was the Office of Customer Advocacy, formed in 2007. While eventually growing into a full-service office with a mission to walk small developers through the entire permitting process, its original task was simply to help small businesses solve conflicts it faced within city hall itself.

"You went to the city development services counter and there might have been six different departments that had a regulatory jurisdiction over your project," explains Esser, who also became a small-scale developer. "They didn't all agree with one another. So you ended up in many cases having to go to a variance hearing to get a waiver from one of them, especially when one of the city department's requirements conflicted with another city department's requirements." A large firm with an army of employees and resources can plow its way through such a maze, but small-scale enterprises often give up. So the Office of Customer Advocacy became a problem-solving tool, assigning case officers to oversee small projects.

Another major result of the task force was an Arts, Culture and Small Business Overlay, the first zoning overlay in the city's history. It relaxed a variety of counterproductive regulations, the most important of which was eliminating the prohibition against on-street parking. This restriction, designed to accelerate car traffic from the business district to the suburbs, was killing off customer traffic for small businesses. The zoning overlay also relaxed parking requirements for repurposed buildings so that a new small business could open without having to purchase and raze adjacent property for parking lots.

A sign of this new era was a live/work project directly across Roosevelt Street from the art galleries that Esser, Lanning, and others had started. Called the Artisan Village, it was a row of live/work lofts built on what had been a dirt lot. In that watershed year of 2005, it was the first live/work project ever permitted in the city. For an approachable price point of $185,000, artists and craftspeople could buy a street-front building, live upstairs, and start a retail business below. As owner-occupied businesses, the Village brought in a population with long-term vested interests in the community. Today its shops range from cafés and galleries to retail boutiques.

To aid and abet the pioneering small developers—for they were still just that, pioneers in an urban wilderness—Mayor Gordon and the city council also launched several foundational changes to foster the return of people to the downtown. Whereas the Phoenix Partnership—the consortium of major employers that spearheaded the sports arenas—had emphasized blanket high-rise rezoning to increase urban density, the Gordon administration instead pushed for education infrastructure and public transportation.

The first project was to accelerate the development of the biomedical campus, a far better use of the demolished Evans-Churchill neighborhood than a football stadium. As of 2015, the thirty-acre campus was well on its way to being built out, with a cluster of academic and research facilities that included ASU's School of Nutrition, the Phoenix Union Bioscience High School, the International

Genomics Consortium, Northern Arizona University, the National Institute of Diabetes, the Barrow Neurological Institute, and the University of Arizona's College of Medicine and College of Pharmacy. At the same time, ASU—whose main campus remains in nearby Tempe—moved its schools for media, health care, government, and most recently law to a new Downtown Phoenix campus, repurposing old office buildings and creating new facilities for 11,500 students.

A big catalyst for the downtown ASU campus was another feather in the cap of the Gordon administration—the creation of a twenty-mile-long light rail project that ran from Mesa on the east to the outskirts of Glendale on the west, passing through the core downtown.

"The twenty miles of the light rail was built all in 2008, the largest single light rail project ever built all at once in the country," says Curt Upton, director of Reinvent Phoenix, a planning organization that was created in 2011 to accelerate the development of walkable neighborhoods around the light rail stations.

"The [installation of the rail] was moving so fast we hadn't done much land use planning," says Upton, another of the young pioneers brought in under the city's new administration. "Most cities have DOT [Department of Transportation] plans years, maybe decades, ahead of the light rail. We knew we had some catching up to do . . . Our goal from the beginning was to create the most walkable environment in Phoenix, which is a drivable, not a walkable, city." Upton's conclusion? "It's hard to create a movement from a government-led initiative."

Indeed, the idea that you could create a lean urban scenario by pushing for it top-down was to prove more difficult than expected. As it turned out, the bureaucracy of Phoenix—let alone the vested interests of its old-boy business community—had spent too many years entrenched in ossified ways of thinking. It was going to take some serious effort to disrupt the ways things were done.

WHERE THE TIRE MEETS THE ROAD

In its struggle to reinvent itself as a city fostering small-scale projects and individualistic, walkable neighborhoods, Phoenix—similar to cities such as New Orleans and Starkville—began returning to older vernacular forms, solutions that had been forgotten in the rush to modernity. "We used to have a streetcar system here in Phoenix," says Upton, "and a funny story about that came out in the media when we started building the light rail and ripping up the street. The old streetcar tracks were right where we were building."

Nothing reflected this return to the solutions of yesteryear better than an exemplary initiative that came out of the Office of Customer Advocacy: the Adaptive Reuse Program.

Cindy Stotler was the city's assistant director of Planning & Development at the time the Office of Customer Advocacy came into being, and she became its first director. While Stotler had worked in city hall for years in its budget and finance departments, she had only recently joined the planning department, so she brought a fresh perspective to the office.

Her first priority was to create a new, compact "infill" district surrounding the light rail corridor. "We wanted to see intense urban development," she says, and that meant getting the public transit, solid waste, and fire departments to buy into the idea of a tighter grid for finer-grain development with, for example, smaller turnarounds for fire and waste trucks. It also meant encouraging smaller-scale building, including mid-rises of four or five stories, which flew in the face of the high-rise vision the Phoenix Partnership had in mind.

Coming to Stotler's aid was the silver lining of the Great Recession. Just as the light rail system was being built, there was simply no market for the kind of soaring towers dreamed of by the old guard. "The good news is that there was demand around the light rail. People wanted to build things besides high-rises on the lots where they thought high-rises were going to go," says Stotler. "But we still had a lot of true believers who wanted high-rises there, big-time, and they just fought it. What they did not understand was that the economy would only support so much of that [high-rise] infill, especially in Phoenix. Phoenix does not have to be a New York. Paris is a beautiful, walkable, mid-rise city with a lot of density and activity. Why couldn't we have that?"

Still, says Stotler, the economic downturn dampened the financial resources even for mid-rise residences, and despite its best efforts to encourage mid-rise development around the light rail, the city saw few projects come in during the early years of the Great Recession. Phoenix needed to drill down even further, and that required lowering the barriers to extremely small-scale projects designed to re-purpose the remaining buildings of the old city. So, with civic pioneers like Esser and Lanning and their band of merry artists pushing to re-purpose historic bungalows, the focus for lowering thresholds became the Adaptive Reuse Program. Its goal: to overcome coding absurdities that made small projects too expensive for small businesses.

"The rules and regulations that we had for infill were not designed for small adaptive reuse, and we had to lighten them," says Stotler. "The smaller the size of the adaptive reuse project, the more regulatory relief we had to offer—like lifting requirements for sprinklers, or for extra bathrooms."

At the Office of Customer Advocacy, the staff at the customer counter was trained so that if a project looked like a case for adaptive reuse it was assigned a special assistant. "Development is for the big guys, and people who know what they are doing and can hire attorneys and design professionals. They've been through this," says Stotler. "But the little guys, the restaurateur, the coffee shop, little guys like that, they don't know what they are doing. They know how to sell coffee, but they don't know how to build anything, they don't know how much permits cost, all that kind of stuff."

For the smallest entry-level scale, the Adaptive Reuse Program provided two things. First was relief from city fees for plan reviews and permits, waivers of up to $7,000 per building. The second—which proved far more important—was providing a project advocate to guide applicants through the code and find its seams. At first, it was a matter of just letting entrepreneurs know what they did and didn't have to bring up to code. But as time passed, the project advocates become code whisperers, able to help urban pioneers bypass or work around regulations.

"The more experience we had with this, the more things we were finding that we could help them with," says Stotler. "We were all becoming experts in the existing building codes, and putting that to use with these old buildings, and getting them out of a lot of regulatory issues." A perfect example was an art project in an empty lot on Roosevelt, down the street from the artisan community. The lot was frequently a staging area for the First Friday art walks, and several artists wanted to use the space to open mini-galleries in empty shipping containers.

"We turned these storage containers into galleries, with insulation and hardwood floors," says Eye Lounge's Esser, who besides running his gallery and a residency program for the ASU art museum founded an Arts District community development corporation to plant trees, remove graffiti, install lighting, and brand area events. The container galleries, by code, were illegal. But with advice from the Adaptive Reuse staff, they simply changed what they were called and got them permitted. "Technically, under the building code, these are storage facilities. They are storing art inside. It just so happens that people can go into the storage area to see the art," he says. "This is another case where the city came and helped us navigate the codes."

Today, the wall outside of Stotler's office in city hall is covered with a gallery of more than a dozen successful adaptive reuse projects her staff helped shepherd through city code. They range from an old mission church that is now the popular Taco Guild eatery, to a former swap mart that is now offices for Grand Canyon University. Stotler's favorite is a place called The Yard, an erstwhile Ducati motorcycle dealership that had been vacant for years. It is now home to the Culinary Dropout restaurant, with a coffee shop in what had been the mechanic's bay. A large outdoor area covered by an awning is now "the play area," with Ping-Pong tables and a bocce ball court. "It's one of the prettiest adaptive reuses we have," says Stotler. "This has become a place to go, and everyone is going there." It also generates more than ten million dollars a year in sales, which means close to one million dollars per year in sales and property taxes for the city and state.

The dollars that adaptive reuse generate are, in the end, the most powerful advocates for small-scale urbanism. Today, whenever activist Lanning organizes her constituency of small businesses and historic readapters, she always admonishes them to have at the ready the facts and figures of their economic impact. Dollars talk.

"I bring studies [to city council meetings] all the time. I try to make them understand it in their own language. I show them what the next generation wants in order to live and work here," says Lanning. "It's not about this neighborhood or that building, it's a blanket look at the city. I tell them that if we are going to be competitive for higher-wage jobs, this is what you have to do."

When Richard Florida came to address the leadership of Phoenix at Lanning's seminal conference about the importance of small, unique developments, one of the examples he used sprang from the streets of the city itself. And it perfectly illustrated the wealth created by the new pioneers of Phoenix.

"What's led the wildfire of support for adaptive reuse has been some very successful demonstration projects," says Reinvent Phoenix director Upton. "When Richard Florida came to Phoenix, one of the places he highlighted was Fortieth and Campbell. He said, 'Look, you're doing it here. Just do more of it.'"

The intersection of 40th and Campbell, in the Arcadia neighborhood of northeast Phoenix, was a commercial cluster originally built in the 1950s. It had become a scuzzy embarrassment for an

otherwise well-kept working-class neighborhood. There was a convenience store that sold lotto tickets, liquor, and pornography, where
kids hung out to play video games. There was a Domino's Pizza and
an old Laundromat, the latter used as a sales headquarters for local
crystal meth dealers. It also had a midcentury US post office that had
since become a mail-order warehouse for musical gear.

In 2001, an entrepreneur named Craig DeMarco leased and renovated the historic post office, turning it into an upscale wine café
called Postino, which created a domino effect in the neighborhood.

What alerted DeMarco to the possibility of creating a new café,
he says, was a coffee stand called the Java Garden that popped up on
a storm-water retention area at the intersection. Operating without
any permits, the cart's owner had placed a few chairs on the corner.
"That was the first spark, a lady who was making espresso drinks," he
says. "This was long before the coffee culture came to Phoenix, but it
was how we found the project, walking our dogs one day, and seeing
this java cart just stuck there in the retention area."

DeMarco figured he could do something similar, so he begged,
borrowed, and hocked his house for the $150,000 he needed to set
up shop. "I was so naïve at the time, and I had no idea [what was
required]. The city called one day and said, 'We heard you were starting a restaurant. Did you know you need a use permit?'" DeMarco
did not know that, nor that he needed public postings, a neighborhood hearing, and ultimately approval by the city council. Of the
$150,000 he had raised for the project, he found himself burning
through the money to hire zoning attorneys—so much so that he
had to raise another $70,000 (advances from a slew of credit cards)
just to cover the legal bills.

Fortunately, DeMarco's district councilperson was Greg Stanton,
the future mayor who was then an early advocate for urban pioneers
trying to gain a foothold. "So, it went our way at the council and
we got it open," says DeMarco. Within a year he and his partners
bought the corner convenience store and repurposed it as La Grande

Orange, a kind of Dean & DeLuca gourmet deli, pizza, and wine store that sold everything from homemade English muffins to sea-salt chocolate cookies.

"Postino created a more authentic sense of place than a brand-new, suburban-oriented building, which is the only thing that Phoenix had produced until then, and because of that one investment the whole area transformed," says Reinvent Phoenix's Upton, who grew up in the neighborhood. "I've never seen a more rapid upgrade of an area like that in Phoenix. It wasn't a real low-income area. It was a pretty solid middle-class kind of neighborhood where people drove Fords and Chevys. But now people drive Mercedes and BMWs." Today valet parkers stand poised at the entrance of Postino, and additional businesses have joined the cluster—including a high-end dermatology clinic that looks straight out of Beverly Hills. The original New Pioneer of the Java Garden ended up relocating to a brick building down the street.

DeMarco realized he had hit upon a formula for success: Phoenicians wanted small, interesting, local places to hang out. He went from Postino to create another dozen adaptive reuse projects. The Windsor, for example, had been a 1950s strip mall in the north-central area of the city. Reconfigured as one long space, it became a hip bar and restaurant, with a patio courtyard out back, lots of room for bicycles to park, and a homemade ice cream shop at one end to serve as an after-dinner dessert destination. Across the street, creating a cluster destination, DeMarco turned an old bank building into Federal Pizza (including using the old teller drive-through for take-out) and converted an adjacent, shuttered post office into another Postino wine café.

By the time DeMarco was creating Windsor, the city's adaptive reuse program was underway. But the concept had yet to penetrate the middle ranks of the city's bureaucracy. Not surprisingly, it still required push-down from the top to lighten up the regulations that made such projects too expensive for entry-level entrepreneurs.

TEETHING PAINS

Lorenzo Perez is one of the principals in Venue Projects, the development firm that built out Windsor for DeMarco. Because it was a change of use, the building was immediately hit with an avalanche of conditions to bring it up to code. One of those, recalls Perez, was the requirement that any canopy extending from any commercial building more than four feet had to have a sprinkler system installed.

"If you change a use, it triggers the need to sprinkle the building, and the fire marshals here carry a lot of weight," says Lorenzo. "The ordinance said anything four foot wide. We had a canopy that was four foot, four inches. But it was made of masonry and steel, and there was no issue of danger [to customers]. It was a front-walk overhang that had been there since 1940 and had never burned. We asked if they could let it go, but they said no, you have to sprinkle that. The fire marshal was holding us hostage on the final inspection. It would have cost us serious dollars. So I had to think, who do I know that is connected?"

All told, it took the combined intervention of the office of land use, the adaptive reuse program, and the mayor's office itself to back down the fire marshal. "In the end we went down with a $250 check for an appeal, and it got resolved," recalls Perez. "But it was a go-around, and that's what you have to do."

In a pattern that has repeated itself in numerous situations, pioneering developers like Perez and small business activists like Lanning find themselves thwarted by mid-level bureaucrats—"burons" in the language of lean—still fixated by the hard rules of city code even when they defy common sense and raise thresholds to prohibitive levels. One tool that small Phoenix developers and business owners have come to rely on from the Lean Urbanism war chest is terminology. Similar to Cottage Square and The Gulf, in the absurd world of hypercoding vs. common sense, it often comes down to the language used.

One example that Lanning cites comes from when she tried to get approval for inexpensive live/work artist spaces that used stacked shipping containers. "We were sitting with a gentleman [from the planning department] who thought I would be impressed when he recited code by section and number," she says. "He said, literally, 'You can't do two-story live/work spaces there.' I asked him what you could do. And he said, 'You can do duplexes.' And I asked, 'Can you do two-story duplexes?' He said yes. So I said, 'Forget the live/work project. We'll do duplexes.' Right in front of him. And he said, 'Okay, great.' All we did was change the language. It's just unbelievable."

In the ongoing sparring match between the pioneers of creative, small-scale development in Phoenix and the implacable, illogical code enforcers, it also became apparent that go-arounds and under-the-radar approaches would work only for the truly small. Anything that approached a mid-sized project—or anything that was highly visible—would require top-down help not only from the Office of Customer Advocacy but from the office of the mayor and those city commissioners who "got it."

Nothing illustrates that better than The Newton, an adaptive reuse by Perez's Venue Projects of a historic steakhouse near one of the light rail stations.

At one point this former Beef Eaters restaurant had been the place for politicians, professionals, and the business elite to meet. It was a classic two-martini lunch spot, as well as a social center where weddings were held and family events celebrated. It had flourished in the '60s, '70s, and even '80s, but with the relentless abandonment of the downtown, the 18,000-square-foot facility could not sustain itself. It finally closed in 2006, and its owner Jay Newton died in poverty.

The building became derelict, eventually used as a cavernous hide-out by a trifecta of drug dealers, prostitutes, and homeless vagrants, who on cold days burned furniture in the still-working fireplace. A developer who bought the building right before the crash of '07

wanted to tear it down, but the community—which still affectionately remembered the building as a social center—wanted it saved.
So did the new administration at city hall. Familiar with the work
that Perez had done at Windsor, the city approached him and Venue
Projects.

Working through a growing network of like-minded "place-
makers," Perez learned that gallery-activist Greg Esser's wife Cindy
Dach was looking to establish a new branch of her highly successful suburban bookstore, Changing Hands. "We are this forty-year-
old bookstore in Tempe. We'd gotten a lot of requests to come to
downtown Phoenix, but we could never find the right fit," says Dach.
"Bookstores are a very difficult model. We kept meeting with developers who didn't understand that we needed a different type of lease,
that we were a different kind of tenant. Lorenzo [Perez] and his partner Jon [Kitchell] got that."

The problem was size. The old Beef Eaters was 18,000 square
feet, way beyond Dach's needs. So Perez followed a page straight
from the Lean Urbanism playbook—that urban revival emerges in
archipelago clusters of small businesses, and that it develops through
patient, successional development over time by owners vested in the
place itself, rather than developers who wish to buy, build, and flip.

"There are developers who come in and buy a dirt lot and plop
down a building to sell," notes Dach. "But developers who live here
understand that you need to develop a node, or even a district . . ."
So Perez brought in chef Justin Beckett, who had an award-winning
but tiny restaurant downtown called Beckett's Table. The final piece
of the puzzle came through an annual event called the Pie Social,
where Dach and Perez met the owners of Southwest Gardener, a
shop whose lease was up.

Open only since May 2014, The Newton is now a model of synergy, with 6,000 square feet taken by the bookstore, 5,000 square feet
taken by Beckett's new restaurant Southern Rail, and 2,500 square
feet taken by the garden shop. Another 500 square feet was taken by a

small consulting firm, while the remaining space—a large room where the old Beef Eaters fireplace still stands (and works)—is a common area (called the commons) with chairs and tables. In order to create a place to hang out, the bookstore also opened a coffee and wine bar that acts as a buffer between the bookstore and the commons—and also provides high-margin sales to sustain the bookshop.

The cluster of businesses has had a synergistic effect—business at the garden store, for example, has quadrupled from their previous location. Another unique factor is that the building is owned not just by Venue Projects, but also by the restaurant and the bookstore—a threshold opportunity for both.

Could the building have been developed without active intervention by key city officials? Perez doubts it. As an adaptive reuse building, its permit fees were waived. It also received an adaptive reuse grant to pay for architectural fees and a loan from a pool of money being used to encourage development along the light rail.

"We used to go to the City of Phoenix, and all they would tell us is why we couldn't do something," says Venue Projects partner Jon Kitchell. "But we had a compelling project, a building that no one in the city of Phoenix wanted erased, with fond memories for politicians as far back as you could go. We said, 'Let's figure out how we can do this in and around all the codes.'" And the city went for it.

Time and again, it was upper-echelon city officials who bent the codes to make the project work, pushing it down through a stubborn bureaucracy. Take parking. Because it was a change of use, the new project triggered current codes for parking, which were written for suburban standards. Never mind that the original use, as an 18,000-square-foot restaurant, had managed just fine with the existing parking. New suburban codes called for far more, enough to kill the project.

"We had been assigned a group of people by the city that were part of the decision makers for the project," recalls Kitchell. "We called a meeting, and we told them we couldn't get the parking to work, that the parking [officials] wouldn't give us credit for the light rail parking across the street and so forth . . . They said, 'Can you leave the room and let us talk among ourselves?' Fifteen minutes later they called us back in and outlined a plan that would get us through their existing code . . . That was real progress."

"The beauty of this project," says Perez, "was that it was high profile, and a priority project. When things looked like they were slowing down I had calls from the mayor's office, the councilmen's office, asking, 'What can we do, how is it going?' Sure, it was still a struggle, but we had political channels. We had to have high-level relationships, because we got a lot of low-level pushback. They were just doing their jobs, so you had to get it pulled up from the top rather than pushed through from the bottom." Even the sign in front of the project, "The Newton," violated an arbitrary signage code that had to be overridden by higher-ups.

In another hallmark of the lean scene, the building itself and its contents were recycled—beginning with peeling off layers of additions, revealing the old roofline and interior ceiling. The original booths from Beef Eaters were reupholstered, for example, while an old kitchen sink from the boiler room became the potting sink for Southwest Gardener. A snarling cluster of palm trees on one corner of the lot were pulled apart and replanted throughout the property.

"We literally deconstructed and harvested the building," says Perez. "My partner, Jon [Kitchell], can spot black walnut, or redwood. The entry was all walnut floors. He took it up and split it so it went farther. The flooring was turned into the walls."

THE CIRCLE OF STRIFE

When it comes to the evolution of the city's appreciation for lean principles, no one mirrors Phoenix better than another of its New Pioneers, Beatrice Moore. Today the largest owner of small, historic buildings on cutting-edge Grand Avenue, Moore has been an artist in Phoenix since the late 1980s.

Originally a resident and studio artist in the warehouse district, Moore was among the few voices that opposed the wholesale leveling of that area in order to put in basketball and baseball stadiums. As one of the first people to renovate and reuse historic structures in the downtown, she experienced firsthand the enormous weight of heavy coding that made such projects Herculean tasks.

As a consequence, she was among the first locals to understand that New Pioneers can usually flourish only under the radar. At the other end of that experience, she was also one of the first small-scale developers to experience relief with the help of the Office of Customer Advocacy.

When Moore first arrived in Phoenix, she moved into an industrial space in the warehouse district. All was well until the Downtown Phoenix Partnership created a business improvement district in the core downtown and decided that gigantic, tax-revenue generating sports stadiums would revive the area. Coincidentally, they would also allow influential property owners to cash out via land purchases for the arenas.

The year before the DPP came into existence, Moore and her fellow artists in the warehouse district had organized the first "art detour," which became the first of the gallery walks revived a decade later as First Friday on Roosevelt.

"We heard rumors that the city was going to put in a [basketball] arena around where we were in the warehouse district," recalls Moore. "We sort of hijacked the mayor and took him for a little trolley ride that first year [of the arts walk]. We tried to convince him to put the stadium east of Seventh Street. That way you could have connectivity to the warehouse district and save all these great buildings. But ultimately they wanted it in the Phoenix Partnership area, right in their [business improvement] district."

Moore and her partner were among the few artists living in their space and, along with other area residents, were forced to relocate. They needed to move again when the almost-adjacent Cardinal baseball stadium was approved a few years later.

"They had already torn down a bunch of the warehouses for the basketball arena. So we fought the baseball stadium, but it was a losing proposition. Among other things, the arts community was split," says Moore. "Many thought it would be a benefit to bring the [baseball] stadium downtown. We told them that it would only raise property values because of speculation, that they were going to get pushed out and wouldn't be able to afford to be downtown. But they thought, 'Oh, we're going to have all these people shopping down here in our studios.'"

Moore realized two things at that point. The first was that you had to be a property owner—and not a renter—to have any clout. The second was that you had to land in an area outside of the path of development. So she ended up buying the old 15,000-square-foot Bragg's Pie Factory building on Grand Avenue, then a dilapidated boulevard with petty street crime and scattered social service centers for the homeless and poor.

"We really liked this neighborhood; we liked the small scale. At the time it felt a long way from downtown," says Moore. "It was a very neglected area. There were no artists. We didn't come here to be part of an artists' community; we just wanted to do our work and be left alone. We just wanted to be creative and not worry about someone tearing down the building that we were in."

What Moore did not understand was that low-cost lean urban pioneering requires more than just moving into an area that has been marginalized. It also requires knowing how to work around city code and how to avoid acting in a transparent way that assumes common sense on the part of code enforcers. What looked like a project that would take a year to eighteen months—repurposing the old Bragg's Pie Factory—ended up taking four years in a process that nearly bankrupted Moore.

"We got snagged by the city on this project because they had a regulation that said if a building was empty for more than a year it automatically triggered a change of use," she says. "If we had known this, we would have occupied it ourselves. It would have been one of those white lies if we knew how it was going to impact us. But we didn't know that, when someone says 'change of use' to you, it's a really ugly thing if you are trying to fix something up."

The reasoning behind a change-of-use upgrade is that a building languishing unused for years and years may have some serious safety issues. But if a building is empty for just a year, that is not necessarily the case. If Moore's building had remained occupied, it would have required no upgrades, since there were no safety or health issues. But once the reuse triggered the city's attention, Moore was required to rip out the concrete flooring in the front of the building to make it handicap accessible, and to replace all the plumbing and wiring, regardless of condition or functionality.

"When we got the escrow on this building there was a tenant here, but they moved out," says Moore. She thought that was a good thing, since it would make remodeling easier as they stripped away the ceiling and other layers to reveal the original structure. But she ended up without a tenant for the entire four years it took to bring the building up to code, which made the project an almost unbearable financial struggle.

By the time the pie factory was up to code in 2008, the Office of Customer Advocacy had come into existence. And that made a critical difference for her next project, a series of inexpensive gallery and studio spaces for artists in a high-profile building on the corner of Grand and Roosevelt. By that time, she had already learned to avoid the city's prying eyes, as had many of her neighbors. (She lives in a building in the area that she dubbed "a storage facility"; a couple of artists in another nearby warehouse raised a family there by calling it "a commercial studio.") When Moore acquired a lot across the street to provide parking for her Bragg's Pie Factory building—now home to eight tenants, including a café—she did not mention it to the city, using instead the new Arts, Culture and Small Business Overlay to get a parking variance; otherwise she would have had to install lighting, drainage, and traffic islands in the parking lot.

But in the case of her high-profile Bikini Lounge at Grand and Roosevelt, she took the official route. "We submitted a site plan, which cost us $5,000 to file, just to have them mark it up with $300,000 to $400,000 worth of things they said we needed to do to bring it up to current code." Moore declared she was simply going to shutter the space when the Office of Customer Advocacy got involved. They led Moore through a process of acquiring certificates of occupancy for the building's various spaces, which obviated the need for a blanket upgrade to code.

"Having to bring it up to current code would have been way too expensive. Back when that property was built in the 1920s, they didn't do things like drainage in the parking lot or in the yards," says Moore. "With the Office of Customer Advocacy, we ended up paying only for things that actually were health or safety-type issues. We ended up spending maybe $10,000 to upgrade the electric box and add a couple of things like exit signs. So this was night and day [difference]."

One thing the Office of Customer Advocacy advised Moore about was language. Specifically: avoid the use of the term "art gallery," which would have required producing sufficient permanent parking for the maximum number of people who might show up once a month for a gallery opening. "They had nothing in their code to address the unique situation of a gallery," says Moore. So galleries were treated with the same occupancy-based regulations as restaurants, even though that made no sense. "These bureaucrats don't want to have to make a commonsense decision if it's not in the code."

Now, says Moore, she understands the New Pioneer game. "You have to be educated enough to know what to say and what not to say. We have learned to say as little as possible and not to answer anything you don't have to. Some people want to be honest, but when you get involved with the city you realize it's a matter of survival—unless you have a ton of money."

A TIME FOR RESURRECTION

On the first Friday of each month, somewhere between 15,000 and 30,000 visitors descend on the Roosevelt arts district of Phoenix. The streets become a circus of people, ranging from suburban families to urban hipsters. Bands play in abandoned lots. Galleries and shops remain open late; in some they sell sculptures and paintings, in others vintage clothing or handmade pipes. In yet others, there are video installations or models undergoing body painting. Trailers become art galleries. Food trucks line the streets. Parking lots become pop-up flea markets. Artists sell paintings on the street.

The scene today is much more than a gallery walk. It is a lollapalooza of Phoenicians in search of the cool, and there is nothing cooler than the bohemian arts district with its crazy little shops and galleries. If nothing else, the First Friday walk is a palpable display of a far-flung suburban city looking for an authentic core of artisanal, local culture. Despite all the self-proclaimed virtues of the American suburban dream, it remains without a soul, and First Fridays are nothing if not a city in search of itself.

Unlike Detroit, which was a victim of economic downturn, Phoenix bore the brunt of deliberate self-destruction. Detroit suffered wholesale abandonment by its major employers—car manufacturers who relocated their plants to states where unions were unknown, taxes lax, and land cheap. In Phoenix, the city's streetscape was consciously dismembered by political leaders who envisioned an antiseptic future featuring wide avenues, setback high-rises, and vast parking garages.

Then came the Great Recession, which created huge opportunities for small-scale entrepreneurs and new urban pioneers who could not have gotten into the game otherwise. When Venue Projects and their bookstore and restaurant partners acquired The Newton, it was a *"Blair Witch* project, a total wreck with all the copper ripped out, dead cats, buckets of urine, and homeless people who were burning the old chairs in the fireplace," says Venue's Perez. But because of the economic downturn, restoration was possible. With the building selling for about half of its price at the market peak, the entry barrier was lowered. "When the economy took a dip, it really gave an opportunity for guys like me to get into spaces like this," says chef Beckett of Newton's Southern Rail restaurant.

Because of projects such as The Newton, Phoenix is now in the process of reworking its suburban codes to reflect urban realities in a city adapting to mass transit and even bike lanes (fully half the employees at The Newton, for example, arrive at work by either light rail or bicycle). The Office of Customer Advocacy, under assistant planning director Stotler, is developing a Walkable Urban Code for the transit corridor along the light rail line. Among other things, the new code will require the return of something that's been absent for a half century—shade, with trees along the entire right-of-way frontage to be paid for by property owners.

Even with its top-down push, ingrained backlash makes the task of creating a leaner Phoenix a Sisyphean stuggle. "Everything we do in walkability is a battle, requiring negotiations with other departments," says Stotler. "Even trees are a battle. Public Works comes by and says they have to be eighteen feet high so their trucks can go under without hitting them." The utility departments present other issues, starting with current codes that prohibit the planting of a tree within ten feet of a water, sewage, or power line—a big problem since these lines were pushed to the sides as the light rail was installed. This is being changed to six feet, with the city council pushing to have it even closer, using special root barriers.

More than anything, the progressive Lean Urbanism movement in Phoenix requires a reeducation of both the public and the bureaucracy. Phoenix has been so inculcated with a suburban mentality that even some of its citizens—in particular the elderly—oppose the adaptive reuse of abandoned buildings because it means more cars parking on their formerly suburban-like streets. "We get a lot of pushback in the neighborhoods from people who don't want change," says Postino's DeMarco, "so we document the increase in land values."

Perceptions need to be changed on the outside as well. Stotler describes how national home-building giant Lennar sent its suburban planning team, not its urban planning team, to work on a project directly across the street from a light rail station. "Lennar has a standard apartment model that looks like a fortress," says Stotler. "We won't let them do that here. I'm trying to give them drawings that show what the sidewalks and shade are going to have to look like. So, design from there. Open your buildings to the street."

But for every building that Stotler redirects, or that the mayor champions—like the Union-on-Roosevelt project so widely extolled by the local press—other inappropriate buildings slip in. One that was approved along Roosevelt a half-dozen blocks from the Union project is a mid-rise monolith with no street interaction—which required the demolition of a locally iconic gallery known as the Green Building.

"We still do not have enough people at the city with vision or oversight or an understanding of the culture," says pioneer-activist Lanning. "Somebody from the city looking at their proposal should have said, 'This is our most walkable street and we don't see how these drawings address the street at all.' Instead they rubber-stamped it." The reaction from the neighborhood included protest marches, even one where demonstrators carried a coffin for the old Green Building, but to no avail. "So we are going to end up with this monolithic piece of crap in the middle of our neighborhood because the guy at the counter didn't approach it differently. We need training . . ."

Lanning's concern is that once the new residence goes up—built by a company whose executives never attended a First Friday—its occupants will begin to complain about the art walk, and that it will begin a slow demise of the arts district.

Meanwhile, lean, urban pioneering—the kind that relies on operating under the radar—is still alive in Phoenix. In the Churchill/arts district neighborhood where so many of the small shops operated for years in violation of code, there are still New Pioneers on the fringes. A mere two blocks from where visiting artists can stay in low-cost apartments attached to an ASU museum annex, a new drinking establishment called the Milk Bar (a reference to *A Clockwork Orange*) opened. Basically an old bungalow painted entirely white, the back wall has been removed to reveal an open, glowing bar, with a wide expanse of steps descending to an open patio. The patio is flanked by two large white statues of cows. It opened without any permits or licensing, and was last seen to be busy with customers.

"If we did not severely bend and break a bunch of rules, these redevelopments would never have happened," says DeMarco. "If you are not pushing it and showing a little civil disobedience, nothing will change."

Down Grand Avenue from Moore's converted pie factory is a small restaurant called ThirdSpace. "We call it that because your first space is home and your second space is work," says proprietor Neil Hounchell. "We wanted this to be your third space." Behind the restaurant/bar (formerly a car repair shop) is a small square formed by five tiny wooden buildings. All were salvaged from Camp Papago, a former Phoenix POW camp for German soldiers during World War II. Each of the barracks is now a business—a coffee shop, a tattoo parlor, an eyeglass shop—with entry-level monthly rents of $400.

Further down Grand is a newly renovated row of three brick buildings, one of the stars of the Adaptive Reuse Program. Originally the 1928 headquarters of the O. S. Stapley equipment manufacturing company, the buildings had not only fallen into disrepair but also had been covered over with layers of paint, plaster, and aluminum siding. Local developer Mark Abromovitz restored them to their original brick façades.

Abromovitz worked with the Center for Customer Advocacy, which granted him waivers for permits—he estimates a $5,000 savings—and with the city's historic preservation board, which gave him a far more significant grant of $300,000. He was also able to avoid the pitfall of change of use thanks to ongoing occupancy—and an adjustment of the code to a trigger of three years without an occupant instead of one. He considers recycling buildings such as his to be essential to restoring the sense of place for Phoenix. It's also good business.

"What is significant about these buildings is that you can't build them like this any more; it's too cost prohibitive," says Abromovitz, pointing out his building's century-old wooden trusses made from Douglas fir trees and its three-brick-wide walls with thermal pockets. These insulate so effectively that utility bills for one of his five 6,000-square-foot spaces run less than $400 a month. And because he can buy old buildings far cheaper than new buildings, he can rent them for lower rates.

Abromovitz does not intend to restore the buildings to sell them, however. In a mark of the successional principles of Lean Urbanism, pioneer developers like Abromovitz and DeMarco are committed to developing their neighborhoods over time. "I approach these [buildings] for what can I do with them now, not what they'll be worth in fifteen years," says Abromovitz. "I don't speculate, I build."

"The people who are doing this sort of stuff today have a higher purpose and become part of the community," says DeMarco. "Blow and go, that was the Phoenix mentality—to scrap it, build it, sell it, and leave. We are fifteen years into this [our projects] and we are looking at another twenty-five to thirty years. Our peer group really believes in this."

The biggest long-run concern is that neighborhoods like the Roosevelt/Churchill and Grand Avenue arts districts will become victims of their own success. The bulldozing of the iconic Green Building for a mid-rise apartment building on Roosevelt Street, for example, or even Abromovitz's O. S. Stapley building—which he intends to rent to professional firms looking for cheaper, trendier places than a downtown office tower—are threatening to liquidate the lean aspects of their neighborhoods.

"A lot of the artists are very naïve," says the pie factory's Moore. "They think, 'We're going to be cool now with a coffee shop and restaurant.' They don't see the correlation between restaurants that can pay a lot of rent and artists who can't. They don't quite get it that most art districts become entertainment districts and they lose the artists because they can't afford to be there anymore."

She continues, "This is why we are reluctant to sell our buildings, because we don't trust that people will do the right thing with them. I'm hoping the people who want to build expensive apartment lofts will not build here, because right now this is a great neighborhood for affordable housing . . . One of the conclusions that I have come to is that to keep a neighborhood balanced you have to have true diversity, and that means economic diversity.

"We have some things in our neighborhood that I embrace psychologically because they protect us," she adds. These include a center for teenage addicts, a shelter for abused women, and an old motel used to house people with mental disabilities. "We've even told developers who are planning on putting in some expensive lofts, 'Well, do you know you are this close to a homeless shelter?' We kind of joke that the prostitutes and drug dealers are our protective coloring because a lot of developers are scared away by that."

chapter eight

CONCLUSIONS: THE LESSONS OF LEAN URBANISM

Strategies for the New Pioneer

One morning, many months after my travels in search of Lean Urbanism, my wife showed me a newspaper article about a woman who had been living in a tree house for several years in North Miami. Thanks to a tip-off from an anonymous source, code-enforcement officers had descended on the property. They declared that the tree house had been built illegally, and that its water and electricity were likewise illegal, having been hooked up without permits. They determined that the tree house could not be brought up to code and therefore must be torn down.

The occupant, a sixty-five-year-old grandmother, was enormously happy with her version of the Swiss Family Robinson lifestyle: a wooden cottage that climbed around the forked trunks of an old oak tree and strangler fig in the front yard of her son's half-acre home. Characterized by the paper as "a claustrophobic flower child with purple streaks in her graying curls," the grandmother swore she would chain herself to the tree house rather than surrender. Her son had passed away some years earlier.

I found the article painful and disturbing. Has America reached the point where you need a permit and building inspectors to construct a tree house in your own yard? I thought of my own boyhood, when I built a clubhouse in my backyard. It had a door, a window, and a peaked roof covered by tar paper. It would be illegal by today's municipal codes. But it was well built and an incredibly important accomplishment for me. It made me feel that I could create anything, anywhere—that the world was mine to transform.

The chapters of this book are about places in America where people are trying to build things—businesses, small structures, communities—with few resources beyond their own ideas, energy, and grit. I call these people the New Pioneers because their experiences are so resonant of what our pioneering predecessors went through. Like the first immigrants to America, and like the homesteaders who pushed the horizon west, they are people whose wealth lies in what they can do, not in what they own. They are makers of new things.

Each chapter of this book, and each of the ten places I visited, revealed another aspect of what it means to be a New Pioneer. They also illustrated the principles of Lean Urbanism, the phenomenon of urban rebirth that takes place when building and zoning codes are lightened. The two ideas are, in effect, opposite sides of the same coin: New Pioneers are drawn to Lean Zones, since they offer the modern equivalent of yesterday's wide-open wilderness. And where the wilderness of yesteryear is absent or long gone, New Pioneers are using the tools of Lean Urbanism—knowingly and unknowingly—to re-create the even playing field that wilderness once provided.

Act First, Ask Later: This bar in the Evans-Churchill district of Phoenix was created without a permit by a homeowner who opened a wall and then opened for business.

INVISIBLE BUILDERS

Looking back over the ten places that I visited, certain patterns became clear. First and foremost was the idea of living below the radar. Detroit was ground zero for this phenomenon, a city with vast swaths of urban wasteland where building inspectors were few and far between. New Pioneers could, and still can, operate with impunity by keeping their heads down.

The Motor City was far from unique in this regard. Other places I visited where New Pioneers could thrive under the radar were also ignored by inspectors: the unzoned rural wilds of Alabama and the Florida panhandle (the Rural Studio and Seaside), a forgotten warehouse neighborhood in Miami (Wynwood), the mill workers' ghetto in Starkville, Mississippi (the Cotton District).

The extreme cases of this "fly under the radar" rule admittedly occurred in cities that had suffered destruction, with few resources for code enforcement. But most US cities today, from Pittsburgh to Los Angeles, have damaged areas in their aging cores where New Pioneers can flourish (and in some cases already have). Even in cities where code enforcement is strong, by and large the inspectors do not hunt for violations. While they cannot ignore flagrant safety offenses, they rarely search for New Pioneers who live and work under the radar.

Indeed, the idea that lightly regulated zones can engender revitalization is so potent that certain cities have deliberately lifted the regulatory load for the sake of economic development. The best examples are what happened in New Orleans East, where the city suspended code enforcement after Katrina so the Vietnamese could swiftly rebuild, and what happened in Phoenix, where a team of mavericks at city hall allowed exemptions for small businesses to repurpose old buildings rather than tear them down.

THE TIME MACHINE

The suburban boom of post–World War II America set the precedent for planned communities. New subdivisions were platted en masse, gridded, and built using as few components (home models) as possible. Older neighborhoods, in contrast, grew more slowly and were constructed by different, individual builders. Older neighborhoods remain, as a consequence, almost universally more interesting and pleasant to walk through than new neighborhoods.

What Dan Camp and Robert Davis did (in Mississippi and the Florida Panhandle) was to build communities over decades, slowly adding new homes to the existing fabric. This is the Lean Urbanism principle of small-scale successional development, which is another way of saying their towns were built one house at a time, in the way of medieval villages.

The result is a more harmonious, diverse, and interesting community. But just as important is how this type of development lowers the entry barriers for New Pioneers. The use of time replaces the need for capital on the front end, enabling young visionaries with very little start-up cash to build wealth gradually. This is a page right out of the old pioneer playbook. You start with a piece of raw wilderness, and over decades you transform it into orchards, or a farm, or a ranch, or a business. For the New Pioneer, this means landing in an economically marginalized area and playing it for the long run, like the early occupants of Wynwood.

USING THE BONES (THE RECYCLING OF MATERIALS)

We think of recycling mostly in terms of the waste we produce as consumers. In the context of Lean Urbanism and the New Pioneers, however, it has more to do with using—or reusing—the detritus of the physical world. In a very real sense, the early pioneers were recyclers—of the trees, rock, and soil of their homesteads. The New Pioneer equivalent is to recycle the old bones of the cities and towns where they land—right down to the boards and beams, the glass and wood, the windows and doors.

This recycling effort was everywhere to be found in Detroit, with its vast stock of abandoned housing, from blacksmithing old iron nails into kitchen utensils to making furniture from the century-old wood of workers' homes. It was also essential for the Gulf project in Orange Beach, which recycled containers, hurricane glass, football turf, and even theater seats. For the innovative structures built by the Rural Studio, the recycling of everything—from carpeting, windshields, and cardboard to license plates, hay bales, and road rubble—became a mantra. In the case of Cottage Square, Seaside, and Phoenix, recycling meant entire buildings.

The trade-off for using recycled rather than new inputs in design and building is that it typically involves more labor. The choice of insulation for the Green Garage in Detroit was a good example. There, the cost of labor to recycle old insulation found in the building attic equaled the price of what new insulation would have cost. That trade-off was welcome in a city with few jobs; however, it also fits aptly into the psyche of Lean Urbanism and the New Pioneer, where the resources are the people.

THINKING LOW-TECH AND LOCAL (THE RECYCLING OF IDEAS)

One of the sketches that Jay Leno did when he used to host *The Tonight Show* was a segment called "The Office of the Future." In this parody, the camera followed Leno into an early twentieth-century office building in New York. First, Leno explained how the modern office tower had something called stairs, which allowed office workers to get exercise on their way to work. Next, he demonstrated how the tall, double-hung windows allowed for something called convection, where hot air escaped at the top and cooler air came in below—not to mention that it was fresh air, absent from today's hermetically sealed buildings. Finally, he showed the wonders of the old desk lamp, which allowed for individual lighting control, rather than the annoying fluorescent bulbs high overhead.

In a similar vein, my visits to towns and cities where New Pioneers were active revealed that time-tested local building solutions—the vernacular architecture of the region, so to speak—usually proved to be as good, if not better, than modern high-tech alternatives. Certainly they were always cheaper. In New Orleans, for example, the old-fashioned use of peaked roofs and ceilings (to draw off heat), large windows (for cross breezes), and overhangs (to deflect sunlight) were incomparably less expensive and more sustainable than the green-gizmo technology of Brad Pitt's experimental Make It Right village. In Seaside, the use of gravel roads (instead of paved streets), a sink basin at the center of town, and the planting of xeriscape native flora solved drainage more effectively, and for far less money, than the cost of a conventional sewage system.

The use of local vernacular is, in fact, a kind of recycling—but of ideas, not materials. And like recycling, the use of low-tech local solutions often requires more labor than modern high-tech solutions.

They require the application of individual energy. The result, as a happy consequence, is more uniquely individual than something produced en masse—yet another reason our cities need low-tech, local solutions if we want to live in interesting and authentic environments. The addition of light rail in Phoenix was a move in this direction, albeit not as charming as the trolleys of San Francisco.

BOTTOM-UP VS. TOP-DOWN

Among the more profound discoveries from my search for Lean Urbanism was how successful the organic, bottom-up revitalization of the New Pioneers was, relative to the top-down, capital-intensive revitalization that comes from big government and corporate coffers.

The top-down thinking was perfectly epitomized by the massive towers of downtown Detroit's Renaissance Center, and its downtown baseball and football stadiums. The same can be said about the basketball arena and baseball stadium in downtown Phoenix. Neither did anything to revive their respective downtowns, which instead were resuscitated through the infiltration of millennials, artists, bohemians, entrepreneurs, and small businesses.

No urban revival better illustrates the power of the bottom-up versus top-down than post-Katrina New Orleans—even when the top-down has far greater financial resources. The Vietnamese neighborhood of New Orleans East turned down help from the government in exchange for a free pass on rebuilding, no permits needed, no inspections required. The decision by the city to let the Vietnamese rebuild as they pleased created the conditions of Lean Urbanism; the Vietnamese already possessed the New Pioneer spirit of immigrants.

In contrast, astonishing sums of federal money were spent in the black community of New Orleans. But rebuilding there proceeded at a snail's pace thanks to the immense bureaucracy created to administer the relief money. And it was not only the money from the top down; it was the required technology from the top down that made everything more expensive. Only those who rebuilt quickly, on their own, escaped the deadening effects of overregulation from above.

MAKING SMALL POSSIBLE

An interesting ripple in the top-down versus bottom-up paradigm was the practice of creating environments for lean start-ups, which I observed in several places. This is where lean conditions were instituted from above—by providing what amounted to a nest for new life.

By their very nature, New Pioneers operate in the realm of the small. Their work is that of the individual, and consequently it produces all of the virtues of individual creativity, from interesting streetscapes to artisan varieties of consumer goods. The opposite is the realm of the large, the industrial scale, where goods are mass-produced—including the places where we live and shop. In our communities, the result is boring and repetitive housing and retail.

In some of the places I visited, where the barriers had become too high for small businesses to launch, this imbalance required the intervention of private and public-sector benefactors. They needed to become curators of new and interesting enterprises.

This was the case in both the Cotton District and Seaside, where inexpensive spaces were made available so that small business start-ups could enjoy the same advantages as those in a low-cost Pink Zone. Goldman Properties did the same in Wynwood, offering below-market spaces to nurture the small and unique. The most obvious example in the public realm was Phoenix, where one unit in the city planning department actively intervened to reduce costs for small-scale builders and businesses.

END ZONE

The overriding discovery I made in my search for Lean Urbanism was that when rules and regulations are lightened or even lifted, people are able to create wealth from work and ingenuity. This is not a siren call to the anarchy of absent rules. We need basic regulations that preserve us from danger—to ensure that food should not contain toxins, for example, or that buildings should not collapse. But the preponderance of regulations and the price tag for compliance with them is neither fair nor reasonable. In the end, they serve only to deaden free enterprise.

The converse of this, which I also discovered, is that top-down solutions for urban revitalization are rarely as successful as organic, bottom-up solutions that come from the citizenry. Indeed, I discovered that our citizens are far more capable of rebuilding this country than our professionally regulated system would give them credit for.

We seem to have forgotten that America was built by immigrants, literally, by individual pioneers who fabricated its towns, cities, farms, and businesses without an official stamp from a professional or licensed expert. When the federal government prohibited homeowners (mostly black) in New Orleans from receiving funds without hiring a licensed contractor—something that made it impossible for thousands to rebuild—they forgot that it was the grandparents and great-grandparents of those same citizens who built their homes in the first place.

This is what makes the advent of the New Pioneer so positive, because it represents a return to our faith in ourselves as builders, creators, and doers. As we move into an increasingly complex future, we are made to feel ever more helpless without the services of professionals and experts. The emergence of the New Pioneer is a call to our inner resources, a return to the virtues of self-reliance and common sense in a world that is in danger of offering its soul to the altar of overregulation.

RESOURCES, CONNECTIONS, COMMUNITY

The quest to codify and systematize the principles of Lean Urbanism is the ongoing mission of the Center for Applied Transect Studies. Its "Project for Lean Urbanism" is supported by grants from the John S. and James L. Knight Foundation and has been incorporated into the agenda of the Congress of New Urbanism.

The best source of information about Lean Urbanism is the Center's official website, leanurbanism.org. The center's theme of "Lean Urbanism: Making Small Possible" is supported by links to publications, articles, and videos about the movement. The Center's website also expands the Lean Urbanism footprint from Lean Building and Lean Development to five more platforms, including Lean Business, Lean Green, Lean Governing, Lean Infrastructure, and Lean Learning.

The second-best source of information about Lean Urbanism is the Congress for New Urbanism (CNU.org), which helps create walkable cities and towns. Lean Urbanism is now officially one of its projects.

INDEX

ABOUT THE AUTHOR

J.P. FABER is an award-winning editor and writer with more than twenty-five years of journalism experience. Most of those years were spent editing business magazines, focusing on stories about how individual business leaders and entrepreneurs succeeded—or failed. Among his past publications, Faber was editor-in-chief of international business magazines *China Trade*, *Latin Trade*, and *Latin CEO*; city regional business publications *South Florida CEO* and *Miami Business*; and city regional lifestyle monthly *South Florida Magazine*. He is currently the editor of *Cuba Trade* magazine.

Mr. Faber is a past recipient of the national Hearst writing award and was nominated for a Pulitzer Prize in investigative journalism while at the *Miami News*. Faber is also the author of *The Peebles Principles*, written about Donahue Peebles, a former Senate page who became one of the wealthiest African American businessmen in the US.

In 2014, Faber was hired by the Knight Foundation to report on the phenomenon of Lean Urbanism, situations in which entrepreneurs and small builders are able to create new businesses because of lighter—and leaner—regulations. That reporting became the basis of *The New Pioneers*.